Beginning Android 2

Mark L. Murphy

Apress®

Beginning Android 2

ISBN-13 (pbk): 978-1-4302-2629-1

ISBN-13 (electronic): 978-1-4302-2630-7

Printed and bound in the United States of America 9 8 7 6 5 4 3 2 1

Trademarked names may appear in this book. Rather than use a trademark symbol with every occurrence of a trademarked name, we use the names only in an editorial fashion and to the benefit of the trademark owner, with no intention of infringement of the trademark.

Java™ and all Java-based marks are trademarks or registered trademarks of Sun Microsystems, Inc., in the US and other countries. Apress, Inc., is not affiliated with Sun Microsystems, Inc., and this book was written without endorsement from Sun Microsystems, Inc.

President and Publisher: Paul Manning
Lead Editor: Steve Anglin
Development Editor: Matthew Moodie
Editorial Board: Clay Andres, Steve Anglin, Mark Beckner, Ewan Buckingham, Gary Cornell, Jonathan Gennick, Jonathan Hassell, Michelle Lowman, Matthew Moodie, Duncan Parkes, Jeffrey Pepper, Frank Pohlmann, Douglas Pundick, Ben Renow-Clarke, Dominic Shakeshaft, Matt Wade, Tom Welsh
Coordinating Editor: Fran Parnell
Copy Editor: Marilyn S. Smith
Compositor: MacPS, LLC
Indexer: John Collin
Artist: April Milne
Cover Designer: Anna Ishchenko

Distributed to the book trade worldwide by Springer-Verlag New York, Inc., 233 Spring Street, 6th Floor, New York, NY 10013. Phone 1-800-SPRINGER, fax 201-348-4505, e-mail orders-ny@springer-sbm.com, or visit www.springeronline.com.

For information on translations, please e-mail rights@apress.com, or visit www.apress.com.

Apress and friends of ED books may be purchased in bulk for academic, corporate, or promotional use. eBook versions and licenses are also available for most titles. For more information, reference our Special Bulk Sales–eBook Licensing web page at www.apress.com/info/bulksales.

The information in this book is distributed on an "as is" basis, without warranty. Although every precaution has been taken in the preparation of this work, neither the author(s) nor Apress shall have any liability to any person or entity with respect to any loss or damage caused or alleged to be caused directly or indirectly by the information contained in this work.

Contents at a Glance

Contents

About the Author

Mark Murphy is the founder of CommonsWare and the author of the *Busy Coder's Guide to Android Development*. A three-time entrepreneur, his experience ranges from consulting on open source and collaborative development for the Fortune 500 to application development on just about anything smaller than a mainframe. He has been a software developer for more than 25 years, from the TRS-80 to the latest crop of mobile devices. A polished speaker, Mark has delivered conference presentations and training sessions on a wide array of topics internationally.

Mark writes the Building 'Droids column for AndroidGuys and the Android Angle column for NetworkWorld.

Outside of CommonsWare, Mark has an avid interest in how the Internet will play a role in citizen involvement with politics and government. He is also a contributor to the Rebooting America essay collection.

Acknowledgments

I would like to thank the Android team, not only for putting out a good product, but for invaluable assistance on the Android Google Groups. In particular, I would like to thank Romain Guy, Justin Mattson, Dianne Hackborn, Jean-Baptiste Queru, Jeff Sharkey, and Xavier Ducrohet.

Icons used in the sample code were provided by the Nuvola icon set: www.icon-king.com/?p=15.

Preface

Welcome to the Book!

Thanks for your interest in developing applications for Android! Increasingly, people will access Internet-based services using so-called "nontraditional" means, such as mobile devices. The more we do in that space now, the more that people will help invest in that space to make it easier to build more powerful mobile applications in the future. Android is new—Android-powered devices first appeared on the scene in late 2008—but it likely will rapidly grow in importance due to the size and scope of the Open Handset Alliance.

And, most of all, thanks for your interest in this book! I sincerely hope you find it useful and at least occasionally entertaining.

Prerequisites

If you are interested in programming for Android, you will need at least a basic understanding of how to program in Java. Android programming is done using Java syntax, plus a class library that resembles a subset of the Java SE library (plus Android-specific extensions). If you have not programmed in Java before, you probably should learn how that works before attempting to dive into programming for Android.

The book does not cover in any detail how to download or install the Android development tools, either the Eclipse IDE flavor or the stand-alone flavor. The Android web site covers this quite nicely. The material in the book should be relevant whether or not you use the IDE. You should download, install, and test the Android development tools from the Android web site before trying any of the examples presented in this book.

Some chapters may reference material in previous chapters. Also, not every sample shown has the complete source code in the book, lest this book get too large. If you wish to compile the samples, download the source code from the Apress web site (www.apress.com).

Editions of This Book

This book is being produced via a partnership between Apress and CommonsWare. You are reading the Apress edition, which is available in print and in digital form from various digital book services, such as Safari.

CommonsWare continually updates the original material and makes it available to members of its Warescription program, under the title *The Busy Coder's Guide to Android Development*.

CommonsWare maintains a FAQ about this partnership at http://commonsware.com/apress.

Source Code and Its License

The source code for this book is available to readers at www.apress.com. All of the Android projects are licensed under the Apache 2.0 License at www.apache.org/licenses/LICENSE-2.0.html, in case you have the desire to reuse any of it.

Chapter 1

The Big Picture

Android devices, by and large, will be mobile phones. While the Android technology is being discussed for use in other areas (e.g., car dashboard "PCs"), for now, the focus is on phone applications. For developers, this has benefits and drawbacks.

Challenges of Smartphone Programming

On the plus side, Android-style smartphones are sexy. Offering Internet services over mobile devices dates back to the mid-1990s and the Handheld Device Markup Language (HDML). However, only in recent years have phones capable of Internet access taken off. Now, thanks to trends like text messaging and products like Apple's iPhone, phones that can serve as Internet-access devices are rapidly gaining popularity. So, working on Android applications gives you experience with an interesting technology (Android) in a fast-moving market segment (Internet-enabled phones), which is always a good thing.

The problem comes when you actually have to program the darn things.

Anyone with experience in programming for PDAs or phones has felt the pain of phones simply being *small* in all sorts of dimensions, such as the following:

- Screens are small (you won't get comments like, "Is that a 24-inch LCD in your pocket, or...?").

- Keyboards, if they exist, are small.

- Pointing devices, if they exist, are annoying (as anyone who has lost a stylus will tell you) or inexact (large fingers and "multitouch" LCDs are not a good mix).

- CPU speed and memory are limited compared with what are available on desktops and servers.

- You can have any programming language and development framework you want, as long as it was what the device manufacturer chose and burned into the phone's silicon.

Moreover, applications running on a phone must deal with the fact that they are *on a phone*.

People with mobile phones tend to get very irritated when those phones don't work, which is why the "Can you hear me now?" ad campaign from Verizon Wireless has been popular for the past few years. Similarly, those same people will get angry with you if your program "breaks" their phone:

- By tying up the CPU so that calls can't be received

- By not quietly fading into the background when a call comes in or needs to be placed, because it does not work properly with the rest of the phone's operating system

- By crashing the phone's operating system, such as by leaking memory like a sieve

Hence, developing programs for a phone is a different experience than developing desktop applications, web sites, or back-end server processes. The tools look different, the frameworks behave differently, and there are more limitations on what you can do with your programs.

What Android tries to do is meet you halfway:

- You get a commonly used programming language (Java) with some commonly used libraries (e.g., some Apache Commons APIs), with support for tools you may be used to using (Eclipse).

- You get a fairly rigid and separate framework in which your programs need to run so they can be "good citizens" on the phone and not interfere with other programs or the operation of the phone itself.

As you might expect, much of this book deals with that framework and how to write programs that work within its confines and take advantage of its capabilities.

What Androids Are Made Of

When you write a desktop application, you are "master of your own domain." You launch your main window and any child windows—like dialog boxes—that are needed. From your standpoint, you are your own world, leveraging features supported by the operating system, but largely ignorant of any other program that may be running on the computer at the same time. If you do interact with other programs, it is typically through an API, such as Java Database Connectivity (JDBC), or frameworks atop it, to communicate with MySQL or another database.

Android has similar concepts, but packaged differently and structured to make phones more crash-resistant. Here are the main components used in an Android application:

- *Activities*: The building block of the user interface is the activity. You can think of an activity as being the Android analogue for the window or dialog box in a desktop application. While it is possible for activities to not have a user interface, most likely your "headless" code will be packaged in the form of content providers or services.

- *Content providers*: Content providers provide a level of abstraction for any data stored on the device that is accessible by multiple applications. The Android development model encourages you to make your own data available to other applications, as well as your own. Building a content provider lets you do that, while maintaining complete control over how your data is accessed.

- *Services*: Activities and content providers are short-lived and can be shut down at any time. Services, on the other hand, are designed to keep running, if needed, independent of any activity. You might use a service for checking for updates to an RSS feed or to play back music even if the controlling activity is no longer operating.

- *Intents*: Intents are system messages, running around the inside of the device, notifying applications of various events, from hardware state changes (e.g., an SD card was inserted), to incoming data (e.g., an SMS message arrived), to application events (e.g., your activity was launched from the device's main menu). Not only can you respond to intents, but you can create your own to launch other activities or to let you know when specific situations arise (e.g., raise such-and-so intent when the user gets within 100 meters of this-and-such location).

Stuff at Your Disposal

Android comes with a number of features to help you develop applications:

- *Storage*: You can package data files with your application, for things that do not change, such as icons or help files. You also can carve out a bit of space on the device itself, for databases or files containing user-entered or retrieved data needed by your application. And, if the user supplies bulk storage, like an SD card, you can read and write files there as needed.

- *Network*: Android devices will generally be Internet-ready, through one communications medium or another. You can take advantage of the Internet access at any level you wish, from raw Java sockets all the way up to a built-in WebKit-based web browser widget you can embed in your application.

- *Multimedia*: Android devices have the ability to play back and record audio and video. While the specifics may vary from device to device, you can query the device to learn its capabilities, and then take advantage of the multimedia capabilities as you see fit—whether that is to play back music, take pictures with the camera, or use the microphone for audio note-taking.

- *Global positioning system (GPS)*: Android devices will frequently have access to location providers, such as a GPS, which can tell your applications where the device is on the face of the Earth. In turn, you can display maps or otherwise take advantage of the location data, such as tracking a device's movements if the device has been stolen.

- *Phone services*: Of course, since Android devices are typically phones, your software can initiate calls, send and receive Short Message Service (SMS) messages, and everything else you expect from a modern bit of telephony technology.

Chapter **2**

Projects and Targets

After you have downloaded and installed the latest Android Software Development Kit (SDK), and perhaps the Android Developer Tools (ADT) plugin for Eclipse (both available from the Android Developers web site), you're ready to get started. This chapter covers what is involved in building an Android application.

Pieces and Parts

To create an Android application, you will need to create a corresponding Android project. This could be an Eclipse project, if you are using Eclipse for Android development. The project will hold all of your source code, resources (e.g., internationalized strings), third-party JARs, and related materials. The Android build tools—whether Eclipse-integrated or stand-alone—will turn the contents of your project into an Android package (APK) file, which is the Android application. Those tools will also help you get your APK file onto an Android emulator or an actual Android device for testing purposes.

One key element of a project is the *manifest* (`AndroidManifest.xml`). This file contains the "table of contents" for your application, listing all of the major application components, permissions, and so on. The manifest is used by Android at runtime to tie your application into the operating system. The manifest contents are also used by the Android Market (and perhaps other independent "app stores"), so applications that need Android 2.0 will not be presented to people with Android 1.5 devices, for example.

To test your application with the emulator, you will need to create an Android Virtual Device, or AVD. Most likely, you will create several of these, as each AVD emulates an Android device with a particular set of hardware. You might have AVDs for different screen sizes, Android versions, and so on.

When creating projects and creating AVDs, you will need to indicate to Android the API level with which you are working. The API level is a simple integer that maps to an Android version; for example, API level 3 means Android 1.5. When creating a project, you will be able to tell Android the minimum and maximum API levels your application supports. When creating an AVD, you will tell Android which API level the AVD should emulate, so you can see how your application runs on various (fake) devices implementing different versions of Android.

All of these concepts are described in greater detail in this chapter.

Creating a Project

To create a project from the command line, for use with the command-line build tools (e.g., ant), you will need to run the android create project command. This command takes a number of switches to indicate the Java package in which the application's code will reside, the API level the application is targeting, and so on. The result of running this command will be a directory containing all of the files necessary to build a "Hello, World!" Android application.

Here is an example of running android create project:

```
android create project --target 2 --path ./FirstApp --activity FirstApp --package apt.tutorial
```

If you intend to develop for Android using Eclipse, rather than android create project, you will use the Eclipse new-project wizard to create a new Android application.

NOTE: The source code that accompanies this book was set up to be built using the command-line build tools. If you prefer to use Eclipse, you can create empty Eclipse Android projects and import the code into those projects.

Project Structure

The Android build system is organized around a specific directory tree structure for your Android project, much like any other Java project. The specifics, though, are fairly unique to Android. Here's a quick primer on the project structure, to help you make sense of it all, particularly for the sample code referenced in this book.

Root Contents

When you create a new Android project (e.g., via android create project), you get several items in the project's root directory, including the following:

- AndroidManifest.xml: An XML file describing the application being built and which components—activities, services, and so on—are being supplied by that application.

- build.xml: An Ant script for compiling the application and installing it on the device.

- `default.properties` and `local.properties`: Property files used by the Ant build script.

- `assets/`: A folder that holds other static files you wish packaged with the application for deployment onto the device.

- `bin/`: A folder that holds the application once it is compiled.

- `gen/`: Where Android's build tools will place source code that they generate.

- `libs/`: A folder that holds any third-party JARs your application requires.

- `src/`: A folder that holds the Java source code for the application.

- `res/`: A folder that holds resources—such as icons, graphic user interface (GUI) layouts, and the like—that are packaged with the compiled Java in the application.

- `tests/`: A folder that holds an entirely separate Android project used for testing the one you created.

The Sweat Off Your Brow

When you create an Android project (e.g., via `android create project`), you supply the fully qualified class name of the main activity for the application (e.g., `com.commonsware.android.SomeDemo`). You will then find that your project's `src/` tree already has the namespace directory tree in place, plus a stub `Activity` subclass representing your main activity (e.g., `src/com/commonsware/android/SomeDemo.java`). You are welcome to modify this file and add others to the `src/` tree as needed to implement your application.

The first time you compile the project (e.g., via `ant`), out in the main activity's namespace directory, the Android build chain will create `R.java`. This contains a number of constants tied to the various resources you placed in the `res/` directory tree. Throughout this book, you will see that many of the examples reference things in `R.java` (e.g., referring to a layout's identifier via `R.layout.main`).

NOTE: You should not modify `R.java` yourself, but instead let the Android tools handle this for you.

And Now, the Rest of the Story

The `res/` directory tree holds resources—static files that are packaged along with your application, either in their original form or, occasionally, in a preprocessed form. These are some of the subdirectories you will find or create under `res/`:

- `res/drawable/`: For images (PNG, JPEG, etc.).

- `res/layout/`: For XML-based UI layout specifications.

- `res/menu/`: For XML-based menu specifications.

- `res/raw/`: For general-purpose files (e.g., a CSV file of account information).

- `res/values/`: For strings, dimensions, and the like.

- `res/xml/`: For other general-purpose XML files you wish to ship.

All of these, as well as other resources, are covered in this book.

What You Get Out of It

When you compile your project (via `ant` or the IDE), the results go into the `bin/` directory under your project root, as follows:

- `bin/classes/`: Holds the compiled Java classes.

- `bin/classes.dex`: Holds the executable created from those compiled Java classes.

- `bin/`*`yourapp`*`.ap_`: Holds your application's resources, packaged as a ZIP file (where *yourapp* is the name of your application).

- `bin/`*`yourapp`*`-debug.apk` or `bin/`*`yourapp`*`-unsigned.apk`: The actual Android application (where *yourapp* is the name of your application).

The `.apk` file is a ZIP archive containing the `.dex` file, the compiled edition of your resources (`resources.arsc`), any uncompiled resources (such as what you put in `res/raw/`), and the `AndroidManifest.xml` file. It is also digitally signed, with the `-debug` portion of the filename indicating it has been signed using a debug key that works with the emulator, or `-unsigned` indicating that you built your application for release (`ant release`), but the APK still needs to be signed using `jarsigner` and an official key.

Inside the Manifest

The foundation for any Android application is the manifest file, `AndroidManifest.xml` in the root of your project. Here is where you declare what is inside your application—the activities, the services, and so on. You also indicate how these pieces attach themselves to the overall Android system; for example, you indicate which activity (or activities) should appear on the device's main menu (a.k.a. the launcher).

When you create your application, a starter manifest will be generated for you automatically. For a simple application, offering a single activity and nothing else, the autogenerated manifest will probably work out fine, or perhaps require a few minor modifications. On the other end of the spectrum, the manifest file for the Android API demo suite is more than 1,000 lines long. Your production Android applications will probably fall somewhere in the middle.

Most of the interesting bits of the manifest will be described in greater detail in the chapters on their associated Android features. For example, the `service` element will be described in greater detail in Chapter 29, which covers creating services. For now, you just need to understand the role of the manifest and its general overall construction.

In the Beginning, There Was the Root, And It Was Good

The root of all manifest files is, not surprisingly, a `manifest` element:

```
<manifest xmlns:android="http://schemas.android.com/apk/res/android"
  package="com.commonsware.android.search">
...
</manifest>
```

Note the namespace declaration. Curiously, the generated manifests apply it only on the attributes, not the elements (e.g., it's `manifest`, not `android:manifest`). Since this pattern works, unless Android changes, you should stick with it.

The biggest piece of information you need to supply on the `manifest` element is the `package` attribute (also curiously not namespaced). Here, you can provide the name of the Java package that will be considered the "base" of your application. Then, everywhere else in the manifest file that needs a class name, you can just substitute a leading dot as shorthand for the package. For example, if you needed to refer to `com.commonsware.android.search.Snicklefritz` in this preceding manifest, you could just use `.Snicklefritz`, since `com.commonsware.android.search` is defined as the application's package.

Permissions, Instrumentations, and Applications (Oh My!)

Underneath the `manifest` element, you may find the following:

- `uses-permission` elements: Indicate the permissions your application will need in order to function properly.

- `permission` elements: Declare permissions that activities or services might require other applications to hold in order to use your application's data or logic.

- `instrumentation` elements: Indicate code that should be invoked on key system events, such as starting up activities, for the purposes of logging or monitoring.

- `uses-library` elements: Hook in optional Android components, such as mapping services.

- `uses-sdk` element: Indicates for which version of the Android SDK the application was built.

■   `application` element: Defines the guts of the application that the manifest describes.

Here's an example:

```
<manifest xmlns:android="http://schemas.android.com/apk/res/android"
  package="com.commonsware.android">
  <uses-permission
    android:name="android.permission.ACCESS_LOCATION" />
  <uses-permission
    android:name="android.permission.ACCESS_GPS" />
  <uses-permission
    android:name="android.permission.ACCESS_ASSISTED_GPS" />
  <uses-permission
    android:name="android.permission.ACCESS_CELL_ID" />
  <application>
...
  </application>
</manifest>
```

In this example, the manifest has `uses-permission` elements to indicate some device capabilities the application will need—in this case, permissions to allow the application to determine its current location. The contents of the `application` element will describe the activities, services, and whatnot that make up the bulk of the application itself.

Permissions will be covered in greater detail in Chapter 28.

Your Application Does Something, Right?

The children of the `application` element represent the core of the manifest file.

By default, when you create a new Android project, you get a single `activity` element:

```
<manifest xmlns:android="http://schemas.android.com/apk/res/android"
    package="com.commonsware.android.skeleton">
    <application>
        <activity android:name=".Now" android:label="Now">
            <intent-filter>
                <action android:name="android.intent.action.MAIN" />
                <category android:name="android.intent.category.LAUNCHER" />
            </intent-filter>
        </activity>
    </application>
</manifest>
```

This element supplies `android:name` for the class implementing the activity, `android:label` for the display name of the activity, and (frequently) an `intent-filter` child element describing under which conditions this activity will be displayed. The stock `activity` element sets up your activity to appear in the launcher, so users can choose to run it. As you'll see later in this book, you can have several activities in one project, if you so choose.

You may have one or more `provider` elements, indicating content providers, which are the components that supply data to your activities and, with your permission, other activities in other applications on the device. These wrap up databases or other data stores into a single API that any application can use. Later, you'll see how to create content providers and how to use content providers that you or others create.

Finally, you may have one or more service elements, describing services, which are long-running pieces of code that can operate independently of any activity. The quintessential example is the MP3 player, where you want the music to keep playing even if the user pops open other activities and the MP3 player's user interface is "misplaced." Chapters 29 and 30 cover how to create and use services.

Achieving the Minimum

Android, like most operating systems, goes through various revisions, versions, and changes. Some of these affect the Android SDK, meaning there are new classes, methods, or parameters you can use that you could not in previous versions of the SDK.

If you want to ensure your application is run only on devices that have a certain version (or higher) of the Android environment, you will add a uses-sdk element, as a child of the root <manifest> element in your AndroidManifest.xml file. The <uses-sdk> element has one attribute, minSdkVersion, indicating which SDK version your application requires:

```
<manifest xmlns:android="http://schemas.android.com/apk/res/android"
  package="com.commonsware.android.search">
  <uses-sdk minSdkVersion="2" />
  ...
</manifest>
```

At the time of this writing, there are five possible minSdkVersion values:

- 1: Android 1.0 SDK

- 2: Android 1.1 SDK

- 3: Android 1.5 SDK

- 4: Android 1.6 SDK

- 5: Android 2.0 SDK

If you omit the <uses-sdk> element, your application will behave as though minSdkVersion is set to 1.

CAUTION: The Android Market seems to insist that you specifically state your minSdkVersion, so be certain to have a proper <uses-sdk> element if you are going to distribute via that channel.

If you set <uses-sdk>, the application will install only on compatible devices. You do not need to specify the latest SDK, but if you choose an older one, it is up to you to ensure your application works on every SDK version you claim is compatible. For example, if you leave out <uses-sdk>, in effect, you are stipulating that your application works on every Android SDK version ever released, and you will need to test your application to determine if this is indeed the case.

Also note that a bug in the Android Market means you should make the `<uses-sdk>` element be the first child of your `<manifest>` element.

Version=Control

Particularly if you are going to distribute your application, via the Android Market or other means, you probably should add a pair of other attributes to the root `<manifest>` element: `android:versionCode` and `android:versionName`. These assist in the process of upgrading applications.

The `android:versionName` attribute is some human-readable label for the version name or number of your application. So, you can use "3.0" or "System V" or "5000" or "3.1" as you see fit.

The `android:versionCode` attribute is a pure integer indication of the version of the application. This is used by the system to determine if one version of your application is newer than another. *Newer* is defined as "has a higher `android:versionCode` value." Whether you attempt to convert your actual version (as found in `android:versionName`) to a number or simply increment this value by one for each release is up to you.

Emulators and Targets

Let's take a moment to discuss the notion of *targets* in Android, since they can be a bit confusing. Targets are important for your long-term application development, particularly when you use the Android emulator for testing your applications.

Virtually There

To use the emulator, you will need to create one or more AVDs. These virtual devices are designed to mimic real Android devices like the T-Mobile G1 or the HTC Magic. You tell the emulator which AVD to use, and the emulator will pretend it is the device described by that AVD.

When you create an AVD, you need to specify a target. The target indicates which class of device the AVD will pretend to be. At the time of this writing, there are five targets:

- 1: An Android 1.1 device, such as a nonupgraded T-Mobile G1.
- 2: An Android 1.5 device that lacks Google Maps support. This is what you might get from a home-brew port of Android onto a device.
- 3: An Android 1.5 device that has Google Maps support.
- 4: An Android 1.6 device that has Google Maps support.
- 5: An Android 2.0 device that has Google Maps support.

TIP: You can find out the available API targets via the `android list targets` command.

If you are building applications that may use Google Maps, you will want to use an AVD that has a target of 3 or higher.

You can create as many AVDs as you need and for which you have disk space. Each AVD behaves as a totally distinct device, so installing your app on one AVD does not affect any other AVDs that you have created.

AVDs can be created through the `android create avd` command, via Eclipse, or via the AVD Manager, a GUI added in Android 1.6. To use the AVD Manager, simply run the `android` command without any arguments. As shown in Figure 2-1, you will be presented with a list of prebuilt AVDs, New and Delete buttons to add and remove AVDs, a Start button to launch an emulator using a selected AVD, and so on.

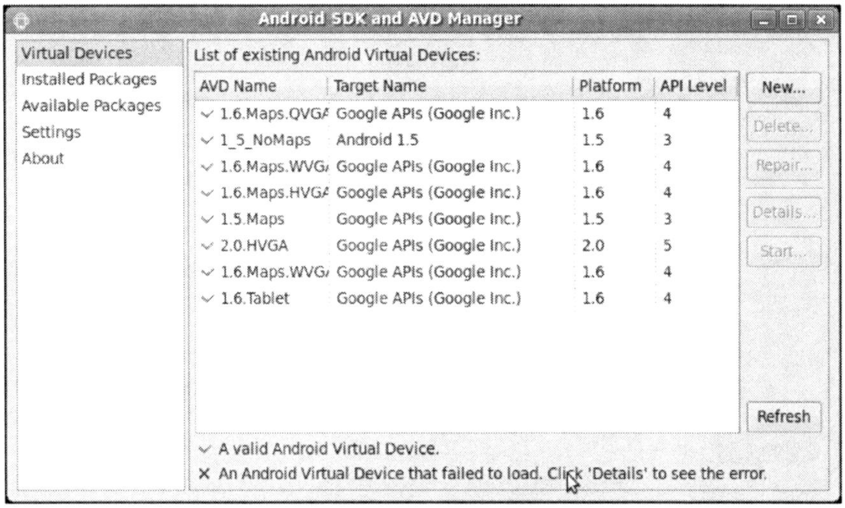

Figure 2-1. *The AVD Manager GUI, showing a list of available AVDs*

When you add an AVD through the GUI (via the New button in the main window), you will be prompted for a name, target API/Google Maps combination, details about an SD card image, and the size of screen you wish to emulate (called the *skin*). Figure 2-2 shows the Create New AVD dialog box.

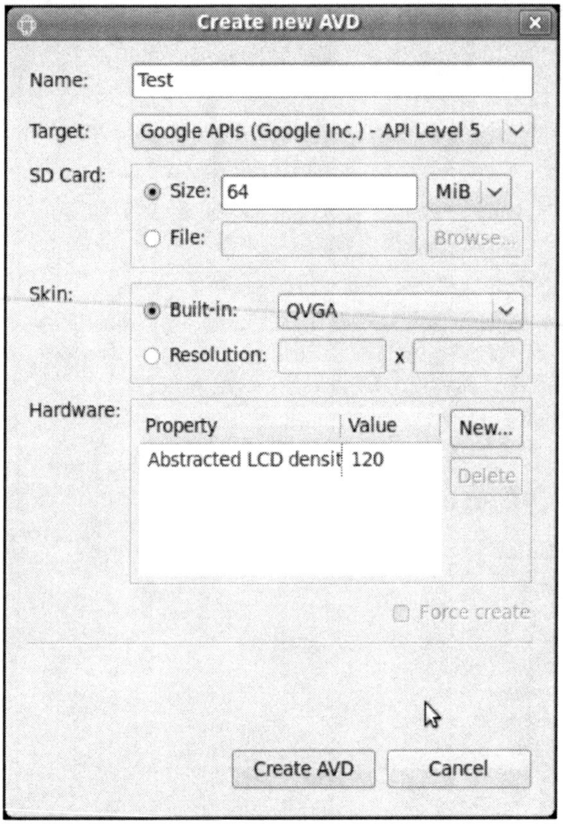

Figure 2-2. *Adding an AVD*

Aiming at a Target

When you create a new project (via android create project or Eclipse), you will need to indicate which class of device this project targets. The same values shown in the previous section apply. For example, creating a project with a target of 3 indicates Android 1.5. Your resulting application will not install on devices that do not meet the specified target.

Here are some rules of thumb for dealing with targets:

- Ask for only what you really need. If you are sticking with Android 1.5 APIs, you may as well ask to build with Android 1.5 APIs and maximize the number of devices on which your program can run.

- Test on as many targets as you can and that are possible. For example, you may be tempted to target 1, to reach the maximum possible range of Android devices. That is fine, but you will need to test on a target 1 AVD, and a target 2 AVD, and so on.

- Check out the new target levels with each Android release. There should be a new values with every Android point-release update (e.g., 2.0 or 1.6), and possibly even for SDK patch levels (e.g., 1.5r1 versus 1.5r2). Be sure to test your application on those new targets whenever you can, as some people may start getting devices with the new Android release soon.

- Testing on AVDs, regardless of target, is no substitute for testing on hardware. AVDs are designed to give you disposable environments that let you test a wide range of environments, even those that may not yet exist in hardware. However, you really need to test your application on at least one actual Android device. If nothing else, the speed of your emulator may not match the speed of the device; the emulator may be faster or slower depending on your system.

Chapter **3**

Creating a Skeleton Application

Every programming language or environment book starts off with the popular "Hello, World!" demonstration. This is just enough of a program to prove you can build things. However, the typical Hello, World! program has no interactivity (e.g., it just dumps the words to a console), and so it's really boring.

This chapter demonstrates a simple project, but one using Advanced Push-Button Technology and the current time, making it a bit more interesting than the typical Hello, World! demo.

Begin at the Beginning

As described in the previous chapter, to work with anything in Android, you need a project. If you are using tools that are not Android-enabled, you can use the `android create project` script, found in the `tools/` directory in your SDK installation. You will need to pass to `android create project` the API target, the directory where you want the skeleton generated, the name of the default activity, and the Java package where all of this should reside:

```
android create project --target 2 \
  --path /path/to/my/project/dir --activity Now \
  --package com.commonsware.android.Now
```

You can also download the project directories of the samples shown in this book in a ZIP file on the Apress web site. These projects are ready for use; you do not need to run `android create project` on those unpacked samples.

Your project's `src/` directory contains the standard Java-style tree of directories based on the Java package you used when you created the project (e.g., `com.commonsware.android` results in `src/com/commonsware/android/`). Inside the innermost directory, you should find a pregenerated source file named `Now.java`, which is where your first activity will go.

This activity will contain a single button that displays the time that the button was last pushed (or the time the application was started if the button has not been pushed).

> **NOTE:** If you downloaded the source files from the Apress web site, you can just use the Skeleton/Now project directly, rather than entering the code.

Open Now.java in your editor and paste in the following code:

```
package com.commonsware.android.skeleton;

import android.app.Activity;
import android.os.Bundle;
import android.view.View;
import android.widget.Button;
import java.util.Date;

public class Now extends Activity implements View.OnClickListener {
  Button btn;

  @Override
  public void onCreate(Bundle icicle) {
    super.onCreate(icicle);

    btn=new Button(this);
    btn.setOnClickListener(this);
    updateTime();
    setContentView(btn);
  }

  public void onClick(View view) {
    updateTime();
  }

  private void updateTime() {
    btn.setText(new Date().toString());
  }
}
```

Let's examine this piece by piece.

Dissecting the Activity

The package declaration needs to be the same as the one you used when creating the project. And, as with any other Java project, you need to import any classes you reference. Most of the Android-specific classes are in the android package.

```
package com.commonsware.android.skeleton;

import android.app.Activity;
import android.os.Bundle;
import android.view.View;
import android.widget.Button;
import java.util.Date;
```

It's worth noting that not every Java SE class is available to Android programs. Visit the Android class reference to see what is and is not available.

```
public class Now extends Activity implements View.OnClickListener {
  Button btn;
```

Activities are public classes, inheriting from the `android.app.Activity` base class. In this case, the activity holds a button (btn).

> **NOTE:** A button, as you can see from the package name, is an Android widget, and widgets are the user interface elements that you use in your application.

Since, for simplicity, we want to trap all button clicks just within the activity itself, we also have the activity class implement `OnClickListener`:

```
@Override
public void onCreate(Bundle icicle) {
  super.onCreate(icicle);

  btn=new Button(this);
  btn.setOnClickListener(this);
  updateTime();
  setContentView(btn);
}
```

The `onCreate()` method is invoked when the activity is started. The first thing you should do is chain upward to the superclass, so the stock Android activity initialization can be done.

In our implementation, we then create the button instance (new `Button(this)`), tell it to send all button clicks to the activity instance itself (via `setOnClickListener()`), call a private `updateTime()` method (shown shortly), and then set the activity's content view to be the button itself (via `setContentView()`).

> **NOTE:** All widgets extend the `View` base class. You usually build the user interface out of a hierarchy of views, but in this example, we are using a single view.

We will discuss that magical `Bundle icicle` in Chapter 16. For the moment, consider it an opaque handle that all activities receive upon creation.

```
public void onClick(View view) {
  updateTime();
}
```

In Swing, a `JButton` click raises an `ActionEvent`, which is passed to the `ActionListener` configured for the button. In Android, a button click causes `onClick()` to be invoked in the `OnClickListener` instance configured for the button. The listener is provided to the view that triggered the click (in this case, the button). All we do here is call that private `updateTime()` method:

```
private void updateTime() {
  btn.setText(new Date().toString());
}
```

When we open the activity (onCreate()), or when the button is clicked (onClick()), we update the button's label to be the current time via setText(), which functions much the same as the JButton equivalent.

Building and Running the Activity

To build the activity, use your integrated development environment's (IDE's) built-in Android packaging tool or run ant in the base directory of your project. Then do the following to run the activity:

1. Launch the emulator by running the android command, choosing an AVD in the AVD Manager, and clicking the Start button. You should be able to accept the defaults in the Launch Options dialog. Figure 3–1 shows the Android home screen.

NOTE: The first time you use an AVD with the emulator, it will take substantially longer to start than it will subsequent times.

Figure 3–1. *The Android home screen*

2. Install the package (e.g., run ant install).

3. View the list of installed applications in the emulator and find the Now application. In Figure 3–2, it's on the bottom row.

Figure 3–2. *The Android application launcher*

4. Open that application. You should see an activity screen similar to the one shown in Figure 3–3.

Figure 3–3. *The Now demonstration activity*

Clicking the button—in other words, clicking pretty much anywhere on the phone's screen—will update the time shown in the button's label.

Note that the label is centered horizontally and vertically, as those are the default styles applied to button captions. You can control that formatting, as described in Chapter 5.

After you are finished gazing at the awesomeness of Advanced Push-Button Technology, you can click the back button on the emulator to return to the launcher.

Chapter 4

Using XML-Based Layouts

While it is technically possible to create and attach widgets to your activity purely through Java code, as we did in the preceding chapter, the more common approach is to use an XML-based layout file. Dynamic instantiation of widgets is reserved for more complicated scenarios, where the widgets are not known at compile time (e.g., populating a column of radio buttons based on data retrieved from the Internet).

With that in mind, it's time to break out the XML and learn how to lay out Android activities that way.

What Is an XML-Based Layout?

As the name suggests, an XML-based layout is a specification of widgets' relationships to each other—and to their containers (which are covered in Chapter 6)—encoded in XML format. Specifically, Android considers XML-based layouts to be resources, and as such, layout files are stored in the res/layout directory inside your Android project.

Each XML file contains a tree of elements specifying a layout of widgets and containers that make up one View hierarchy. The attributes of the XML elements are properties, describing how a widget should look or how a container should behave. For example, if a Button element has an attribute value of android:textStyle = "bold", that means that the text appearing on the face of the button should be rendered in a boldface font style.

Android's SDK ships with a tool (aapt) that uses the layouts. This tool should be automatically invoked by your Android toolchain (e.g., Eclipse or Ant's build.xml). Of particular importance to you as a developer is that aapt generates the R.java source file within your project, allowing you to access layouts and widgets within those layouts directly from your Java code, as will be demonstrated in this chapter.

Why Use XML-Based Layouts?

Most everything you do using XML layout files can be achieved through Java code. For example, you could use setTypeface() to have a button render its text in bold, instead of using a property in an XML layout. Since XML layouts are yet another file for you to keep track of, we need good reasons for using such files.

Perhaps the biggest reason is to assist in the creation of tools for view definition, such as a GUI builder in an IDE like Eclipse or a dedicated Android GUI designer like DroidDraw. Such GUI builders could, in principle, generate Java code instead of XML. The challenge is rereading the UI definition to support edits, which is far simpler when the data is in a structured format like XML rather than in a programming language. Moreover, keeping generated XML definitions separated from handwritten Java code makes it less likely that someone's custom-crafted source will get clobbered by accident when the generated bits are regenerated. XML forms a nice middle ground between something that is convenient for tool writers to use and easy for programmers to work with by hand as needed.

Also, XML as a GUI definition format is becoming more commonplace. Microsoft's Extensible Application Markup Language (XAML), Adobe's Flex, and Mozilla's XML User Interface Language (XUL) all take a similar approach to that of Android: put layout details in an XML file and put programming smarts in source files (e.g., JavaScript for XUL). Many less well-known GUI frameworks, such as ZK, also use XML for view definition. While following the herd is not necessarily the best policy, it does have the advantage of helping to ease the transition to Android from any other XML-centered view description language.

OK, So What Does It Look Like?

Here is the Button from the previous chapter's sample application, converted into an XML layout file, found in the Layouts/NowRedux sample project:

```
<?xml version="1.0" encoding="utf-8"?>
<Button xmlns:android="http://schemas.android.com/apk/res/android"
    android:id="@+id/button"
    android:text=""
    android:layout_width="fill_parent"
    android:layout_height="fill_parent"/>
```

The class name of the widget, Button, forms the name of the XML element. Since Button is an Android-supplied widget, we can just use the bare class name. If you create your own widgets as subclasses of android.view.View, you will need to provide a full package declaration as well (e.g., com.commonsware.android.MyWidget).

The root element needs to declare the Android XML namespace:

```
xmlns:android="http://schemas.android.com/apk/res/android"
```

All other elements will be children of the root and will inherit that namespace declaration.

Because we want to reference this button from our Java code, we need to give it an identifier via the android:id attribute. We will cover this concept in greater detail in the next section.

The remaining attributes are properties of this Button instance:

- ▓ android:text: Indicates the initial text to be displayed on the button face (in this case, an empty string).

- ▓ android:layout_width and android:layout_height: Tell Android to have the button's width and height fill the parent—in this case, the entire screen.

These attributes will be covered in greater detail in Chapter 6.

Since this single widget is the only content in our activity, we need just this single element. Complex UIs will require a whole tree of elements, representing the widgets and containers that control their positioning. All the remaining chapters of this book will use the XML layout form whenever practical, so there are dozens of other examples of more complex layouts for you to peruse.

What's with the @ Signs?

Many widgets and containers need to appear only in the XML layout file and do not need to be referenced in your Java code. For example, a static label (TextView) frequently needs to be in the layout file just to indicate where it should appear. These sorts of elements in the XML file do not need to have the android:id attribute to give them a name.

Anything you *do* want to use in your Java source, though, needs an android:id.

The convention is to use @+id/... as the id value, where the ... represents your locally unique name for the widget in question. In the XML layout example in the preceding section, @+id/button is the identifier for the Button widget.

Android provides a few special android:id values, of the form @android:id/.... You will see some of these in various examples throughout this book.

And How Do We Attach These to the Java?

Given that you have painstakingly set up the widgets and containers in an XML layout file named main.xml stored in res/layout, all you need is one statement in your activity's onCreate() callback to use that layout:

```
setContentView(R.layout.main);
```

This is the same setContentView() we used earlier, passing it an instance of a View subclass (in that case, a Button). The Android-built View, constructed from our layout, is accessed from that code-generated R class. All of the layouts are accessible under

R.layout, keyed by the base name of the layout file; for example, res/layout/main.xml results in R.layout.main.

To access your identified widgets, use findViewById(), passing in the numeric identifier of the widget in question. That numeric identifier was generated by Android in the R class as R.id.something (where something is the specific widget you are seeking). Those widgets are simply subclasses of View, just like the Button instance we created in the previous chapter.

The Rest of the Story

In the original Now demo, the button's face would show the current time, which would reflect when the button was last pushed (or when the activity was first shown, if the button had not yet been pushed). Most of that logic still works, even in this revised demo (NowRedux). However, rather than instantiating the Button in our activity's onCreate() callback, we can reference the one from the XML layout:

```
package com.commonsware.android.layouts;

import android.app.Activity;
import android.os.Bundle;
import android.view.View;
import android.widget.Button;
import java.util.Date;

public class NowRedux extends Activity
  implements View.OnClickListener {
  Button btn;

  @Override
  public void onCreate(Bundle icicle) {
    super.onCreate(icicle);

    setContentView(R.layout.main);

    btn=(Button)findViewById(R.id.button);
    btn.setOnClickListener(this);
    updateTime();
  }

  public void onClick(View view) {
    updateTime();
  }

  private void updateTime() {
    btn.setText(new Date().toString());
  }
}
```

The first difference is that, rather than setting the content view to be a view we created in Java code, we set it to reference the XML layout (setContentView(R.layout.main)).

The R.java source file will be updated when we rebuild this project to include a reference to our layout file (stored as main.xml in our project's res/layout directory).

The other difference is that we need to get our hands on our Button instance, for which we use the findViewById() call. Since we identified our button as @+id/button, we can reference the button's identifier as R.id.button. Now, with the Button instance in hand, we can set the callback and set the label as needed.

The results look the same as with the original Now demo, as shown in Figure 4–1.

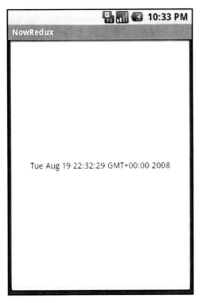

Figure 4–1. *The NowRedux sample activity*

Chapter 5

Employing Basic Widgets

Every GUI toolkit has some basic widgets: fields, labels, buttons, and so on. Android's toolkit is no different in scope, and the basic widgets will provide a good introduction to how widgets work in Android activities.

Assigning Labels

The simplest widget is the label, referred to in Android as a TextView. As in most GUI toolkits, labels are bits of text that cannot be edited directly by users. Typically, they are used to identify adjacent widgets (e.g., a "Name:" label next to a field where you fill in a name).

In Java, you can create a label by creating a TextView instance. More commonly, though, you will create labels in XML layout files by adding a TextView element to the layout, with an android:text property to set the value of the label itself. If you need to swap labels based on certain criteria, such as internationalization, you may wish to use a resource reference in the XML instead, as will be described in Chapter 20.

TextView has numerous other properties of relevance for labels, such as the following:

  ▪ android:typeface: Sets the typeface to use for the label (e.g., monospace).

  ▪ android:textStyle: Indicates that the typeface should be made bold (bold), italic (italic), or bold and italic (bold_italic).

  ▪ android:textColor: Sets the color of the label's text, in RGB hex format (e.g., #FF0000 for red).

For example, in the Basic/Label project, you will find the following layout file:

```
<?xml version="1.0" encoding="utf-8"?>
<TextView xmlns:android="http://schemas.android.com/apk/res/android"
  android:layout_width="fill_parent"
  android:layout_height="wrap_content"
  android:text="You were expecting something profound?"
  />
```

Just that layout alone, with the stub Java source provided by Android's project builder (e.g., android create project), gives you the demo shown in Figure 5–1.

Figure 5–1. *The LabelDemo sample application*

Button, Button, Who's Got the Button?

You have already seen the use of the Button widget in the previous two chapters. As it turns out, Button is a subclass of TextView, so everything discussed in the preceding section also applies to formatting the face of the button.

However, Android 1.6 adds a new feature for the declaration of the "on-click" listener for a Button. In addition to the classic approach of defining some object (such as the activity) as implementing the View.OnClickListener interface, you can now take a somewhat simpler approach:

- Define some method on your Activity that holds the button that takes a single View parameter, has a void return value, and is public.

- In your layout XML, on the Button element, include the android:onClick attribute with the name of the method you defined in the previous step.

For example, you might have a method on your Activity that looks like this:

```
public void someMethod(View theButton) {
  // do something useful here
}
```

Then you could use this XML declaration for the Button itself, including android:onClick:

```
<Button
 android:onClick="someMethod"
 ...
/>
```

This is enough for Android to wire together the `Button` with the click handler.

Fleeting Images

Android has two widgets to help you embed images in your activities: `ImageView` and `ImageButton`. As the names suggest, they are image-based analogues to `TextView` and `Button`, respectively.

Each widget takes an `android:src` attribute (in an XML layout) to specify which picture to use. These usually reference a drawable resource, described in greater detail in Chapter 20. You can also set the image content based on a `Uri` from a content provider via `setImageURI()`.

`ImageButton`, a subclass of `ImageView`, mixes in the standard `Button` behaviors, for responding to clicks and whatnot. For example, take a peek at the `main.xml` layout from the `Basic/ImageView` sample project:

```
<?xml version="1.0" encoding="utf-8"?>
<ImageView xmlns:android="http://schemas.android.com/apk/res/android"
    android:id="@+id/icon"
    android:layout_width="fill_parent"
    android:layout_height="fill_parent"
    android:adjustViewBounds="true"
    android:src="@drawable/molecule"
    />
```

The result, just using the code-generated activity, is simply the image shown in Figure 5–2.

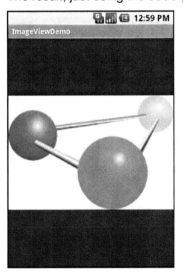

Figure 5–2. *The ImageViewDemo sample application*

Fields of Green. Or Other Colors.

Along with buttons and labels, fields are the third anchor of most GUI toolkits. In Android, they are implemented via the `EditText` widget, which is a subclass of the `TextView` used for labels.

Along with the standard `TextView` properties (e.g., `android:textStyle`), `EditText` has many other properties that will be useful to you in constructing fields, including the following:

- `android:autoText`: Controls if the field should provide automatic spelling assistance.

- `android:capitalize`: Controls if the field should automatically capitalize the first letter of entered text (useful for name or city fields, for example).

- `android:digits`: Configures the field to accept only certain digits.

- `android:singleLine`: Controls if the field is for single-line input or multiple-line input (e.g., does pressing Enter move you to the next widget or add a newline?).

Most of these properties are also available from the new `android:inputType` attribute, introduced in Android 1.5 as part of adding "soft keyboards" to Android (discussed in Chapter 10).

For example, from the `Basic/Field` project, here is an XML layout file showing an `EditText` widget:

```
<?xml version="1.0" encoding="utf-8"?>
<EditText xmlns:android="http://schemas.android.com/apk/res/android"
  android:id="@+id/field"
  android:layout_width="fill_parent"
  android:layout_height="fill_parent"
  android:singleLine="false"
  />
```

Note that `android:singleLine` is set to `"false"`, so users will be able to enter in several lines of text.

For this project, the `FieldDemo.java` file populates the input field with some prose:

```
package com.commonsware.android.field;

import android.app.Activity;
import android.os.Bundle;
import android.widget.EditText;

public class FieldDemo extends Activity {
  @Override
  public void onCreate(Bundle icicle) {
    super.onCreate(icicle);
    setContentView(R.layout.main);
```

```
    EditText fld=(EditText)findViewById(R.id.field);
    fld.setText("Licensed under the Apache License, Version 2.0 " +
            "(the \"License\"); you may not use this file " +
            "except in compliance with the License. You may " +
            "obtain a copy of the License at " +
            "http://www.apache.org/licenses/LICENSE-2.0");
  }
}
```

The result, once built and installed into the emulator, is shown in Figure 5–3.

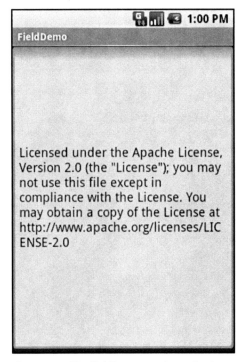

Figure 5–3. *The FieldDemo sample application*

Another flavor of field is one that offers autocompletion, to help users supply a value without typing in the whole entry. That is provided in Android as the AutoCompleteTextView widget, discussed in greater detail in Chapter 9.

Just Another Box to Check

The classic check box has two states: checked and unchecked. Clicking the check box toggles between those states to indicate a choice (e.g., "Add rush delivery to my order").

In Android, there is a CheckBox widget to meet this need. It has TextView as an ancestor, so you can use TextView properties like android:textColor to format the widget.

Within Java, you can invoke the following:

- `isChecked()`: Determines if the check box has been checked.
- `setChecked()`: Forces the check box into a checked or unchecked state.
- `toggle()`: Toggles the check box as if the user checked it.

Also, you can register a listener object (in this case, an instance of OnCheckedChangeListener) to be notified when the state of the check box changes.

For example, from the Basic/CheckBox project, here is a simple check box layout:

```xml
<?xml version="1.0" encoding="utf-8"?>
<CheckBox xmlns:android="http://schemas.android.com/apk/res/android"
    android:id="@+id/check"
    android:layout_width="wrap_content"
    android:layout_height="wrap_content"
    android:text="This checkbox is: unchecked" />
```

The corresponding CheckBoxDemo.java retrieves and configures the behavior of the check box:

```java
public class CheckBoxDemo extends Activity
  implements CompoundButton.OnCheckedChangeListener {
  CheckBox cb;

  @Override
  public void onCreate(Bundle icicle) {
    super.onCreate(icicle);
    setContentView(R.layout.main);

    cb=(CheckBox)findViewById(R.id.check);
    cb.setOnCheckedChangeListener(this);
  }

  public void onCheckedChanged(CompoundButton buttonView,
                               boolean isChecked) {
    if (isChecked) {
      cb.setText("This checkbox is: checked");
    }
    else {
      cb.setText("This checkbox is: unchecked");
    }
  }
}
```

Note that the activity serves as its own listener for check box state changes, since it implements the OnCheckedChangeListener interface (via cb.setOnCheckedChangeListener(this)). The callback for the listener is onCheckedChanged(), which receives the check box whose state has changed and the new state. In this case, we update the text of the check box to reflect what the actual box contains.

What's the result? Clicking the check box immediately updates its text, as shown in Figures 5–4 and 5–5.

Figure 5–4. *The CheckBoxDemo sample application, with the check box unchecked*

Figure 5–5. *The same application, with the check box checked*

Turn the Radio Up

As with other implementations of radio buttons in other toolkits, Android's radio buttons are two-state, like check boxes, but can be grouped such that only one radio button in the group can be checked at any time.

Like CheckBox, RadioButton inherits from CompoundButton, which in turn inherits from TextView. Hence, all the standard TextView properties for font face, style, color, and so on are available for controlling the look of radio buttons. Similarly, you can call isChecked() on a RadioButton to see if it is selected, toggle() to select it, and so on, as you can with a CheckBox.

Most times, you will want to put your RadioButton widgets inside a RadioGroup. The RadioGroup indicates a set of radio buttons whose state is tied, meaning only one button in that group can be selected at any time. If you assign an android:id to your RadioGroup in your XML layout, you can access the group from your Java code and invoke the following:

- check(): Checks a specific radio button via its ID (e.g., group.check(R.id.radio1)).

- clearCheck(): Clears all radio buttons, so none in the group are checked.

- getCheckedRadioButtonId(): Gets the ID of the currently checked radio button (or -1 if none are checked).

For example, from the Basic/RadioButton sample application, here is an XML layout showing a RadioGroup wrapping a set of RadioButton widgets:

```xml
<?xml version="1.0" encoding="utf-8"?>
<RadioGroup
  xmlns:android="http://schemas.android.com/apk/res/android"
  android:orientation="vertical"
  android:layout_width="fill_parent"
  android:layout_height="fill_parent"
  >
    <RadioButton android:id="@+id/radio1"
      android:layout_width="wrap_content"
      android:layout_height="wrap_content"
      android:text="Rock" />

    <RadioButton android:id="@+id/radio2"
      android:layout_width="wrap_content"
      android:layout_height="wrap_content"
      android:text="Scissors" />

    <RadioButton android:id="@+id/radio3"
      android:layout_width="wrap_content"
      android:layout_height="wrap_content"
      android:text="Paper" />
</RadioGroup>
```

Using the stock Android-generated Java for the project and this layout, you get the result shown in Figure 5–6.

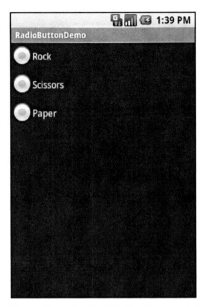

Figure 5–6. *The RadioButtonDemo sample application*

Note that the radio button group is initially set so that none of the buttons are checked at the outset. To preset one of the radio buttons to be checked, use either setChecked() on the RadioButton or check() on the RadioGroup from within your onCreate() callback in your activity.

It's Quite a View

All widgets, including the ones shown in the preceding sections, extend View, and as such, give all widgets an array of useful properties and methods beyond those already described.

Useful Properties

Some of the properties on View most likely to be used include the following, which control the focus sequence:

- android:nextFocusDown
- android:nextFocusLeft
- android:nextFocusRight
- android:nextFocusUp

Another useful property is android:visibility, which controls whether the widget is initially visible.

Useful Methods

You can toggle whether or not a widget is enabled via `setEnabled()` and see if it is enabled via `isEnabled()`. One common use pattern for this is to disable some widgets based on a `CheckBox` or `RadioButton` selection.

You can give a widget focus via `requestFocus()` and see if it is focused via `isFocused()`. You might use this in concert with disabling widgets, to ensure the proper widget has the focus once your disabling operation is complete.

To help navigate the tree of widgets and containers that make up an activity's overall view, you can use the following:

- `getParent()`: Finds the parent widget or container.
- `findViewById()`: Finds a child widget with a certain ID.
- `getRootView()`: Gets the root of the tree (e.g., what you provided to the activity via `setContentView()`).

Colors

There are two types of color attributes in Android widgets. Some, like `android:background`, take a single color (or a graphic image to serve as the background). Others, like `android:textColor` on `TextView` (and subclasses), can take a `ColorStateList`, including via the Java accessor (in this case, `setTextColor()`).

A `ColorStateList` allows you to specify different colors for different conditions. For example, a `TextView` can have one text color when it is the selected item in a list and another color when it is not selected (selection widgets are discussed in Chapter 7). This is handled via the default `ColorStateList` associated with `TextView`.

If you wish to change the color of a `TextView` widget in Java code, you have two main choices:

- Use `ColorStateList.valueOf()`, which returns a `ColorStateList` in which all states are considered to have the same color, which you supply as the parameter to the `valueOf()` method. This is the Java equivalent of the `android:textColor` approach, to make the `TextView` always a specific color, regardless of circumstances.
- Create a `ColorStateList` with different values for different states, either via the constructor or via an XML document.

Chapter 6

Working with Containers

Containers pour a collection of widgets (and possibly child containers) into specific structures. If you want a form with labels on the left and fields on the right, you need a container. If you want OK and Cancel buttons to be beneath the rest of the form, next to one another, and flush to the right side of the screen, you need a container. Just from a pure XML perspective, if you have multiple widgets (beyond RadioButton widgets in a RadioGroup), you need a container just to have a root element to place the widgets inside.

Most GUI toolkits have some notion of layout management, frequently organized into containers. In Java/Swing, for example, you have layout managers like BoxLayout and containers that use them (e.g., Box). Some toolkits, such as XUL and Flex, stick strictly to the box model, figuring that any desired layout can be achieved through the correct combination of nested boxes. Android, through LinearLayout, also offers a box model. In addition, Android supports a range of containers that provide different layout rules.

In this chapter, we will look at several commonly used containers: LinearLayout (the box model), RelativeLayout (a rule-based model), TableLayout (the grid model), and ScrollView, a container designed to assist with implementing scrolling containers.

Thinking Linearly

LinearLayout is a box model, in which widgets or child containers are lined up in a column or row, one after the next. This works in a similar manner to FlowLayout in Java/Swing, and vbox and hbox in Flex and XUL.

Flex and XUL use the box as their primary unit of layout. If you want, you can use LinearLayout in much the same way, eschewing some of the other containers. Getting the visual representation you want is mostly a matter of identifying where boxes should nest and which properties those boxes should have, such as their alignment in relation to other boxes.

LinearLayout Concepts and Properties

To configure a LinearLayout, you have five main areas of control: the orientation, the fill model, the weight, the gravity, and the padding.

Orientation

Orientation indicates whether the LinearLayout represents a row or a column. Just add the android:orientation property to your LinearLayout element in your XML layout, setting the value to be horizontal for a row or vertical for a column.

The orientation can be modified at runtime by invoking setOrientation() on the LinearLayout, supplying it either HORIZONTAL or VERTICAL.

Fill Model

Let's imagine a row of widgets, such as a pair of radio buttons. These widgets have a "natural" size based on their text. Their combined sizes probably do not exactly match the width of the Android device's screen, particularly since screens come in various sizes. You then have the issue of what to do with the remaining space.

All widgets inside a LinearLayout must supply android:layout_width and android:layout_height properties to help address this issue. These properties' values have three flavors:

- You can provide a specific dimension, such as 125px to indicate the widget should take up exactly 125 pixels.

- You can provide wrap_content, which means the widget should fill up its natural space, unless that is too big, in which case Android can use word-wrap as needed to make it fit.

- You can provide fill_parent, which means the widget should fill up all available space in its enclosing container, after all other widgets are handled.

The latter two flavors are the most common, as they are independent of screen size, allowing Android to adjust your view to fit the available space.

Weight

But what happens if you have two widgets that should split the available free space? For example, suppose you have two multiline fields in a column, and you want them to take up the remaining space in the column after all other widgets have been allocated their space. To make this work, in addition to setting android:layout_width (for rows) or android:layout_height (for columns) to fill_parent, you must also set android:layout_weight.

The android:layout_weight property indicates the proportion of the free space that should go to that widget. For example, if you set android:layout_weight to be the same nonzero value for a pair of widgets (e.g., 1), the free space will be split evenly between them. If you set it to be 1 for one widget and 2 for the other widget, the second widget will use up twice the free space that the first widget does. The weight for a widget is zero by default.

Another pattern for using weights is if you want to allocate sizes on a percentage basis. To use this technique for, say, a horizontal layout:

- Set all the android:layout_width values to be 0 for the widgets in the layout.

- Set the android:layout_weight values to be the desired percentage size for each widget in the layout.

- Make sure all those weights add up to 100.

Gravity

By default, everything in a LinearLayout is left- and top-aligned. So, if you create a row of widgets via a horizontal LinearLayout, the row will start flush on the left side of the screen. If that is not what you want, you need to specify a gravity value. Using android:layout_gravity on a widget (or calling setGravity() at runtime on the widget's Java object), you can tell the widget and its container how to align it in on the screen.

For a column of widgets, common gravity values are left, center_horizontal, and right for left-aligned, centered, and right-aligned widgets, respectively.

For a row of widgets, the default is for them to be aligned so their text is aligned on the baseline (the invisible line that letters seem to "sit on"). You can specify a gravity of center_vertical to center the widgets along the row's vertical midpoint.

Padding

By default, widgets are tightly packed next to each other. If you want to increase the whitespace between widgets, you will want to use the android:padding property (or call setPadding() at runtime on the widget's Java object). The padding specifies how much space there is between the boundaries of the widget's "cell" and the actual widget contents, as shown in Figure 6-1.

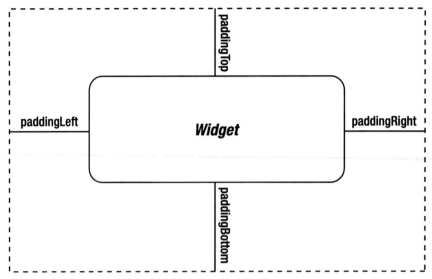

Figure 6-1. *The relationship between a widget, its cell, and the padding values*

The android:padding property allows you to set the same padding on all four sides of the widget, with the widget's contents centered within that padded-out area. If you want the padding to vary on different sides, use android:paddingLeft, android:paddingRight, android:paddingTop, and android:paddingBottom. The value of the padding is a dimension, such as 5px for 5 pixels' worth of padding.

If you apply a custom background to a widget (e.g., via the android:background attribute), the background will be behind both the widget and the padding area. To avoid this, rather than using padding, you can establish margins, which add whitespace without extending the intrinsic size of the widget. You can set margins via android:layout_marginTop and related attributes.

LinearLayout Example

Let's look at an example (Containers/Linear) that shows LinearLayout properties set both in the XML layout file and at runtime. Here is the layout:

```
<?xml version="1.0" encoding="utf-8"?>
<LinearLayout
  xmlns:android="http://schemas.android.com/apk/res/android"
  android:orientation="vertical"
  android:layout_width="fill_parent"
  android:layout_height="fill_parent"
  >
  <RadioGroup android:id="@+id/orientation"
    android:orientation="horizontal"
    android:layout_width="wrap_content"
    android:layout_height="wrap_content"
    android:padding="5px">
    <RadioButton
```

```
        android:id="@+id/horizontal"
        android:text="horizontal" />
      <RadioButton
        android:id="@+id/vertical"
        android:text="vertical" />
    </RadioGroup>
    <RadioGroup android:id="@+id/gravity"
      android:orientation="vertical"
      android:layout_width="fill_parent"
      android:layout_height="wrap_content"
      android:padding="5px">
      <RadioButton
        android:id="@+id/left"
        android:text="left" />
      <RadioButton
        android:id="@+id/center"
        android:text="center" />
      <RadioButton
        android:id="@+id/right"
        android:text="right" />
    </RadioGroup>
</LinearLayout>
```

Note that we have a LinearLayout wrapping two RadioGroup sets. RadioGroup is a subclass of LinearLayout, so our example demonstrates nested boxes as if they were all LinearLayout containers.

The top RadioGroup sets up a row (android:orientation = "horizontal") of RadioButton widgets. The RadioGroup has 5px of padding on all sides, separating it from the other RadioGroup. The width and height are both set to wrap_content, so the radio buttons will take up only the space that they need.

The bottom RadioGroup is a column (android:orientation = "vertical") of three RadioButton widgets. Again, we have 5px of padding on all sides and a natural height (android:layout_height = "wrap_content"). However, we have set android:layout_width to be fill_parent, meaning the column of radio buttons claims the entire width of the screen.

To adjust these settings at runtime based on user input, we need some Java code:

```
package com.commonsware.android.linear;

import android.app.Activity;
import android.os.Bundle;
import android.view.Gravity;
import android.text.TextWatcher;
import android.widget.LinearLayout;
import android.widget.RadioGroup;
import android.widget.EditText;

public class LinearLayoutDemo extends Activity
  implements RadioGroup.OnCheckedChangeListener {
  RadioGroup orientation;
  RadioGroup gravity;

  @Override
```

```
public void onCreate(Bundle icicle) {
  super.onCreate(icicle);
  setContentView(R.layout.main);

  orientation=(RadioGroup)findViewById(R.id.orientation);
  orientation.setOnCheckedChangeListener(this);
  gravity=(RadioGroup)findViewById(R.id.gravity);
  gravity.setOnCheckedChangeListener(this);
}

public void onCheckedChanged(RadioGroup group, int checkedId) {
  switch (checkedId) {
    case R.id.horizontal:
      orientation.setOrientation(LinearLayout.HORIZONTAL);
      break;

    case R.id.vertical:
      orientation.setOrientation(LinearLayout.VERTICAL);
      break;

    case R.id.left:
      gravity.setGravity(Gravity.LEFT);
      break;

    case R.id.center:
      gravity.setGravity(Gravity.CENTER_HORIZONTAL);
      break;

    case R.id.right:
      gravity.setGravity(Gravity.RIGHT);
      break;
  }
}
}
```

In onCreate(), we look up our two RadioGroup containers and register a listener on each, so we are notified when the radio buttons change state (setOnCheckedChangeListener(this)). Since the activity implements OnCheckedChangeListener, the activity itself is the listener.

In onCheckedChanged() (the callback for the listener), we see which RadioGroup had a state change. If it was the orientation group, we adjust the orientation based on the user's selection. If it was the gravity group, we adjust the gravity based on the user's selection.

Figure 6-2 shows the result when the layout demo is first launched inside the emulator.

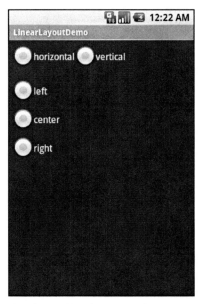

Figure 6-2. *The LinearLayoutDemo sample application, as initially launched*

If we toggle on the vertical radio button, the top RadioGroup adjusts to match, as shown in Figure 6-3.

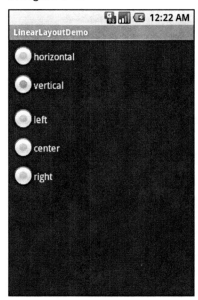

Figure 6-3. *The same application, with the vertical radio button selected*

If we toggle the center or right radio button, the bottom RadioGroup adjusts to match, as shown in Figures 6-4 and 6-5.

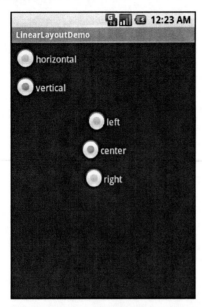

Figure 6-4. *The same application, with the vertical and center radio buttons selected*

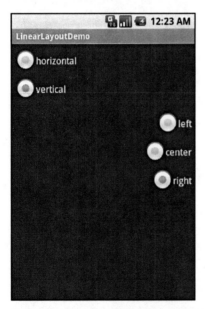

Figure 6-5. *The same application, with the vertical and right radio buttons selected*

All Things Are Relative

RelativeLayout, as the name suggests, lays out widgets based on their relationship to other widgets in the container and the parent container. You can place widget X below and to the left of widget Y, have widget Z's bottom edge align with the bottom of the container, and so on. This is reminiscent of James Elliot's RelativeLayout for use with Java/Swing.

RelativeLayout Concepts and Properties

To make your RelativeLayout work, you need ways to reference other widgets within an XML layout file, plus ways to indicate the relative positions of those widgets.

Positions Relative to Container

The easiest relationships to set up are those that tie a widget's position to that of its container:

- android:layout_alignParentTop: Aligns the widget's top with the top of the container.

- android:layout_alignParentBottom: Aligns the widget's bottom with the bottom of the container.

- android:layout_alignParentLeft: Aligns the widget's left side with the left side of the container.

- android:layout_alignParentRight: Aligns the widget's right side with the right side of the container.

- android:layout_centerHorizontal: Positions the widget horizontally at the center of the container.

- android:layout_centerVertical: Positions the widget vertically at the center of the container.

- android:layout_centerInParent: Positions the widget both horizontally and vertically at the center of the container.

All of these properties take a simple Boolean value (true or false).

> **NOTE:** The padding of the widget is taken into account when performing the various alignments. The alignments are based on the widget's overall cell (combination of its natural space plus the padding).

Relative Notation in Properties

The remaining properties of relevance to RelativeLayout take as a value the identity of a widget in the container. To do this:

- Put identifiers (android:id attributes) on all elements that you will need to address, of the form @+id/....

- Reference other widgets using the same identifier value without the plus sign (@id/...).

For example, if widget A is identified as @+id/widget_a, widget B can refer to widget A in one of its own properties via the identifier @id/widget_a.

Positions Relative to Other Widgets

Four properties control the position of a widget in relation to other widgets:

- android:layout_above: Indicates that the widget should be placed above the widget referenced in the property.

- android:layout_below: Indicates that the widget should be placed below the widget referenced in the property.

- android:layout_toLeftOf: Indicates that the widget should be placed to the left of the widget referenced in the property.

- android:layout_toRightOf: Indicates that the widget should be placed to the right of the widget referenced in the property.

Beyond those four, five additional properties can control one widget's alignment relative to another:

- android:layout_alignTop: Indicates that the widget's top should be aligned with the top of the widget referenced in the property.

- android:layout_alignBottom: Indicates that the widget's bottom should be aligned with the bottom of the widget referenced in the property.

- android:layout_alignLeft: Indicates that the widget's left should be aligned with the left of the widget referenced in the property.

- android:layout_alignRight: Indicates that the widget's right should be aligned with the right of the widget referenced in the property.

- android:layout_alignBaseline: Indicates that the baselines of the two widgets should be aligned (where the baseline is the invisible line that text appears to sit on).

The android:layout_alignBaseline property is useful for aligning labels and fields so that the text appears natural. Since fields have a box around them and labels do not, android:layout_alignTop would align the top of the field's box with the top of the label, which will cause the text of the label to be higher on the screen than the text entered into the field.

So, if you want widget B to be positioned to the right of widget A, in the XML element for widget B, you need to include android:layout_toRightOf = "@id/widget_a" (assuming @id/widget_a is the identity of widget A).

Order of Evaluation

It used to be that Android would use a single pass to process `RelativeLayout`-defined rules. That meant you could not reference a widget (e.g., via `android:layout_above`) until it had been declared in the XML. This made defining some layouts a bit complicated. Starting in Android 1.6, Android uses two passes to process the rules, so you can now safely have forward references to as-yet-undefined widgets.

RelativeLayout Example

Now let's examine a typical "form" with a field, a label, and a pair of buttons labeled OK and Cancel. Here is the XML layout, pulled from the `Containers/Relative` sample project:

```xml
<?xml version="1.0" encoding="utf-8"?>
<RelativeLayout
  xmlns:android="http://schemas.android.com/apk/res/android"
  android:layout_width="fill_parent"
  android:layout_height="wrap_content"
  android:padding="5px">
  <TextView android:id="@+id/label"
    android:layout_width="wrap_content"
    android:layout_height="wrap_content"
    android:text="URL:"
    android:paddingTop="15px"/>
  <EditText
    android:id="@+id/entry"
    android:layout_width="fill_parent"
    android:layout_height="wrap_content"
    android:layout_toRightOf="@id/label"
    android:layout_alignBaseline="@id/label"/>
  <Button
    android:id="@+id/ok"
    android:layout_width="wrap_content"
    android:layout_height="wrap_content"
    android:layout_below="@id/entry"
    android:layout_alignRight="@id/entry"
    android:text="OK" />
  <Button
    android:id="@+id/cancel"
    android:layout_width="wrap_content"
    android:layout_height="wrap_content"
    android:layout_toLeftOf="@id/ok"
    android:layout_alignTop="@id/ok"
    android:text="Cancel" />
</RelativeLayout>
```

First, we open the `RelativeLayout`. In this case, we want to use the full width of the screen (`android:layout_width` = `"fill_parent"`), only as much height as we need (`android:layout_height` = `"wrap_content"`), and have 5 pixels of padding between the boundaries of the container and its contents (`android:padding` = `"5px"`).

Next, we define the label, which is fairly basic, except for its own 15-pixel padding (`android:padding` = `"15px"`). More on that in a moment.

After that, we add in the field. We want the field to be to the right of the label and have the text aligned along the baseline. Also, the field should take up the rest of this "row" in the layout. These requirements are handled by three properties:

- `android:layout_toRightOf = "@id/label"`
- `android:layout_alignBaseline = "@id/label"`
- `android:layout_width = "fill_parent"`

If we skipped the 15-pixel padding on the label, we would find that the top of the field was clipped off. That's because of the 5-pixel padding on the container itself. The `android:layout_alignBaseline = "@id/label"` simply aligns the baselines of the label and field. The label, by default, has its top aligned with the top of the parent. But the label is shorter than the field because of the field's box. Since the field is dependent on the label's position, and the label's position is already defined (because it appeared first in the XML), the field winds up being too high and has the top of its box clipped off by the container's padding.

You may find yourself running into these sorts of problems as you try to get your `RelativeLayout` to behave the way you want it to.

The solution to this conundrum, used in the XML layout shown above, is to give the label 15 pixels' worth of padding on the top This pushes the label down far enough that the field will not get clipped.

The OK button is set to be below the field (`android:layout_below = "@id/entry"`) and have its right side align with the right side of the field (`android:layout_alignRight = "@id/entry"`). The Cancel button is set to be to the left of the OK button (`android:layout_toLeft = "@id/ok"`) and have its top aligned with the OK button (`android:layout_alignTop = "@id/ok"`).

Of course, that 15px of padding is a bit of a hack. A better solution, for Android 1.6 and beyond, is to anchor the `EditText` to the top of the screen and have the `TextView` say it is aligned with the `EditText` widget's baseline, as shown in the following example. (In Android 1.5 and earlier, this was not possible, because of the single-pass rule interpretation mentioned earlier.)

```xml
<?xml version="1.0" encoding="utf-8"?>
<RelativeLayout
        xmlns:android="http://schemas.android.com/apk/res/android"
        android:layout_width="fill_parent"
        android:layout_height="wrap_content"
        android:padding="5px">
    <TextView android:id="@+id/label"
            android:layout_width="wrap_content"
            android:layout_height="wrap_content"
            android:text="URL:"
            android:layout_alignBaseline="@+id/entry"
            android:layout_alignParentLeft="true"/>
    <EditText
            android:id="@id/entry"
            android:layout_width="fill_parent"
            android:layout_height="wrap_content"
```

```
        android:layout_toRightOf="@id/label"
        android:layout_alignParentTop="true"/>
<Button
        android:id="@+id/ok"
        android:layout_width="wrap_content"
        android:layout_height="wrap_content"
        android:layout_below="@id/entry"
        android:layout_alignRight="@id/entry"
        android:text="OK" />
<Button
        android:id="@+id/cancel"
        android:layout_width="wrap_content"
        android:layout_height="wrap_content"
        android:layout_toLeftOf="@id/ok"
        android:layout_alignTop="@id/ok"
        android:text="Cancel" />
</RelativeLayout>
```

With no changes to the autogenerated Java code, the emulator gives us the result
shown in Figure 6-6.

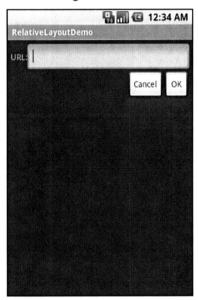

Figure 6-6. *The RelativeLayoutDemo sample application*

Tabula Rasa

If you like HTML tables, spreadsheet grids, and the like, you will appreciate Android's
TableLayout, which allows you to position your widgets in a grid to your specifications.
You control the number of rows and columns, which columns might shrink or stretch to
accommodate their contents, and so on.

TableLayout works in conjunction with TableRow. TableLayout controls the overall behavior of the container, with the widgets themselves poured into one or more TableRow containers, one per row in the grid.

TableLayout Concepts and Properties

For your table layout, you need to figure out how widgets work with rows and columns, plus how to handle widgets that reside outside rows.

Putting Cells in Rows

Rows are declared by you, the developer, by putting widgets as children of a TableRow inside the overall TableLayout. You, therefore, control directly how many rows appear in the table.

The number of columns is determined by Android; you control the number of columns in an indirect fashion. First, there will be at least one column per widget in your longest row. So if you have three rows—one with two widgets, one with three widgets, and one with four widgets—there will be at least four columns. However, a widget can take up more than one column by including the android:layout_span property, indicating the number of columns the widget spans. This is akin to the colspan attribute one finds in table cells in HTML. In this XML layout fragment, the field spans three columns:

```
<TableRow>
  <TextView android:text="URL:" />
  <EditText
    android:id="@+id/entry"
    android:layout_span="3"/>
</TableRow>
```

Ordinarily, widgets are put into the first available column. In the preceding fragment, the label would go in the first column (column 0, as columns are counted starting from 0), and the field would go into a spanned set of three columns (columns 1 through 3). However, you can put a widget into a different column via the android:layout_column property, specifying the 0-based column the widget belongs to:

```
<TableRow>
  <Button
    android:id="@+id/cancel"
    android:layout_column="2"
    android:text="Cancel" />
  <Button android:id="@+id/ok" android:text="OK" />
</TableRow>
```

In the preceding XML layout fragment, the Cancel button goes in the third column (column 2). The OK button then goes into the next available column, which is the fourth column.

Other Children of TableLayout

Normally, TableLayout contains only TableRow elements as immediate children. However, it is possible to put other widgets in between rows. For those widgets, TableLayout behaves a bit like LinearLayout with vertical orientation. The widgets automatically have their width set to fill_parent, so they will fill the same space that the longest row does.

One pattern for this is to use a plain View as a divider. For example, you could use <View android:layout_height = "2px" android:background = "#0000FF" /> for a 2-pixel-high blue bar across the width of the table.

Stretch, Shrink, and Collapse

By default, each column will be sized according to the natural size of the widest widget in that column (taking spanned columns into account). Sometimes, though, that does not work out very well, and you need more control over column behavior.

You can place an android:stretchColumns property on the TableLayout. The value should be a single column number (again, 0-based) or a comma-delimited list of column numbers. Those columns will be stretched to take up any available space on the row. This helps if your content is narrower than the available space.

Conversely, you can place a android:shrinkColumns property on the TableLayout. Again, this should be a single column number or a comma-delimited list of column numbers. The columns listed in this property will try to word-wrap their contents to reduce the effective width of the column. By default, widgets are not word-wrapped. This helps if you have columns with potentially wordy content that might cause some columns to be pushed off the right side of the screen.

You can also leverage an android:collapseColumns property on the TableLayout, again with a column number or comma-delimited list of column numbers. These columns will start out collapsed, meaning that they will be part of the table information but will be invisible. Programmatically, you can collapse and uncollapse columns by calling setColumnCollapsed() on the TableLayout. You might use this to allow users to control which columns are of importance to them and should be shown versus which ones are less important and can be hidden.

You can also control stretching and shrinking at runtime via setColumnStretchable() and setColumnShrinkable().

TableLayout Example

The XML layout fragments shown earlier, when combined, give us a TableLayout rendition of the form we created for RelativeLayout, with the addition of a divider line between the label/field and the two buttons (found in the Containers/Table demo):

```xml
<?xml version="1.0" encoding="utf-8"?>
<TableLayout
  xmlns:android="http://schemas.android.com/apk/res/android"
  android:layout_width="fill_parent"
  android:layout_height="fill_parent"
  android:stretchColumns="1">
  <TableRow>
    <TextView
        android:text="URL:" />
    <EditText android:id="@+id/entry"
      android:layout_span="3"/>
  </TableRow>
  <View
    android:layout_height="2px"
    android:background="#0000FF" />
  <TableRow>
    <Button android:id="@+id/cancel"
      android:layout_column="2"
      android:text="Cancel" />
    <Button android:id="@+id/ok"
      android:text="OK" />
  </TableRow>
</TableLayout>
```

When compiled against the generated Java code and run on the emulator, we get the result shown in Figure 6-7.

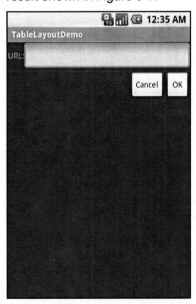

Figure 6-7. *The TableLayoutDemo sample application*

Scrollwork

Phone screens tend to be small, which requires developers to use some tricks to present a lot of information in the limited available space. One trick for doing this is to use scrolling, so only part of the information is visible at one time, and the rest is available via scrolling up or down.

ScrollView is a container that provides scrolling for its contents. You can take a layout that might be too big for some screens, wrap it in a ScrollView, and still use your existing layout logic. It just so happens that the user can see only part of your layout at one time.

For example, here is a ScrollView used in an XML layout file (from the Containers/Scroll demo):

```
<?xml version="1.0" encoding="utf-8"?>
<ScrollView
  xmlns:android="http://schemas.android.com/apk/res/android"
  android:layout_width="fill_parent"
  android:layout_height="wrap_content">
  <TableLayout
    android:layout_width="fill_parent"
    android:layout_height="fill_parent"
    android:stretchColumns="0">
    <TableRow>
      <View
        android:layout_height="80px"
        android:background="#000000"/>
      <TextView android:text="#000000"
        android:paddingLeft="4px"
        android:layout_gravity="center_vertical" />
    </TableRow>
    <TableRow>
      <View
        android:layout_height="80px"
        android:background="#440000" />
      <TextView android:text="#440000"
        android:paddingLeft="4px"
        android:layout_gravity="center_vertical" />
    </TableRow>
    <TableRow>
      <View
        android:layout_height="80px"
        android:background="#884400" />
      <TextView android:text="#884400"
        android:paddingLeft="4px"
        android:layout_gravity="center_vertical" />
    </TableRow>
    <TableRow>
      <View
        android:layout_height="80px"
        android:background="#aa8844" />
      <TextView android:text="#aa8844"
        android:paddingLeft="4px"
        android:layout_gravity="center_vertical" />
    </TableRow>
    <TableRow>
      <View
        android:layout_height="80px"
        android:background="#ffaa88" />
      <TextView android:text="#ffaa88"
```

```
        android:paddingLeft="4px"
        android:layout_gravity="center_vertical" />
    </TableRow>
    <TableRow>
      <View
        android:layout_height="80px"
        android:background="#ffffaa" />
      <TextView android:text="#ffffaa"
        android:paddingLeft="4px"
        android:layout_gravity="center_vertical" />
    </TableRow>
    <TableRow>
      <View
        android:layout_height="80px"
        android:background="#ffffff" />
      <TextView android:text="#ffffff"
        android:paddingLeft="4px"
        android:layout_gravity="center_vertical" />
    </TableRow>
  </TableLayout>
</ScrollView>
```

Without the ScrollView, the table would take up at least 560 pixels (seven rows at 80 pixels each, based on the View declarations). There may be some devices with screens capable of showing that much information, but many will be smaller. The ScrollView lets us keep the table as is, but present only part of it at a time.

On the stock Android emulator, when the activity is first viewed, you see the result shown in Figure 6-8.

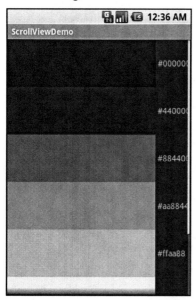

Figure 6-8. *The ScrollViewDemo sample application*

Notice how only five rows and part of the sixth are visible. By pressing the up/down buttons on the D-pad, you can scroll up and down to see the remaining rows. Also note how the right side of the content is clipped by the scrollbar. Be sure to put some padding on that side or otherwise ensure your content does not get clipped in this fashion.

Android 1.5 introduced `HorizontalScrollView`, which works like `ScrollView`, but horizontally. This can be useful for forms that might be too wide rather than too tall. Note that neither `ScrollView` nor `HorizontalScrollView` will give you bidirectional scrolling; you need to choose vertical or horizontal.

Chapter 7

Using Selection Widgets

Back in Chapter 5, you saw how fields could have constraints placed on them to limit possible input, such as only digits. These sorts of constraints help users "get it right" when entering information, particularly on mobile devices with cramped keyboards.

Of course, the ultimate in constrained input is to allow selection only from a set of items, such as a radio button group (also discussed in Chapter 5). Classic UI toolkits have list boxes, combo boxes, drop-down lists, and the like for that very purpose. Android provides many of the same sorts of widgets, plus others of particular interest for mobile devices (e.g., the Gallery for examining saved photos).

Moreover, Android offers a flexible framework for determining which choices are available in these widgets. Specifically, Android offers a framework of data adapters that provide a common interface for selection lists, ranging from static arrays to database contents. Selection views—widgets for presenting lists of choices—are handed an adapter to supply the actual choices.

This chapter begins with a look at Android's adapters, and then introduces its selection widgets.

Adapting to the Circumstances

In the abstract, adapters provide a common interface to multiple disparate APIs. More specifically, in Android's case, adapters provide a common interface to the data model behind a selection-style widget, such as a list box. This use of Java interfaces is fairly common (e.g., Java/Swing's model adapters for JTable), and Java is far from the only environment offering this sort of abstraction (e.g., Flex's XML data-binding framework accepts XML inlined as static data or retrieved from the Internet).

Android's adapters are responsible for providing the roster of data for a selection widget, as well as for converting individual elements of data into specific views to be displayed inside the selection widget. The latter facet of the adapter system may sound a little odd, but in reality, it is not that different from other GUI toolkits' ways of overriding default display behavior. For example, in Java/Swing, if you want a JList-backed list box to actually be a checklist (where individual rows are a check box plus label, and clicks adjust the state of the check box), you inevitably wind up calling setCellRenderer() to supply your own ListCellRenderer, which in turn converts strings for the list into JCheckBox-plus-JLabel composite widgets.

The easiest adapter to use is ArrayAdapter. All you need to do is wrap one of these around a Java array or java.util.List instance, and you have a fully functioning adapter:

```
String[] items={"this", "is", "a",
                "really", "silly", "list"};
new ArrayAdapter<String>(this,
  android.R.layout.simple_list_item_1, items);
```

The ArrayAdapter constructor takes three parameters:

- The Context to use (typically this will be your activity instance)

- The resource ID of a view to use (such as a built-in system resource ID, as shown in the preceding example)

- The actual array or list of items to show

By default, the ArrayAdapter will invoke toString() on the objects in the list and wrap each of those strings in the view designated by the supplied resource. android.R.layout.simple_list_item_1 simply turns those strings into TextView objects. Those TextView widgets, in turn, will be shown in the list, spinner, or whatever widget uses this ArrayAdapter. In Chapter 8, you'll see how to subclass Adapter and override row creation, to give you greater control over how rows appear.

Here are two other adapters in Android that you may want to use:

- CursorAdapter: Converts a Cursor, typically from a content provider, into something that can be displayed in a selection view. (We'll look at CursorAdapter in greater detail in Chapter 22, which covers databases.)

- SimpleAdapter: Converts data found in XML resources.

Lists of Naughty and Nice

The classic list box widget in Android is known as ListView. Include one of these in your layout, invoke setAdapter() to supply your data and child views, and attach a listener via setOnItemSelectedListener() to find out when the selection has changed. With that, you have a fully functioning list box.

However, if your activity is dominated by a single list, you might consider creating your activity as a subclass of ListActivity, rather than the regular Activity base class. If your main view is just the list, you do not even need to supply a layout; ListActivity will construct a full-screen list for you. If you do want to customize the layout, you can, as long as you identify your ListView as @android:id/list, so ListActivity knows which widget is the main list for the activity.

For example, here is a layout pulled from the Selection/List sample project, which is simply a list with a label on top to show the current selection:

```xml
<?xml version="1.0" encoding="utf-8"?>
<LinearLayout
  xmlns:android="http://schemas.android.com/apk/res/android"
  android:orientation="vertical"
  android:layout_width="fill_parent"
  android:layout_height="fill_parent" >
  <TextView
    android:id="@+id/selection"
    android:layout_width="fill_parent"
    android:layout_height="wrap_content"/>
  <ListView
    android:id="@android:id/list"
    android:layout_width="fill_parent"
    android:layout_height="fill_parent"
    android:drawSelectorOnTop="false"
    />
</LinearLayout>
```

The Java code to configure the list and connect the list with the label is as follows:

```java
public class ListViewDemo extends ListActivity {
  TextView selection;
  String[] items={"lorem", "ipsum", "dolor", "sit", "amet",
          "consectetuer", "adipiscing", "elit", "morbi", "vel",
          "ligula", "vitae", "arcu", "aliquet", "mollis",
          "etiam", "vel", "erat", "placerat", "ante",
          "porttitor", "sodales", "pellentesque", "augue", "purus"};

  @Override
  public void onCreate(Bundle icicle) {
    super.onCreate(icicle);
    setContentView(R.layout.main);
    setListAdapter(new ArrayAdapter<String>(this,
                      android.R.layout.simple_list_item_1,
                      items));
    selection=(TextView)findViewById(R.id.selection);
  }

  public void onListItemClick(ListView parent, View v, int position,
                              long id) {
    selection.setText(items[position]);
  }
}
```

With ListActivity, you can set the list adapter via setListAdapter()—in this case, providing an ArrayAdapter wrapping an array of nonsense strings. To find out when the list selection changes, override onListItemClick() and take appropriate steps based on the supplied child view and position—in this case, updating the label with the text for that position. The results are shown in Figure 7–1.

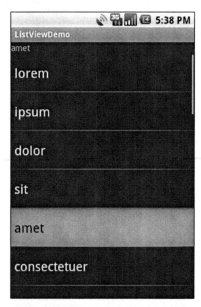

Figure 7–1. *The ListViewDemo sample application*

The second parameter to our ArrayAdapter, android.R.layout.simple_list_item_1, controls the appearance of the rows. The value used in the preceding example provides the standard Android list row: big font, a lot of padding, and white text.

By default, ListView is set up to simply collect clicks on list entries. If you want a list that tracks a user's selection, or possibly multiple selections, ListView can handle that as well, but it requires a few changes:

- Call setChoiceMode() on the ListView in Java code to set the choice mode, supplying either CHOICE_MODE_SINGLE or CHOICE_MODE_MULTIPLE as the value. You can get your ListView from a ListActivity via getListView().

- Rather than using android.R.layout.simple_list_item_1 as the layout for the list rows in your ArrayAdapter constructor, use either android.R.layout.simple_list_item_single_choice or android.R.layout.simple_list_item_multiple_choice for single-choice (see Figure 7–2) or multiple-choice (see Figure 7–3) lists.

- To determine which ones the user checked, call getCheckedItemPositions() on your ListView.

Figure 7–2. *Single-select mode*

Figure 7–3. *Multiple-select mode*

Spin Control

In Android, the Spinner is the equivalent of the drop-down selector you might find in other toolkits (e.g., JComboBox in Java/Swing). Pressing the center button on the D-pad pops up a selection dialog box from which the user can choose an item. You basically get the ability to select from a list without taking up all the screen space of a ListView, at the cost of an extra click or screen tap to make a change.

As with ListView, you provide the adapter for data and child views via setAdapter(), and hook in a listener object for selections via setOnItemSelectedListener().

If you want to tailor the view used when displaying the drop-down perspective, you need to configure the adapter, not the Spinner widget. Use the setDropDownViewResource() method to supply the resource ID of the view to use.

For example, culled from the Selection/Spinner sample project, here is an XML layout for a simple view with a Spinner:

```xml
<?xml version="1.0" encoding="utf-8"?>
<LinearLayout
  xmlns:android="http://schemas.android.com/apk/res/android"
  android:orientation="vertical"
  android:layout_width="fill_parent"
  android:layout_height="fill_parent"
  >
  <TextView
    android:id="@+id/selection"
    android:layout_width="fill_parent"
    android:layout_height="wrap_content"
    />
  <Spinner android:id="@+id/spinner"
    android:layout_width="fill_parent"
    android:layout_height="wrap_content"
    android:drawSelectorOnTop="true"
  />
</LinearLayout>
```

This is the same view as shown in the previous section, but with a Spinner instead of a ListView. The Spinner property android:drawSelectorOnTop controls whether the arrow is drawn on the selector button on the right side of the Spinner UI.

To populate and use the Spinner, we need some Java code:

```java
public class SpinnerDemo extends Activity
  implements AdapterView.OnItemSelectedListener {
  TextView selection;
  String[] items={"lorem", "ipsum", "dolor", "sit", "amet",
        "consectetuer", "adipiscing", "elit", "morbi", "vel",
        "ligula", "vitae", "arcu", "aliquet", "mollis",
        "etiam", "vel", "erat", "placerat", "ante",
        "porttitor", "sodales", "pellentesque", "augue", "purus"};

  @Override
  public void onCreate(Bundle icicle) {
    super.onCreate(icicle);
    setContentView(R.layout.main);
    selection=(TextView)findViewById(R.id.selection);

    Spinner spin=(Spinner)findViewById(R.id.spinner);
    spin.setOnItemSelectedListener(this);
```

```
    ArrayAdapter<String> aa=new ArrayAdapter<String>(this,
                          android.R.layout.simple_spinner_item,
                          items);

  aa.setDropDownViewResource(
    android.R.layout.simple_spinner_dropdown_item);
  spin.setAdapter(aa);
}

public void onItemSelected(AdapterView<?> parent,
                        View v, int position, long id) {
  selection.setText(items[position]);
}

public void onNothingSelected(AdapterView<?> parent) {
  selection.setText("");
  }
}
```

Here, we attach the activity itself as the selection listener
(spin.setOnItemSelectedListener(this)). This works because the activity implements
the OnItemSelectedListener interface. We configure the adapter not only with the list of
fake words, but also with a specific resource to use for the drop-down view (via
aa.setDropDownViewResource()). Also notice the use of
android.R.layout.simple_spinner_item as the built-in View for showing items in the
spinner itself.

Finally, we implement the callbacks required by OnItemSelectedListener to adjust the
selection label based on user input. Figures 7–4 and 7–5 show the results.

Figure 7–4. *The SpinnerDemo sample application, as initially launched*

Figure 7–5. *The same application, with the spinner drop-down list displayed*

Grid Your Lions (or Something Like That...)

As the name suggests, GridView gives you a two-dimensional grid of items from which to choose. You have moderate control over the number and size of the columns; the number of rows is dynamically determined based on the number of items the supplied adapter says are available for viewing.

When combined, a few properties determine the number of columns and their sizes:

- android:numColumns: Specifies how many columns there are, or, if you supply a value of auto_fit, Android will compute the number of columns based on the available space and the following properties.

- android:verticalSpacing and android:horizontalSpacing: Indicate how much whitespace there should be between items in the grid.

- android:columnWidth: Indicates how many pixels wide each column should be.

- android:stretchMode: Indicates, for grids with auto_fit for android:numColumns, what should happen for any available space not taken up by columns or spacing. This can be columnWidth, to have the columns take up available space, or spacingWidth, to have the whitespace between columns absorb extra space.

For example, suppose the screen is 320 pixels wide, and you have android:columnWidth set to 100px and android:horizontalSpacing set to 5px. Three columns would use 310 pixels (three columns of 100 pixels and two whitespace areas of 5 pixels). With android:stretchMode set to columnWidth, the three columns will each expand by 3 to 4 pixels to use up the remaining 10 pixels. With android:stretchMode set to spacingWidth, the two whitespace areas will each grow by 5 pixels to consume the remaining 10 pixels.

Otherwise, the GridView works much like any other selection widget: use setAdapter() to provide the data and child views, invoke setOnItemSelectedListener() to register a selection listener, and so on.

For example, here is a XML layout from the Selection/Grid sample project, showing a GridView configuration:

```xml
<?xml version="1.0" encoding="utf-8"?>
<LinearLayout
  xmlns:android="http://schemas.android.com/apk/res/android"
  android:orientation="vertical"
  android:layout_width="fill_parent"
  android:layout_height="fill_parent"
  >
  <TextView
    android:id="@+id/selection"
    android:layout_width="fill_parent"
    android:layout_height="wrap_content"
    />
  <GridView
    android:id="@+id/grid"
    android:layout_width="fill_parent"
    android:layout_height="fill_parent"
    android:verticalSpacing="35px"
    android:horizontalSpacing="5px"
    android:numColumns="auto_fit"
    android:columnWidth="100px"
    android:stretchMode="columnWidth"
    android:gravity="center"
    />
</LinearLayout>
```

For this grid, we take up the entire screen except for what our selection label requires. The number of columns is computed by Android (android:numColumns = "auto_fit") based on 5-pixel horizontal spacing (android:horizontalSpacing = "5px") and 100-pixel columns (android:columnWidth = "100px"), with the columns absorbing any "slop" width left over (android:stretchMode = "columnWidth").

The Java code to configure the GridView is as follows:

```java
public class GridDemo extends Activity
  implements AdapterView.OnItemSelectedListener {
  TextView selection;
  String[] items={"lorem", "ipsum", "dolor", "sit", "amet",
          "consectetuer", "adipiscing", "elit", "morbi", "vel",
          "ligula", "vitae", "arcu", "aliquet", "mollis",
          "etiam", "vel", "erat", "placerat", "ante",
          "porttitor", "sodales", "pellentesque", "augue", "purus"};

  @Override
  public void onCreate(Bundle icicle) {
```

```
    super.onCreate(icicle);
    setContentView(R.layout.main);
    selection=(TextView)findViewById(R.id.selection);

    GridView g=(GridView) findViewById(R.id.grid);
    g.setAdapter(new FunnyLookingAdapter(this,
                      android.R.layout.simple_list_item_1,
                      items));
    g.setOnItemSelectedListener(this);
  }

  public void onItemSelected(AdapterView<?> parent, View v,
                              int position, long id) {
    selection.setText(items[position]);
  }

  public void onNothingSelected(AdapterView<?> parent) {
    selection.setText("");
  }

  private class FunnyLookingAdapter extends ArrayAdapter {
    Context ctxt;

    FunnyLookingAdapter(Context ctxt, int resource,
                        String[] items) {
      super(ctxt, resource, items);

      this.ctxt=ctxt;
    }

    public View getView(int position, View convertView,
                        ViewGroup parent) {
      TextView label=(TextView)convertView;

      if (convertView==null) {
        convertView=new TextView(ctxt);
        label=(TextView)convertView;
      }

      label.setText(items[position]);

      return(convertView);
    }
  }
}
```

For the grid cells, rather than using autogenerated TextView widgets as in the previous sections, we create our own views, by subclassing ArrayAdapter and overriding getView(). In this case, we wrap the funny-looking strings in our own TextView widgets, just to be different. If getView() receives a TextView, we just reset its text; otherwise, we create a new TextView instance and populate it.

With the 35-pixel vertical spacing from the XML layout (android:verticalSpacing = "35"), the grid overflows the boundaries of the emulator's screen, as shown in Figures 7–6 and 7–7.

Figure 7–6. *The GridDemo sample application, as initially launched*

Figure 7–7. *The same application, scrolled to the bottom of the grid*

Fields: Now with 35% Less Typing!

The AutoCompleteTextView is sort of a hybrid between the EditText (field) and the Spinner. With autocompletion, as the user types, the text is treated as a prefix filter, comparing the entered text as a prefix against a list of candidates. Matches are shown in a selection list that, as with Spinner, drops down from the field. The user can either type the full entry (e.g., something not in the list) or choose an item from the list to be the value of the field.

AutoCompleteTextView subclasses EditText, so you can configure all the standard look-and-feel aspects, such as font face and color. In addition, AutoCompleteTextView has an android:completionThreshold property, to indicate the minimum number of characters a user must enter before the list filtering begins.

You can give AutoCompleteTextView an adapter containing the list of candidate values via setAdapter(). However, since the user could type something that is not in the list, AutoCompleteTextView does not support selection listeners. Instead, you can register a TextWatcher, as you can with any EditText widget, to be notified when the text changes. These events will occur either because of manual typing or from a selection from the drop-down list.

The following is a familiar XML layout, this time containing an AutoCompleteTextView (pulled from the Selection/AutoComplete sample application):

```xml
<?xml version="1.0" encoding="utf-8"?>
<LinearLayout
  xmlns:android="http://schemas.android.com/apk/res/android"
  android:orientation="vertical"
  android:layout_width="fill_parent"
  android:layout_height="fill_parent"
  >
  <TextView
    android:id="@+id/selection"
    android:layout_width="fill_parent"
    android:layout_height="wrap_content"
    />
  <AutoCompleteTextView android:id="@+id/edit"
      android:layout_width="fill_parent"
      android:layout_height="wrap_content"
      android:completionThreshold="3"/>
</LinearLayout>
```

The corresponding Java code is as follows:

```java
public class AutoCompleteDemo extends Activity
  implements TextWatcher {
  TextView selection;
  AutoCompleteTextView edit;
  String[] items={"lorem", "ipsum", "dolor", "sit", "amet",
          "consectetuer", "adipiscing", "elit", "morbi", "vel",
          "ligula", "vitae", "arcu", "aliquet", "mollis",
          "etiam", "vel", "erat", "placerat", "ante",
          "porttitor", "sodales", "pellentesque", "augue", "purus"};

  @Override
  public void onCreate(Bundle icicle) {
    super.onCreate(icicle);
    setContentView(R.layout.main);
    selection=(TextView)findViewById(R.id.selection);
    edit=(AutoCompleteTextView)findViewById(R.id.edit);
```

```
      edit.addTextChangedListener(this);

      edit.setAdapter(new ArrayAdapter<String>(this,
                       android.R.layout.simple_dropdown_item_1line,
                       items));
  }

  public void onTextChanged(CharSequence s, int start, int before,
                            int count) {
    selection.setText(edit.getText());
  }

  public void beforeTextChanged(CharSequence s, int start,
                                int count, int after) {
    // needed for interface, but not used
  }

  public void afterTextChanged(Editable s) {
    // needed for interface, but not used
  }
}
```

This time, our activity implements TextWatcher, which means our callbacks are onTextChanged() and beforeTextChanged(). In this case, we are interested in only the former, and we update the selection label to match the AutoCompleteTextView's current contents.

Figures 7–8, 7–9, and 7–10 show the results.

Figure 7–8. *The AutoCompleteDemo sample application, as initially launched*

Figure 7–9. *The same application, after a few matching letters were entered, showing the autocomplete drop-down*

Figure 7–10. *The same application, after the autocomplete value was selected*

Galleries, Give or Take the Art

The Gallery widget is not one ordinarily found in GUI toolkits. It is, in effect, a list box that is horizontally laid out. One choice follows the next across the horizontal plane, with the currently selected item highlighted. On an Android device, the user rotates through the options via the left and right D-pad buttons.

Compared to the ListView, the Gallery takes up less screen space, while still showing multiple choices at one time (assuming they are short enough). Compared to the Spinner, the Gallery always shows more than one choice at a time.

The quintessential example use for the Gallery is image preview. Given a collection of photos or icons, the Gallery lets people preview the pictures in the process of choosing one.

Code-wise, the Gallery works much like a Spinner or GridView. In your XML layout, you have a few properties at your disposal:

- android:spacing: Controls the number of pixels between entries in the list.

- android:spinnerSelector: Controls what is used to indicate a selection. This can either be a reference to a Drawable (see Chapter 20) or an RGB value in #AARRGGBB or similar notation.

- android:drawSelectorOnTop: Indicates if the selection bar (or Drawable) should be drawn before (false) or after (true) drawing the selected child. If you choose true, be sure that your selector has sufficient transparency to show the child through the selector; otherwise, users will not be able to read the selection.

Chapter 8

Getting Fancy with Lists

The humble `ListView` is one of the most important widgets in all of Android, simply because it is used so frequently. Whether choosing a contact to call, an e-mail message to forward, or an e-book to read, `ListView` widgets are employed in a wide range of activities. Of course, it would be nice if they were more than just plain text. The good news is that Android lists can be as fancy as you want (within the limitations of a mobile device's screen, obviously). However, making them fancy takes some work, as you will learn in this chapter.

Getting to First Base

The classic Android `ListView` is a plain list of text—solid but uninspiring. We hand the `ListView` a bunch of words in an array, and then tell Android to use a simple built-in layout for pouring those words into a list.

However, you can have a list whose rows are made up of icons, icons and text, check boxes and text, or whatever you want. It is merely a matter of supplying enough data to the adapter and helping the adapter to create a richer set of `View` objects for each row.

For example, suppose we want a `ListView` whose entries are made up of an icon, followed by some text. We could construct a layout for the row that looks like this, found in the `FancyLists/Static` sample project:

```xml
<?xml version="1.0" encoding="utf-8"?>
<LinearLayout xmlns:android="http://schemas.android.com/apk/res/android"
  android:layout_width="fill_parent"
  android:layout_height="wrap_content"
  android:orientation="horizontal"
>
  <ImageView
    android:id="@+id/icon"
    android:layout_width="22px"
    android:paddingLeft="2px"
    android:paddingRight="2px"
    android:paddingTop="2px"
    android:layout_height="wrap_content"
    android:src="@drawable/ok"
```

```
    />
    <TextView
      android:id="@+id/label"
      android:layout_width="wrap_content"
      android:layout_height="wrap_content"
      android:textSize="44sp"
    />
</LinearLayout>
```

This layout uses a LinearLayout to set up a row, with the icon on the left and the text (in a nice big font) on the right.

However, by default, Android has no idea that we want to use this layout with our ListView. To make the connection, we need to supply our Adapter with the resource ID of our custom layout:

```
public class StaticDemo extends ListActivity {
  TextView selection;
  String[] items={"lorem", "ipsum", "dolor", "sit", "amet",
          "consectetuer", "adipiscing", "elit", "morbi", "vel",
          "ligula", "vitae", "arcu", "aliquet", "mollis",
          "etiam", "vel", "erat", "placerat", "ante",
          "porttitor", "sodales", "pellentesque", "augue",
          "purus"};

  @Override
  public void onCreate(Bundle icicle) {
    super.onCreate(icicle);
    setContentView(R.layout.main);
    setListAdapter(new ArrayAdapter<String>(this,
                     R.layout.row, R.id.label,
                     items));
    selection=(TextView)findViewById(R.id.selection);
  }

  public void onListItemClick(ListView parent, View v,
                       int position,  long id) {
    selection.setText(items[position]);
  }
}
```

This follows the general structure for the previous ListView sample. The key difference is that we have told ArrayAdapter that we want to use our custom layout (R.layout.row) and that the TextView where the word should go is known as R.id.label within that custom layout.

> **NOTE:** Remember that to reference a layout (row.xml), use R.layout as a prefix on the base name of the layout XML file (R.layout.row).

The result is a ListView with icons down the left side. In this case, all the icons are the same, as shown in Figure 8–1.

Figure 8–1. *The StaticDemo application*

A Dynamic Presentation

Supplying an alternate layout to use for rows, as in the preceding example, handles simple cases very nicely. However, it falls down when you have more complicated scenarios for your rows, such as the following:

■ Not every row uses the same layout (e.g., some rows one line of text and others have two).

■ You need to configure the widgets in the rows (e.g., use different icons for different cases).

In those cases, the better option is to create your own subclass of your desired Adapter, override getView(), and construct your rows yourself. The getView() method is responsible for returning a View, representing the row for the supplied position in the adapter data.

As an example, let's rework the code shown in the previous section to use getView(), so we can show different icons for rows. We'll use one icon for short words and one for long words (from the FancyLists/Dynamic sample project).

```
public class DynamicDemo extends ListActivity {
  TextView selection;
  String[] items={"lorem", "ipsum", "dolor", "sit", "amet",
          "consectetuer", "adipiscing", "elit", "morbi", "vel",
          "ligula", "vitae", "arcu", "aliquet", "mollis",
          "etiam", "vel", "erat", "placerat", "ante",
          "porttitor", "sodales", "pellentesque", "augue",
          "purus"};
```

```java
@Override
public void onCreate(Bundle icicle) {
  super.onCreate(icicle);
  setContentView(R.layout.main);
  setListAdapter(new IconicAdapter());
  selection=(TextView)findViewById(R.id.selection);
}

public void onListItemClick(ListView parent, View v,
                            int position, long id) {
  selection.setText(items[position]);
}

class IconicAdapter extends ArrayAdapter {
  IconicAdapter() {
    super(DynamicDemo.this, R.layout.row, items);
  }

  public View getView(int position, View convertView,
                      ViewGroup parent) {
    LayoutInflater inflater=getLayoutInflater();
    View row=inflater.inflate(R.layout.row, parent, false);
    TextView label=(TextView)row.findViewById(R.id.label);

    label.setText(items[position]);

    ImageView icon=(ImageView)row.findViewById(R.id.icon);

    if (items[position].length()>4) {
      icon.setImageResource(R.drawable.delete);
    }
    else {
      icon.setImageResource(R.drawable.ok);
    }

    return(row);
  }
}
}
```

The theory is that we override getView() and return rows based on which object is being displayed, where the object is indicated by a position index into the Adapter. However, if you look at the preceding implementation, you will see a reference to a LayoutInflater class, which requires a bit of an explanation.

In this case, "inflation" means the act of converting an XML layout specification into the actual tree of View objects the XML represents. This is undoubtedly a tedious bit of code: take an element, create an instance of the specified View class, walk the attributes, convert those into property setter calls, iterate over all child elements, lather, rinse, and repeat. The good news is that the fine folks on the Android team wrapped up all that into a class called LayoutInflater, which we can use ourselves. For our fancy list, we want to inflate a View for each row shown in the list, so we can use the convenient shorthand of the XML layout to describe what the rows are supposed to look like.

In our example, we inflate the R.layout.row layout we created. This gives us a View object, which, in reality, is our LinearLayout with an ImageView and a TextView, just as R.layout.row specifies. However, rather than needing to create all those objects ourselves and wire them together, the XML and LayoutInflater handle the "heavy lifting" for us.

So, we have used LayoutInflater to give us a View representing the row. This row is "empty," since the static layout file has no idea what actual data goes into the row. It is our job to customize and populate the row as we see fit before returning it, as follows:

- Fill in the text label for our label widget, using the word at the supplied position.

- See if the word is longer than four characters and, if so, find our ImageView icon widget and replace the stock resource with a different one.

Now, we have a ListView with different icons based on the context of the specific entry in the list, as shown in Figure 8–2.

Figure 8–2. *The DynamicDemo application*

Obviously, this was a fairly contrived example, but you can see where this technique could be used to customize rows based on any sort of criteria, such as other columns in a returned Cursor.

Better. Stronger. Faster.

The getView() implementation shown in the preceding section works, but it's inefficient. Every time the user scrolls, we must create a bunch of new View objects to accommodate the newly shown rows. This is bad.

It might be bad for the immediate user experience, if the list appears to be sluggish. More likely, though, it will be bad due to battery usage—every bit of CPU that is used eats up the battery. This is compounded by the extra work the garbage collector needs to do to get rid of all those extra objects we create. So the less efficient our code, the more quickly the phone's battery will be drained, and the less happy the user will be. And we want happy users, right?

So, let's take a look at a few tricks to make your fancy ListView widgets more efficient.

Using convertView

The getView() method receives, as one of its parameters, a View named, by convention, convertView. Sometimes, convertView will be null. In those cases, you need to create a new row View from scratch (e.g., via inflation), just as in the previous example. However, if convertView is not null, then it is actually one of your previously created View objects. This will happen primarily when the user scrolls the ListView. As new rows appear, Android will attempt to recycle the views of the rows that scrolled off the other end of the list, to save you from needing to rebuild them from scratch.

Assuming that each of your rows has the same basic structure, you can use findViewById() to get at the individual widgets that make up your row and change their contents, and then return convertView from getView(), rather than create a whole new row. For example, here is the getView() implementation from the previous example, now optimized via convertView (from the FancyLists/Recycling project):

```
public class RecyclingDemo extends ListActivity {
  TextView selection;
  String[] items={"lorem", "ipsum", "dolor", "sit", "amet",
        "consectetuer", "adipiscing", "elit", "morbi", "vel",
        "ligula", "vitae", "arcu", "aliquet", "mollis",
        "etiam", "vel", "erat", "placerat", "ante",
        "porttitor", "sodales", "pellentesque", "augue",
        "purus"};

  @Override
  public void onCreate(Bundle icicle) {
    super.onCreate(icicle);
    setContentView(R.layout.main);
    setListAdapter(new IconicAdapter());
    selection=(TextView)findViewById(R.id.selection);
  }

  public void onListItemClick(ListView parent, View v,
                              int position, long id) {
    selection.setText(items[position]);
```

```
}

class IconicAdapter extends ArrayAdapter {
  IconicAdapter() {
    super(RecyclingDemo.this, R.layout.row, items);
  }

  public View getView(int position, View convertView,
                      ViewGroup parent) {
    View row=convertView;

    if (row==null) {
      LayoutInflater inflater=getLayoutInflater();

      row=inflater.inflate(R.layout.row, parent, false);
    }

    TextView label=(TextView)row.findViewById(R.id.label);

    label.setText(items[position]);

    ImageView icon=(ImageView)row.findViewById(R.id.icon);

    if (items[position].length()>4) {
      icon.setImageResource(R.drawable.delete);
    }
    else {
      icon.setImageResource(R.drawable.ok);
    }

    return(row);
  }
}
}
```

Here, we check to see if the convertView is null. If so, we inflate our row; otherwise, we just reuse it. The work to fill in the contents (icon image and text) is the same in either case. The advantage is that we avoid the potentially expensive inflation step.

Using the Holder Pattern

Another somewhat expensive operation commonly done with fancy views is calling findViewById(). This dives into your inflated row and pulls out widgets by their assigned identifiers, so you can customize the widget contents (e.g., to change the text of a TextView or change the icon in an ImageView). Since findViewById() can find widgets anywhere in the tree of children of the row's root View, this could take a fair number of instructions to execute, particularly if you need to find the same widgets repeatedly.

In some GUI toolkits, this problem is avoided by having the composite View objects, like rows, be declared totally in program code (in this case, Java). Then accessing individual widgets is merely a matter of calling a getter or accessing a field. And you can certainly do that with Android, but the code gets rather verbose.

What would be nice is a way where you can still use the layout XML, yet cache your row's key child widgets so you need to find them only once. That's where the holder pattern comes into play. All View objects have getTag() and setTag() methods. These allow you to associate an arbitrary object with the widget. The holder pattern uses that "tag" to hold an object that, in turn, holds each of the child widgets of interest. By attaching that holder to the row View, every time you use the row, you already have access to the child widgets you care about, without needing to call findViewById() again.

So, let's take a look at one of these holder classes (taken from the FancyLists/ViewWrapper sample project):

```
class ViewWrapper {
  View base;
  TextView label=null;
  ImageView icon=null;

  ViewWrapper(View base) {
    this.base=base;
  }

  TextView getLabel() {
    if (label==null) {
      label=(TextView)base.findViewById(R.id.label);
    }

    return(label);
  }

  ImageView getIcon() {
    if (icon==null) {
      icon=(ImageView)base.findViewById(R.id.icon);
    }

    return(icon);
  }
}
```

ViewWrapper not only holds onto the child widgets, but it also lazy-finds the child widgets. If you create a wrapper and don't need a specific child, you never go through the findViewById() operation for it, and never have to pay for those CPU cycles.

The holder pattern has some other advantages:

- It allows you to consolidate all your per-widget type casting in one place, rather than needing to cast everywhere you call findViewById().

- You could use it to track other information about the row, such as state information you are not yet ready to flush to the underlying model.

Using ViewWrapper is a matter of creating an instance whenever we inflate a row and attaching said instance to the row View via setTag(), as shown in this rewrite of getView():

```
public class ViewWrapperDemo extends ListActivity {
  TextView selection;
  String[] items={"lorem", "ipsum", "dolor", "sit", "amet",
          "consectetuer", "adipiscing", "elit", "morbi", "vel",
          "ligula", "vitae", "arcu", "aliquet", "mollis",
          "etiam", "vel", "erat", "placerat", "ante",
          "porttitor", "sodales", "pellentesque", "augue",
          "purus"};

  @Override
  public void onCreate(Bundle icicle) {
    super.onCreate(icicle);
    setContentView(R.layout.main);
    setListAdapter(new IconicAdapter());
    selection=(TextView)findViewById(R.id.selection);
  }

  private String getModel(int position) {
    return(((IconicAdapter)getListAdapter()).getItem(position));
  }

  public void onListItemClick(ListView parent, View v,
                          int position, long id) {
   selection.setText(getModel(position));
  }

  class IconicAdapter extends ArrayAdapter<String> {
    IconicAdapter() {
      super(ViewWrapperDemo.this, R.layout.row, items);
    }

    public View getView(int position, View convertView,
                    ViewGroup parent) {
      View row=convertView;
      ViewWrapper wrapper=null;

      if (row==null) {
        LayoutInflater inflater=getLayoutInflater();

        row=inflater.inflate(R.layout.row, parent, false);
        wrapper=new ViewWrapper(row);
        row.setTag(wrapper);
      }
      else {
        wrapper=(ViewWrapper)row.getTag();
      }

      wrapper.getLabel().setText(getModel(position));

      if (getModel(position).length()>4) {
        wrapper.getIcon().setImageResource(R.drawable.delete);
```

```
      }
      else {
        wrapper.getIcon().setImageResource(R.drawable.ok);
      }

      return(row);
    }
  }
}
```

Just as we check `convertView` to see if it is null in order to create the row `View` objects as needed, we also pull out (or create) the corresponding row's `ViewWrapper`. Then accessing the child widgets is merely a matter of calling their associated methods on the wrapper.

Making a List...

Lists with pretty icons next to them are all fine and well. But can we create `ListView` widgets whose rows contain interactive child widgets instead of just passive widgets like `TextView` and `ImageView`? For example, there is a `RatingBar` widget that allows users to assign a rating by clicking on a set of star icons. Could we combine the `RatingBar` with text in order to allow people to scroll a list of, say, songs and rate them directly inside the list?

There is good news and bad news.

The good news is that interactive widgets in rows work just fine. The bad news is that it is a little tricky, specifically when it comes to taking action when the interactive widget's state changes (e.g., a value is typed into a field). You need to store that state somewhere, since your `RatingBar` widget will be recycled when the `ListView` is scrolled. You need to be able to set the `RatingBar` state based on the actual word you are viewing as the `RatingBar` is recycled, and you need to save the state when it changes so it can be restored when this particular row is scrolled back into view.

What makes this interesting is that, by default, the `RatingBar` has absolutely no idea which model in the `ArrayAdapter` it is looking at. After all, the `RatingBar` is just a widget, used in a row of a `ListView`. You need to teach the rows which model they are currently displaying, so when their rating bar is checked, they know which model's state to modify.

So, let's see how this is done, using the activity in the `FancyLists/RateList` sample project. We'll use the same basic classes as our previous demo, showing a list of nonsense words that you can rate. In addition, words given a top rating are put in all uppercase.

```
public class RateListDemo extends ListActivity {
  String[] items={"lorem", "ipsum", "dolor", "sit", "amet",
          "consectetuer", "adipiscing", "elit", "morbi", "vel",
          "ligula", "vitae", "arcu", "aliquet", "mollis",
          "etiam", "vel", "erat", "placerat", "ante",
          "porttitor", "sodales", "pellentesque", "augue",
          "purus"};
```

```
@Override
public void onCreate(Bundle icicle) {
  super.onCreate(icicle);

  ArrayList<RowModel> list=new ArrayList<RowModel>();

  for (String s : items) {
    list.add(new RowModel(s));
  }

  setListAdapter(new RatingAdapter(list));
}

private RowModel getModel(int position) {
  return(((RatingAdapter)getListAdapter()).getItem(position));
}

class RatingAdapter extends ArrayAdapter<RowModel> {
  RatingAdapter(ArrayList<RowModel> list) {
    super(RateListDemo.this, R.layout.row, list);
  }

  public View getView(int position, View convertView,
                      ViewGroup parent) {
    View row=convertView;
    ViewWrapper wrapper;
    RatingBar rate;

    if (row==null) {
      LayoutInflater inflater=getLayoutInflater();

      row=inflater.inflate(R.layout.row, parent, false);
      wrapper=new ViewWrapper(row);
      row.setTag(wrapper);
      rate=wrapper.getRatingBar();

      RatingBar.OnRatingBarChangeListener l=
                  new RatingBar.OnRatingBarChangeListener() {
        public void onRatingChanged(RatingBar ratingBar,
                                    float rating,
                                    boolean fromTouch)  {
          Integer myPosition=(Integer)ratingBar.getTag();
          RowModel model=getModel(myPosition);

          model.rating=rating;

          LinearLayout parent=(LinearLayout)ratingBar.getParent();
          TextView label=(TextView)parent.findViewById(R.id.label);

          label.setText(model.toString());
        }
      };

      rate.setOnRatingBarChangeListener(l);
    }
    else {
      wrapper=(ViewWrapper)row.getTag();
```

```
        rate=wrapper.getRatingBar();
      }

      RowModel model=getModel(position);

      wrapper.getLabel().setText(model.toString());
      rate.setTag(new Integer(position));
      rate.setRating(model.rating);

      return(row);
    }
  }

  class RowModel {
    String label;
    float rating=2.0f;

    RowModel(String label) {
      this.label=label;
    }

    public String toString() {
      if (rating>=3.0) {
        return(label.toUpperCase());
      }

      return(label);
    }
  }
}
```

Here are the differences in this activity and getView() implementation compared with
the previous examples:

■ While we are still using String[] items as the list of nonsense words,
rather than pour that String array straight into an ArrayAdapter, we
turn it into a list of RowModel objects. RowModel is the mutable model. It
holds the nonsense word plus the current checked state. In a real
system, these might be objects populated from a Cursor, and the
properties would have more business meaning.

■ Utility methods like onListItemClick() needed to be updated to
reflect the change from a pure String model to use a RowModel.

■ The ArrayAdapter subclass (RatingAdapter), in getView(), looks to see
if convertView is null. If so, we create a new row by inflating a simple
layout and also attach a ViewWrapper. For the row's RatingBar, we add
an anonymous onRatingChanged() listener that looks at the row's tag
(getTag()) and converts that into an Integer, representing the position
within the ArrayAdapter that this row is displaying. Using that, the
rating bar can get the actual RowModel for the row and update the
model based on the new state of the rating bar. It also updates the
text adjacent to the RatingBar when checked to match the rating bar
state.

- We make sure that the RatingBar has the proper contents and has a tag (via setTag()) pointing to the position in the adapter the row is displaying.

The row layout is just a RatingBar and a TextView inside a LinearLayout:

```xml
<?xml version="1.0" encoding="utf-8"?>
<LinearLayout xmlns:android="http://schemas.android.com/apk/res/android"
  android:layout_width="fill_parent"
  android:layout_height="wrap_content"
  android:orientation="horizontal"
>
  <RatingBar
    android:id="@+id/rate"
    android:layout_width="wrap_content"
    android:layout_height="wrap_content"
    android:numStars="3"
    android:stepSize="1"
    android:rating="2" />
  <TextView
    android:id="@+id/label"
    android:paddingLeft="2px"
    android:paddingRight="2px"
    android:paddingTop="2px"
    android:textSize="40sp"
    android:layout_width="fill_parent"
    android:layout_height="wrap_content"/>
</LinearLayout>
```

The ViewWrapper simply extracts the RatingBar and the TextView from the row View:

```java
class ViewWrapper {
  View base;
  RatingBar rate=null;
  TextView label=null;

  ViewWrapper(View base) {
    this.base=base;
  }

  RatingBar getRatingBar() {
    if (rate==null) {
      rate=(RatingBar)base.findViewById(R.id.rate);
    }

    return(rate);
  }

  TextView getLabel() {
    if (label==null) {
      label=(TextView)base.findViewById(R.id.label);
    }

    return(label);
  }
}
```

And the visual result is what you would expect, as shown in Figure 8–3. This includes the toggled rating bars turning their words into all uppercase, as shown in Figure 8–4.

Figure 8–3. *The RateListDemo application, as initially launched*

Figure 8–4. *The same application, showing a top-rated word*

...And Checking It Twice

The rating list in the previous section works, but implementing it was very tedious. Worse, much of that tedium would not be reusable, except in very limited circumstances. We can do better.

What we would really like is to be able to create a layout like this:

```
<?xml version="1.0" encoding="utf-8"?>
<com.commonsware.android.fancylists.seven.RateListView
  xmlns:android="http://schemas.android.com/apk/res/android"
  android:id="@android:id/list"
  android:layout_width="fill_parent"
  android:layout_height="fill_parent"
  android:drawSelectorOnTop="false"
/>
```

In our code, almost all of the logic that might have referred to a ListView before "just works" with the RateListView we put in the layout:

```
String[] items={"lorem", "ipsum", "dolor", "sit", "amet",
        "consectetuer", "adipiscing", "elit", "morbi", "vel",
        "ligula", "vitae", "arcu", "aliquet", "mollis",
        "etiam", "vel", "erat", "placerat", "ante",
        "porttitor", "sodales", "pellentesque", "augue",
        "purus"};

@Override
public void onCreate(Bundle icicle) {
  super.onCreate(icicle);
  setContentView(R.layout.main);

  setListAdapter(new ArrayAdapter<String>(this,
                  android.R.layout.simple_list_item_1,
                  items));
  }
}
```

Where things get a wee bit challenging is when you stop and realize that, in everything up to this point in this chapter, we never actually changed the ListView itself. All our work was with the adapters, overriding getView() and inflating our own rows.

So, if we want RateListView to take in any ordinary ListAdapter and just work—putting rating bars on the rows as needed—we are going to need to do some fancy footwork. Specifically, we need to wrap the "raw" ListAdapter in some other ListAdapter that knows how to put the rating bars on the rows and track the state of those rating bars.

First, we need to establish the pattern of one ListAdapter augmenting another. Here is the code for AdapterWrapper, which takes a ListAdapter and delegates all of the interface's methods to the delegate (from the FancyLists/RateListView sample project):

```
public class AdapterWrapper implements ListAdapter {
  ListAdapter delegate=null;

  public AdapterWrapper(ListAdapter delegate) {
    this.delegate=delegate;
```

```
    }
    public int getCount() {
      return(delegate.getCount());
    }

    public Object getItem(int position) {
      return(delegate.getItem(position));
    }

    public long getItemId(int position) {
      rcturn(delegate.getItemId(position));
    }

    public View getView(int position, View convertView,
                        ViewGroup parent) {
      return(delegate.getView(position, convertView, parent));
    }

    public void registerDataSetObserver(DataSetObserver observer) {
      delegate.registerDataSetObserver(observer);
    }

    public boolean hasStableIds() {
      return(delegate.hasStableIds());
    }

    public boolean isEmpty() {
      return(delegate.isEmpty());
    }

    public int getViewTypeCount() {
      return(delegate.getViewTypeCount());
    }

    public int getItemViewType(int position) {
      return(delegate.getItemViewType(position));
    }

    public void unregisterDataSetObserver(DataSetObserver observer) {
      delegate.unregisterDataSetObserver(observer);
    }

    public boolean areAllItemsEnabled() {
      return(delegate.areAllItemsEnabled());
    }

    public boolean isEnabled(int position) {
      return(delegate.isEnabled(position));
    }
}
```

We can then subclass AdapterWrapper to create RateableWrapper, overriding the default getView() but otherwise allowing the delegated ListAdapter to do the real work:

```
public class RateableWrapper extends AdapterWrapper {
  Context ctxt=null;
  float[] rates=null;
```

```
public RateableWrapper(Context ctxt, ListAdapter delegate) {
  super(delegate);

  this.ctxt=ctxt;
  this.rates=new float[delegate.getCount()];

  for (int i=0;i<delegate.getCount();i++) {
    this.rates[i]=2.0f;
  }
}

public View getView(int position, View convertView,
                    ViewGroup parent) {
  ViewWrapper wrap=null;
  View row=convertView;

  if (convertView==null) {
    LinearLayout layout=new LinearLayout(ctxt);
    RatingBar rate=new RatingBar(ctxt);

    rate.setNumStars(3);
    rate.setStepSize(1.0f);

    View guts=delegate.getView(position, null, parent);

    layout.setOrientation(LinearLayout.HORIZONTAL);

    rate.setLayoutParams(new LinearLayout.LayoutParams(
        LinearLayout.LayoutParams.WRAP_CONTENT,
        LinearLayout.LayoutParams.FILL_PARENT));
    guts.setLayoutParams(new LinearLayout.LayoutParams(
        LinearLayout.LayoutParams.FILL_PARENT,
        LinearLayout.LayoutParams.FILL_PARENT));

    RatingBar.OnRatingBarChangeListener l=
                new RatingBar.OnRatingBarChangeListener() {
      public void onRatingChanged(RatingBar ratingBar,
                                  float rating,
                                  boolean fromTouch)  {
        rates[(Integer)ratingBar.getTag()]=rating;
      }
    };

    rate.setOnRatingBarChangeListener(l);

    layout.addView(rate);
    layout.addView(guts);

    wrap=new ViewWrapper(layout);
    wrap.setGuts(guts);
    layout.setTag(wrap);

    rate.setTag(new Integer(position));
    rate.setRating(rates[position]);
```

```
      row=layout;
    }
    else {
      wrap=(ViewWrapper)convertView.getTag();
      wrap.setGuts(delegate.getView(position, wrap.getGuts(),
                               parent));
      wrap.getRatingBar().setTag(new Integer(position));
      wrap.getRatingBar().setRating(rates[position]);
    }

    return(row);
  }
}
```

The idea is that RateableWrapper is where most of our rate-list logic resides. It puts the rating bars on the rows, and it tracks the rating bars' states as they are adjusted by the user. For the states, it has a float[] sized to fit the number of rows that the delegate says are in the list.

RateableWrapper's implementation of getView() is reminiscent of the one from RateListDemo, except that rather than use LayoutInflater, we need to manually construct a LinearLayout to hold our RatingBar and the "guts" (a.k.a., whatever view the delegate created that we are decorating with the rating bar). LayoutInflater is designed to construct a View from raw widgets. In our case, we don't know in advance what the rows will look like, other than that we need to add a rating bar to them. However, the rest is similar to the one from RateListDemo, including using a ViewWrapper, hooking up onRatingBarChanged() to have the rating bar update the state, and so forth:

```
class ViewWrapper {
  ViewGroup base;
  View guts=null;
  RatingBar rate=null;

  ViewWrapper(ViewGroup base) {
    this.base=base;
  }

  RatingBar getRatingBar() {
    if (rate==null) {
      rate=(RatingBar)base.getChildAt(0);
    }

    return(rate);
  }

  void setRatingBar(RatingBar rate) {
    this.rate=rate;
  }

  View getGuts() {
    if (guts==null) {
      guts=base.getChildAt(1);
    }

    return(guts);
```

```
  }

  void setGuts(View guts) {
    this.guts=guts;
  }
}
```

With all that in place, RateListView is comparatively simple:

```
public class RateListView extends ListView {
  public RateListView(Context context) {
    super(context);
  }

  public RateListView(Context context, AttributeSet attrs) {
    super(context, attrs);
  }

  public RateListView(Context context, AttributeSet attrs,
                      int defStyle) {
    super(context, attrs, defStyle);
  }

  public void setAdapter(ListAdapter adapter) {
    super.setAdapter(new RateableWrapper(getContext(), adapter));
  }
}
```

We simply subclass ListView and override setAdapter() so we can wrap the supplied ListAdapter in our own RateableWrapper.

Visually, the results are similar to the RateListDemo, albeit without top-rated words appearing in all uppercase, as shown in Figure 8–5.

Figure 8–5. *The RateListViewDemo sample application*

The difference is in reusability. We could package RateListView in its own JAR and plop it into any Android project where we need it. So while RateListView is somewhat complicated to write, we need to write it only once, and the rest of the application code is blissfully simple.

> **NOTE:** Of course, the sample RateListView could use some more features, such as programmatically changing states (updating both the float[] and the actual RatingBar itself) and allowing other application logic to be invoked when a RatingBar state is toggled (via some sort of callback). These and other enhancements are left as exercises for the reader.

Adapting Other Adapters

All adapter classes can follow the ArrayAdapter pattern of overriding getView() to define the rows. However, CursorAdapter and its subclasses have a default implementation of getView().

The getView() method inspects the supplied View to recycle. If it is null, getView() calls newView(), then bindView(). If it is not null, getView() just calls bindView().

If you are extending CursorAdapter, which is used for displaying results of a database or content provider query, you should override newView() and bindView(), instead of getView(). All this does is remove your if() test you would have in getView() and put each branch of that test in an independent method, akin to the following:

```
public View newView(Context context, Cursor cursor,
                    ViewGroup parent) {
  LayoutInflater inflater=context.getLayoutInflater();
  View row=inflater.inflate(R.layout.row, null);
  ViewWrapper wrapper=new ViewWrapper(row);

  row.setTag(wrapper);

  return(row);
}

public void bindView(View row, Context context, Cursor cursor) {
  ViewWrapper wrapper=(ViewWrapper)row.getTag();

  // actual logic to populate row from Cursor goes here
}
```

Chapter 22 provides details about using a Cursor.

Chapter **9**

Employing Fancy Widgets and Containers

The widgets and containers covered so far are not only found in many GUI toolkits (in one form or fashion), but also are widely used in building GUI applications—whether web-based, desktop, or mobile. The widgets and containers described in this chapter are a little less widely used, though you will likely find many to be quite useful.

Pick and Choose

With limited-input devices like phones, having widgets and dialogs that are aware of the type of stuff someone is supposed to be entering is very helpful. These elements minimize keystrokes and screen taps, as well as reduce the chance of making some sort of error (e.g., entering a letter somewhere only numbers are expected).

As shown in Chapter 5, EditText has content-aware flavors for entering numbers and text. Android also supports widgets (DatePicker and TimePicker) and dialogs (DatePickerDialog and TimePickerDialog) for helping users enter dates and times.

DatePicker and DatePickerDialog allow you to set the starting date for the selection, in the form of a year, month, and day of month value. Note that the month runs from 0 for January through 11 for December. Each lets you provide a callback object (OnDateChangedListener or OnDateSetListener) where you are informed of a new date selected by the user. It is up to you to store that date someplace, particularly if you are using the dialog, since there is no other way for you to get at the chosen date later.

Similarly, TimePicker and TimePickerDialog let you set the initial time the user can adjust, in the form of an hour (0 through 23) and a minute (0 through 59). You can indicate if the selection should be in 12-hour mode with an AM/PM toggle or in 24-hour mode (what in the United States is thought of as "military time" and in the rest of the world as "the way times are supposed to be"). You can also provide a callback object (OnTimeChangedListener or OnTimeSetListener) to be notified of when the user has chosen a new time, which is supplied to you in the form of an hour and minute.

For example, from the Fancy/Chrono sample project, here's a trivial layout containing a label and two buttons, which will pop up the dialog flavors of the date and time pickers:

```xml
<?xml version="1.0" encoding="utf-8"?>
<LinearLayout
  xmlns:android="http://schemas.android.com/apk/res/android"
  android:orientation="vertical"
  android:layout_width="fill_parent"
  android:layout_height="fill_parent"
  >
  <TextView android:id="@+id/dateAndTime"
    android:layout_width="fill_parent"
    android:layout_height="wrap_content"
    />
  <Button android:id="@+id/dateBtn"
    android:layout_width="fill_parent"
    android:layout_height="wrap_content"
    android:text="Set the Date"
    />
  <Button android:id="@+id/timeBtn"
    android:layout_width="fill_parent"
    android:layout_height="wrap_content"
    android:text="Set the Time"
    />
</LinearLayout>
```

The more interesting stuff comes in the Java source:

```java
public class ChronoDemo extends Activity {
  DateFormat fmtDateAndTime=DateFormat.getDateTimeInstance();
  TextView dateAndTimeLabel;
  Calendar dateAndTime=Calendar.getInstance();
  DatePickerDialog.OnDateSetListener d=new DatePickerDialog.OnDateSetListener() {
    public void onDateSet(DatePicker view, int year, int monthOfYear,
                int dayOfMonth) {
      dateAndTime.set(Calendar.YEAR, year);
      dateAndTime.set(Calendar.MONTH, monthOfYear);
      dateAndTime.set(Calendar.DAY_OF_MONTH, dayOfMonth);
      updateLabel();
    }
  };
  TimePickerDialog.OnTimeSetListener t=new TimePickerDialog.OnTimeSetListener() {
    public void onTimeSet(TimePicker view, int hourOfDay,
                      int minute) {
      dateAndTime.set(Calendar.HOUR_OF_DAY, hourOfDay);
      dateAndTime.set(Calendar.MINUTE, minute);
      updateLabel();
    }
  };

  @Override
  public void onCreate(Bundle icicle) {
    super.onCreate(icicle);
    setContentView(R.layout.main);

    Button btn=(Button)findViewById(R.id.dateBtn);
```

```
    btn.setOnClickListener(new View.OnClickListener() {
      public void onClick(View v) {
        new DatePickerDialog(ChronoDemo.this,
            d,
            dateAndTime.get(Calendar.YEAR),
            dateAndTime.get(Calendar.MONTH),
            dateAndTime.get(Calendar.DAY_OF_MONTH)).show();
      }
    });

    btn=(Button)findViewById(R.id.timeBtn);

    btn.setOnClickListener(new View.OnClickListener() {
      public void onClick(View v) {
        new TimePickerDialog(ChronoDemo.this,
                    t,
                    dateAndTime.get(Calendar.HOUR_OF_DAY),
                    dateAndTime.get(Calendar.MINUTE),
                    true).show();
      }
    });

    dateAndTimeLabel=(TextView)findViewById(R.id.dateAndTime);

    updateLabel();
  }

  private void updateLabel() {
    dateAndTimeLabel.setText(fmtDateAndTime
                        .format(dateAndTime.getTime()));
  }
}
```

The model for this activity is just a Calendar instance, initially set to be the current date and time. We pour it into the view via a DateFormat formatter. In the updateLabel() method, we take the current Calendar, format it, and put it in the TextView.

Each button is given an OnClickListener callback object. When the button is clicked, either a DatePickerDialog or a TimePickerDialog is shown. In the case of the DatePickerDialog, we give it an OnDateSetListener callback that updates the Calendar with the new date (year, month, and day of month). We also give the dialog the last-selected date, getting the values from the Calendar. In the case of the TimePickerDialog, it gets an OnTimeSetListener callback to update the time portion of the Calendar, the last-selected time, and a true indicating we want 24-hour mode on the time selector.

With all this wired together, the resulting activity looks like Figures 9–1, 9–2, and 9–3.

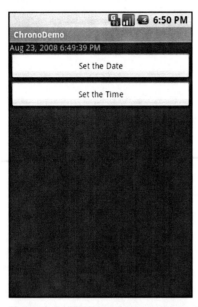

Figure 9–1. *The ChronoDemo sample application, as initially launched*

Figure 9–2. *The same application, showing the date picker dialog*

Figure 9–3. *The same application, showing the time picker dialog*

Time Keeps Flowing Like a River

If you want to display the time, rather than have users enter it, you may wish to use the DigitalClock or AnalogClock widgets. These are extremely easy to use, as they automatically update with the passage of time. All you need to do is put them in your layout and let them do their thing.

For example, from the Fancy/Clocks sample application, here is an XML layout containing both DigitalClock and AnalogClock widgets:

```xml
<?xml version="1.0" encoding="utf-8"?>
<RelativeLayout xmlns:android="http://schemas.android.com/apk/res/android"
  android:orientation="vertical"
  android:layout_width="fill_parent"
  android:layout_height="fill_parent"
  >
  <AnalogClock android:id="@+id/analog"
    android:layout_width="fill_parent"
    android:layout_height="wrap_content"
    android:layout_centerHorizontal="true"
    android:layout_alignParentTop="true"
    />
  <DigitalClock android:id="@+id/digital"
    android:layout_width="wrap_content"
    android:layout_height="wrap_content"
    android:layout_centerHorizontal="true"
    android:layout_below="@id/analog"
    />
</RelativeLayout>
```

Without any Java code other than the generated stub, we can build this project and get the activity shown in Figure 9–4.

Figure 9–4. *The ClocksDemo sample application*

If you are looking for more of a timer, Chronometer may be of interest. With a Chronometer, you can track elapsed time from a starting point. You simply tell it when to start() and stop(), and possibly override the format string that displays the text. Figure 9–5 shows an example.

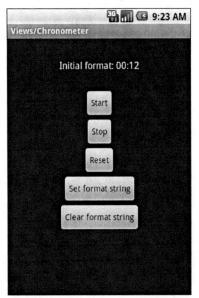

Figure 9–5. *The Views/Chronometer API demo from the Android 2.0 SDK*

Making Progress

If you need to be doing something for a long period of time, you owe it to your users to do two things:

- Use a background thread.

- Keep them apprised of your progress, lest they think your activity has wandered away and will never come back.

The typical approach to keeping users informed of progress is to display some form of progress bar, or "throbber" (like the animated graphic that appears near the upper-right corner of many web browsers). Android supports this through the ProgressBar widget.

A ProgressBar widget keeps track of progress, defined as an integer, with 0 indicating no progress has been made. You can define the maximum end of the range—the value that indicates progress is complete—via setMax(). By default, ProgressBar starts with a progress of 0, though you can start from some other position via setProgress().

If you prefer your progress bar to be indeterminate, use setIndeterminate(), setting it to true.

In your Java code, you can either positively set the amount of progress that has been made (via setProgress()) or increment the progress from its current amount (via incrementProgressBy()). You can find out how much progress has been made via getProgress().

Since the ProgressBar is tied closely to the use of threads—a background thread doing work, updating the UI thread with new progress information—its use is demonstrated in Chapter 15.

Seeking Resolution

A subclass of ProgressBar is SeekBar. A ProgressBar is an output widget, telling the user how much progress has been made. Conversely, the SeekBar is an input widget, allowing the user to select a value along a range of possible values, as shown in Figure 9–6.

Figure 9–6. *The Views/SeekBar API demo from the Android 2.0 SDK*

The user can drag the thumb or click either side of it to reposition the thumb. The thumb then points to a particular value along a range. That range will be 0 to some maximum value, 100 by default, which you control via a call to setMax(). You can determine the current position via getProgress(), or find out when the user makes a change to the thumb's position by registering a listener via setOnSeekBarChangeListener().

You saw a variation on this theme with the RatingBar example in Chapter 8.

Put It on My Tab

The general Android philosophy is to keep activities short and sweet. If there is more information than can reasonably fit on one screen, albeit perhaps with scrolling, then it perhaps belongs in another activity kicked off via an Intent, as will be described in Chapter 18. However, that can be complicated to set up. Moreover, sometimes there legitimately is a lot of information that needs to be collected to be processed as an atomic operation.

In a traditional UI, you might use tabs to hold the information, such as a JTabbedPane in Java/Swing. In Android, you now have the option of using a TabHost container in much the same way. In this setup, a portion of your activity's screen is taken up with tabs, which, when clicked, swap out part of the view and replace it with something else. For example, you might have an activity with a tab for entering a location and a second tab for showing a map of that location.

Some GUI toolkits refer to tabs as just the things a user clicks to toggle from one view to another. Others refer to tabs as the combination of the clickable buttonlike element and the content that appears when it is chosen. Android treats the tab buttons and contents as discrete entities, which I'll refer to as "tab buttons" and "tab contents" in this section.

The Pieces

You need to use the following items to set up a tabbed portion of a view:

- TabHost is the overarching container for the tab buttons and tab contents.

- TabWidget implements the row of tab buttons, which contain text labels and, optionally, icons.

- FrameLayout is the container for the tab contents. Each tab content is a child of the FrameLayout.

This is similar to the approach that Mozilla's XUL takes. In XUL's case, the tabbox element corresponds to Android's TabHost, the tabs element corresponds to TabWidget, and tabpanels corresponds to FrameLayout.

The Idiosyncrasies

There are a few rules to follow, at least in this milestone edition of the Android toolkit, in order to make the three tab pieces work together:

- You must give the TabWidget an android:id of @android:id/tabs.

- If you wish to use the TabActivity, you must give the TabHost an android:id of @android:id/tabhost.

TabActivity, like ListActivity, wraps a common UI pattern (an activity made up entirely of tabs) into a pattern-aware activity subclass. You do not necessarily have to use TabActivity—a plain activity can use tabs as well.

For example, here is a layout definition for a tabbed activity, from Fancy/Tab:

```xml
<?xml version="1.0" encoding="utf-8"?>
<TabHost xmlns:android="http://schemas.android.com/apk/res/android"
  android:id="@+id/tabhost"
  android:layout_width="fill_parent"
  android:layout_height="fill_parent">
  <LinearLayout
    android:orientation="vertical"
    android:layout_width="fill_parent"
    android:layout_height="fill_parent">
    <TabWidget android:id="@android:id/tabs"
      android:layout_width="fill_parent"
      android:layout_height="wrap_content"
    />
    <FrameLayout android:id="@android:id/tabcontent"
      android:layout_width="fill_parent"
      android:layout_height="fill_parent">
      <AnalogClock android:id="@+id/tab1"
```

```
            android:layout_width="fill_parent"
            android:layout_height="fill_parent"
            android:layout_centerHorizontal="true"
        />
        <Button android:id="@+id/tab2"
            android:layout_width="fill_parent"
            android:layout_height="fill_parent"
            android:text="A semi-random button"
        />
    </FrameLayout>
  </LinearLayout>
</TabHost>
```

Note that the TabWidget and FrameLayout are immediate children of the TabHost, and the FrameLayout itself has children representing the various tabs. In this case, there are two tabs: a clock and a button. In a more complicated scenario, the tabs could be some form of container (e.g., LinearLayout) with their own contents.

Wiring It Together

The Java code needs to tell the TabHost which views represent the tab contents and what the tab buttons should look like. This is all wrapped up in TabSpec objects. You get a TabSpec instance from the host via newTabSpec(), fill it out, and then add it to the host in the proper sequence.

TabSpec has two key methods:

- setContent(): Indicates what goes in the tab content for this tab, typically the android:id of the view you want shown when this tab is selected.

- setIndicator(): Sets the caption for the tab button and, in some flavors of this method, supplies a Drawable to represent the icon for the tab.

Note that tab "indicators" can actually be views in their own right, if you need more control than a simple label and optional icon.

Also note that you must call setup() on the TabHost before configuring any of these TabSpec objects. The call to setup() is not needed if you are using the TabActivity base class for your activity.

For example, here is the Java code to wire together the tabs from the preceding layout example:

```
package com.commonsware.android.fancy;

import android.app.Activity;
import android.os.Bundle;
import android.widget.TabHost;

public class TabDemo extends Activity {
  @Override
  public void onCreate(Bundle icicle) {
```

```
      super.onCreate(icicle);
      setContentView(R.layout.main);

      TabHost tabs=(TabHost)findViewById(R.id.tabhost);

      tabs.setup();

      TabHost.TabSpec spec=tabs.newTabSpec("tag1");

      spec.setContent(R.id.tab1);
      spec.setIndicator("Clock");
      tabs.addTab(spec);

      spec=tabs.newTabSpec("tag2");
      spec.setContent(R.id.tab2);
      spec.setIndicator("Button");
      tabs.addTab(spec);
  }
}
```

We find our TabHost via the familiar findViewById() method, and then have it setup().
After that, we get a TabSpec via newTabSpec(), supplying a tag whose purpose is
unknown at this time. Given the spec, we call setContent() and setIndicator(), and
then call addTab() back on the TabHost to register the tab as available for use. Finally,
we can choose which tab is the one to show via setCurrentTab(), providing the 0-based
index of the tab.

The results are shown in Figures 9–7 and 9–8.

Figure 9–7. *The TabDemo sample application, showing the first tab*

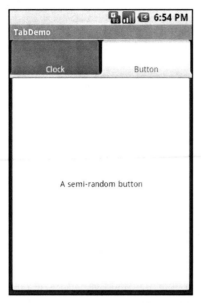

Figure 9–8. *The same application, showing the second tab*

Adding Them Up

TabWidget is set up to allow you to easily define tabs at compile time. However, sometimes, you want to add tabs to your activity during runtime. For example, imagine an e-mail client where individual messages are opened in their own tab, for easy toggling between messages. In this case, you don't know how many tabs you will need or what their contents will be until runtime, when the user chooses to open a message. Fortunately, Android also supports adding tabs dynamically at runtime.

Adding tabs dynamically at runtime works much like the compile-time tabs described in the previous section, except you use a different flavor of setContent()—one that takes a TabHost.TabContentFactory instance. This is just a callback that will be invoked. You provide an implementation of createTabContent(), and use it to build and return the View that becomes the content of the tab.

Let's take a look at an example (Fancy/DynamicTab). First, here is some layout XML for an activity that sets up the tabs and defines one tab, containing a single button:

```xml
<?xml version="1.0" encoding="utf-8"?>
<LinearLayout xmlns:android="http://schemas.android.com/apk/res/android"
  android:orientation="vertical"
  android:layout_width="fill_parent"
  android:layout_height="fill_parent">
  <TabHost android:id="@+id/tabhost"
    android:layout_width="fill_parent"
    android:layout_height="fill_parent">
    <TabWidget android:id="@android:id/tabs"
      android:layout_width="fill_parent"
      android:layout_height="wrap_content"
```

```
        />
        <FrameLayout android:id="@android:id/tabcontent"
          android:layout_width="fill_parent"
          android:layout_height="fill_parent"
          android:paddingTop="62px">
          <Button android:id="@+id/buttontab"
            android:layout_width="fill_parent"
            android:layout_height="fill_parent"
            android:text="A semi-random button"
          />
        </FrameLayout>
      </TabHost>
</LinearLayout>
```

Now we want to add new tabs whenever the button is clicked. That can be accomplished with the following code:

```
public class DynamicTabDemo extends Activity {
  @Override
  public void onCreate(Bundle icicle) {
    super.onCreate(icicle);
    setContentView(R.layout.main);

    final TabHost tabs=(TabHost)findViewById(R.id.tabhost);

    tabs.setup();

    TabHost.TabSpec spec=tabs.newTabSpec("buttontab");
    spec.setContent(R.id.buttontab);
    spec.setIndicator("Button");
    tabs.addTab(spec);

    Button btn=(Button)tabs.getCurrentView().findViewById(R.id.buttontab);

    btn.setOnClickListener(new View.OnClickListener() {
      public void onClick(View view) {
        TabHost.TabSpec spec=tabs.newTabSpec("tag1");

        spec.setContent(new TabHost.TabContentFactory() {
          public View createTabContent(String tag) {
            return(new AnalogClock(DynamicTabDemo.this));
          }
        });
        spec.setIndicator("Clock");
        tabs.addTab(spec);
      }
    });
  }
}
```

In our button's setOnClickListener() callback, we create a TabHost.TabSpec object and give it an anonymous TabHost.TabContentFactory. The factory, in turn, returns the View to be used for the tab—in this case, just an AnalogClock. The logic for constructing the tab's View could be much more elaborate, such as using LayoutInflater to construct a view from layout XML.

Initially, when the activity is launched, we have just the one tab, as shown in Figure 9–9. Figure 9–10 shows all three tabs.

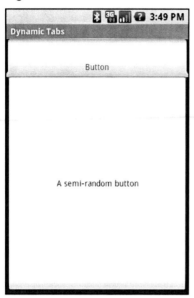

Figure 9–9. *The DynamicTab application, with the single initial tab*

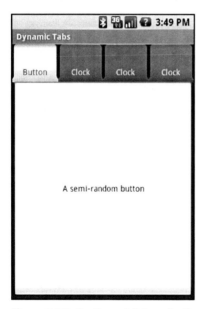

Figure 9–10. *The DynamicTab application, with three dynamically created tabs*

Intents and Views

In the preceding examples, the contents of each tab were set to be a View, such as a Button. This is easy and straightforward, but it is not the only option. You can also integrate another activity from your application via an Intent.

Intents are ways of specifying something you want accomplished, and then telling Android to go find something to accomplish it. Frequently, these are used to cause activities to spawn. For example, whenever you launch an application from the main Android application launcher, the launcher creates an Intent and has Android open the activity associated with that Intent. This whole concept, and how activities can be placed in tabs, is described in Chapter 18.

Flipping Them Off

Sometimes, you want the overall effect of tabs (only some Views visible at a time), but you do not want the actual UI implementation of tabs. Maybe the tabs take up too much screen space. Maybe you want to switch between perspectives based on a gesture or a device shake. Or maybe you just like being different.

The good news is that the guts of the view-flipping logic from tabs can be found in the ViewFlipper container, which can be used in other ways than the traditional tab.

ViewFlipper inherits from FrameLayout, in the same way you use it to describe the innards of a TabWidget. However, initially, the ViewFlipper container just shows the first child view. It is up to you to arrange for the views to flip, either manually by user interaction or automatically via a timer.

For example, here is a layout for a simple activity (Fancy/Flipper1) using a Button and a ViewFlipper:

```xml
<?xml version="1.0" encoding="utf-8"?>
<LinearLayout xmlns:android="http://schemas.android.com/apk/res/android"
    android:orientation="vertical"
    android:layout_width="fill_parent"
    android:layout_height="fill_parent"
    >
  <Button android:id="@+id/flip_me"
      android:layout_width="fill_parent"
      android:layout_height="wrap_content"
      android:text="Flip Me!"
      />
  <ViewFlipper android:id="@+id/details"
    android:layout_width="fill_parent"
    android:layout_height="fill_parent"
    >
    <TextView
      android:layout_width="fill_parent"
      android:layout_height="wrap_content"
      android:textStyle="bold"
      android:textColor="#FF00FF00"
      android:text="This is the first panel"
```

```
      />
      <TextView
        android:layout_width="fill_parent"
        android:layout_height="wrap_content"
        android:textStyle="bold"
        android:textColor="#FFFF0000"
        android:text="This is the second panel"
      />
      <TextView
        android:layout_width="fill_parent"
        android:layout_height="wrap_content"
        android:textStyle="bold"
        android:textColor="#FFFFFF00"
        android:text="This is the third panel"
      />
  </ViewFlipper>
</LinearLayout>
```

Notice that the layout defines three child views for the ViewFlipper, each a TextView with a simple message. Of course, you could have very complicated child views, if you so chose.

Manual Flipping

To manually flip the views, we need to hook into the Button and flip them ourselves when the button is clicked:

```
public class FlipperDemo extends Activity {
  ViewFlipper flipper;

  @Override
  public void onCreate(Bundle icicle) {
    super.onCreate(icicle);
    setContentView(R.layout.main);

    flipper=(ViewFlipper)findViewById(R.id.details);

    Button btn=(Button)findViewById(R.id.flip_me);

    btn.setOnClickListener(new View.OnClickListener() {
      public void onClick(View view) {
        flipper.showNext();
      }
    });
  }
}
```

This is just a matter of calling showNext() on the ViewFlipper, as you can on any ViewAnimator class.

The result is a trivial activity: click the button, and the next TextView in sequence is displayed, wrapping around to the first after viewing the last, as shown in Figures 9–11 and 9–12.

Figure 9–11. *The Flipper1 application, showing the first panel*

Figure 9–12. *The same application, after switching to the second panel*

Of course, this could be handled more simply by having a single TextView and changing the text and color on each click. However, you can imagine that the ViewFlipper contents could be much more complicated, like the contents you might put into a TabView.

Adding Contents on the Fly

As with the TabWidget, sometimes, your ViewFlipper contents may not be known at compile time. And as with TabWidget, you can add new contents on the fly with ease.

For example, let's look at another sample activity (Fancy/Flipper2), using this layout:

```xml
<?xml version="1.0" encoding="utf-8"?>
<LinearLayout xmlns:android="http://schemas.android.com/apk/res/android"
    android:orientation="vertical"
    android:layout_width="fill_parent"
    android:layout_height="fill_parent"
    >
  <ViewFlipper android:id="@+id/details"
    android:layout_width="fill_parent"
    android:layout_height="fill_parent"
    >
  </ViewFlipper>
</LinearLayout>
```

Notice that the ViewFlipper has no contents at compile time. Also notice that there is no Button for flipping between the contents—more on this in the next section.

For the ViewFlipper contents, we will create large Button widgets, each containing one of the random words used in many chapters in this book. Then we will set up the ViewFlipper to automatically rotate between the Button widgets, using an animation for transition.

```java
public class FlipperDemo2 extends Activity {
  static String[] items={"lorem", "ipsum", "dolor", "sit", "amet",
                         "consectetuer", "adipiscing", "elit",
                         "morbi", "vel", "ligula", "vitae",
                         "arcu", "aliquet", "mollis", "etiam",
                         "vel", "erat", "placerat", "ante",
                         "porttitor", "sodales", "pellentesque",
                         "augue", "purus"};
  ViewFlipper flipper;

  @Override
  public void onCreate(Bundle icicle) {
    super.onCreate(icicle);
    setContentView(R.layout.main);

    flipper=(ViewFlipper)findViewById(R.id.details);

    flipper.setInAnimation(AnimationUtils.loadAnimation(this,
                                     R.anim.push_left_in));
    flipper.setOutAnimation(AnimationUtils.loadAnimation(this,
                                     R.anim.push_left_out));

    for (String item : items) {
      Button btn=new Button(this);

      btn.setText(item);

      flipper.addView(btn,
```

```
            new ViewGroup.LayoutParams(
                    ViewGroup.LayoutParams.FILL_PARENT,
                    ViewGroup.LayoutParams.FILL_PARENT));
    }

    flipper.setFlipInterval(2000);
    flipper.startFlipping();
  }
}
```

After getting our `ViewFlipper` widget from the layout, we first set up the "in" and "out" animations. In Android terms, an animation is a description of how a widget leaves (out) or enters (in) the viewable area. Animations are resources, stored in res/anim/ in your project. For this example, we are using a pair of animations supplied by the SDK samples, available under the Apache 2.0 license. As their names suggest, widgets are "pushed" to the left, either to enter or leave the viewable area.

> **NOTE:** Animation is a complex beast. I cover it in my book *The Busy Coder's Guide to Advanced Android Development* (CommonsWare LLC, 2009).

Automatic Flipping

After iterating over the funky words, turning each into a `Button`, and adding the `Button` as a child of the `ViewFlipper`, we set up the flipper to automatically flip between children (`flipper.setFlipInterval(2000);`) and to start flipping (`flipper.startFlipping();`).

The result is an endless series of buttons. Each appears and then slides out to the left after 2 seconds, being replaced by the next button in sequence, wrapping around to the first after the last has been shown. Figure 9–13 shows an example.

Figure 9–13. *The Flipper2 application, showing an animated transition*

The auto-flipping ViewFlipper is useful for status panels or other situations where you have a lot of information to display, but not much room. The caveat is that, since it automatically flips between views, expecting users to interact with individual views is dicey, because the view might switch away partway through their interaction.

Getting in Someone's Drawer

For a long time, Android developers yearned for a sliding-drawer container that worked like the one on the home screen, containing the icons for launching applications. The official implementation was in the open source code but was not part of the SDK, until Android 1.5, when the developers released SlidingDrawer for others to use.

Unlike most other Android containers, SlidingDrawer moves, switching from a closed to an open position. This puts some restrictions on which container holds the SlidingDrawer. It needs to be in a container that allows multiple widgets to sit atop each other. RelativeLayout and FrameLayout satisfy this requirement; FrameLayout is a container purely for stacking widgets atop one another. On the flip side, LinearLayout does not allow widgets to stack (they fall one after another in a row or column), and so you should not have a SlidingDrawer as an immediate child of a LinearLayout.

Here is a layout showing a SlidingDrawer in a FrameLayout, from the Fancy/DrawerDemo project:

```
<?xml version="1.0" encoding="utf-8"?>
<FrameLayout xmlns:android="http://schemas.android.com/apk/res/android"
    android:layout_width="fill_parent"
    android:layout_height="fill_parent"
    android:background="#FF4444CC"
    >
  <SlidingDrawer
    android:id="@+id/drawer"
    android:layout_width="fill_parent"
    android:layout_height="fill_parent"
    android:handle="@+id/handle"
    android:content="@+id/content">
    <ImageView
      android:id="@id/handle"
      android:layout_width="wrap_content"
      android:layout_height="wrap_content"
      android:src="@drawable/tray_handle_normal"
    />
    <Button
      android:id="@id/content"
      android:layout_width="fill_parent"
      android:layout_height="fill_parent"
      android:text="I'm in here!"
    />
  </SlidingDrawer>
</FrameLayout>
```

The SlidingDrawer should contain two things:

- A handle, frequently an ImageView or something along those lines, such as the one used here, pulled from the Android open source project

- The contents of the drawer itself, usually some sort of container, but a Button in this case

Moreover, SlidingDrawer needs to know the android:id values of the handle and contents, via the android:handle and android:content attributes, respectively. This tells the drawer how to animate itself as it slides open and closed.

Figure 9–14 shows what the SlidingDrawer looks like closed, using the supplied handle, and Figure 9–15 shows it open.

Figure 9–14. *A SlidingDrawer, closed*

Figure 9–15. *A SlidingDrawer, open*

As you might expect, you can open and close the drawer from Java code, as well as via user touch events (which are handled by the widget, so that's not something you need to worry about). However, you have two sets of these methods: ones that take place instantaneously (open(), close(), and toggle()) and ones that use the animation (animateOpen(), animateClose(), animateToggle()).

You can lock() and unlock() the drawer; while locked, the drawer will not respond to touch events.

You can also register three types of callbacks if you wish:

- A listener to be invoked when the drawer is opened

- A listener to be invoked when the drawer is closed

- A listener to be invoked when the drawer is "scrolled" (i.e., the user drags or flings the handle)

For example, the launcher's SlidingDrawer toggles the icon on the handle from open to closed to "delete" (if you long-tap something on the desktop). It accomplishes this, in part, through callbacks like these.

SlidingDrawer can be vertical or horizontal. Note, though, that it keeps its orientation despite the screen orientation. In other words, if you rotate the Android device or emulator running DrawerDemo, the drawer always opens from the bottom—it does not always stick to the original side from which it opened. This means that if you want the drawer to always open from the same side, as the launcher does, you will need separate layouts for portrait versus landscape, a topic discussed in Chapter 20.

Other Good Stuff

Android offers AbsoluteLayout, where the contents are laid out based on specific coordinate positions. You tell AbsoluteLayout where to place a child in precise x and y coordinates, and Android puts it that location, no questions asked.

On the plus side, AbsoluteLayout gives you precise positioning. On the minus side, it means your views will look right only on screens of a certain dimension, or you will need to write a bunch of code to adjust the coordinates based on screen size. Since Android screens might run the gamut of sizes, and new sizes crop up periodically, using AbsoluteLayout could get quite annoying.

> **NOTE:** AbsoluteLayout is officially deprecated, meaning that while it is available to you, its use is discouraged.

Android also has the ExpandableListView. This provides a simplified tree representation, supporting two levels of depth: groups and children. Groups contain children; children are "leaves" of the tree. This requires a new set of adapters, since the ListAdapter family does not provide any sort of group information for the items in the list.

Chapter 10

The Input Method Framework

Android 1.5 introduced the input method framework (IMF), which is commonly referred to as *soft keyboards*. However, the *soft keyboard* term is not necessarily accurate, as IMF could be used for handwriting recognition or other means of accepting text input via the screen.

This chapter describes how to use the IMF to tailor software keyboards to your application's needs.

Keyboards, Hard and Soft

Some Android devices, like the HTC Magic, do not have a hardware keyboard. Other Android devices, like the T-Mobile G1, have a hardware keyboard that is visible some of the time (when it is slid out). It is likely that in the future, there will be Android devices that always have a hardware keyboard available (such as netbooks and phones with an always-available QWERTY keyboard beneath the screen). The IMF handles all of these scenarios. In short, if there is no hardware keyboard, an input method editor (IME) will be available to users when they tap an enabled EditText.

This does not require any code changes to your application, as long as the default functionality of the IME is what you want. Fortunately, Android is fairly smart about guessing what you want, so it may be you can just test with the IME, but otherwise make no specific code changes.

But the keyboard may not quite behave how you would like to work for your application. For example, in the Basic/Field sample project, the FieldDemo activity has the IME overlaying the multiple-line EditText, as shown in Figure 10–1. It would be nice to have more control over how this appears, as well as to specify other behavior of the IME. Fortunately, the framework as a whole gives you many options for this, as is described in this chapter.

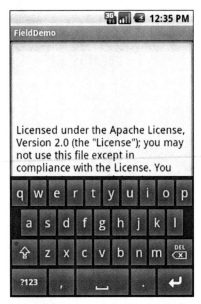

Figure 10–1. *The input method editor, as seen in the FieldDemo sample application*

Tailored to Your Needs

Android 1.1 and earlier offered many attributes on EditText widgets to control their style of input, such as android:password to indicate a field should be for password entry (shrouding the password keystrokes from prying eyes). In Android 1.5, with the IMF, many of these attributes have been combined into a single android:inputType attribute.

The android:inputType attribute takes a class plus modifiers, in a pipe-delimited format (where | is the pipe character). The class generally describes what the user is allowed to input, and this determines the basic set of keys available on the soft keyboard. The following classes are available:

- text (the default)
- number
- phone
- datetime
- date
- time

Many of these classes offer one or more modifiers to further refine what the user will be entering. To help understand these modifiers, take a look at the res/layout/main.xml file from the InputMethod/IMEDemo1 project:

```
<?xml version="1.0" encoding="utf-8"?>
<TableLayout xmlns:android="http://schemas.android.com/apk/res/android"
  android:layout_width="fill_parent"
```

```
  android:layout_height="fill_parent"
  android:stretchColumns="1"
  >
  <TableRow>
    <TextView
      android:text="No special rules:"
    />
    <EditText
    />
  </TableRow>
  <TableRow>
    <TextView
      android:text="Email address:"
    />
    <EditText
      android:inputType="text|textEmailAddress"
    />
  </TableRow>
  <TableRow>
    <TextView
      android:text="Signed decimal number:"
    />
    <EditText
      android:inputType="number|numberSigned|numberDecimal"
    />
  </TableRow>
  <TableRow>
    <TextView
      android:text="Date:"
    />
    <EditText
      android:inputType="date"
    />
  </TableRow>
  <TableRow>
    <TextView
      android:text="Multi-line text:"
    />
    <EditText
      android:inputType="text|textMultiLine|textAutoCorrect"
      android:minLines="3"
      android:gravity="top"
    />
  </TableRow>
</TableLayout>
```

Here, you will see a TableLayout containing five rows, each demonstrating a slightly different flavor of EditText:

- The first row does not have any attributes at all on the EditText, meaning you get a plain text-entry field.

- The second row has android:inputType = "text|textEmailAddress", meaning it is text entry, but specifically seeks an e-mail address.

- The third row allows for signed decimal numeric input, via android:inputType = "number|numberSigned|numberDecimal".

- The fourth row is set up to allow for data entry of a date (android:inputType = "date").

- The last row allows for multiline input with autocorrection of probable spelling errors (android:inputType = "text|textMultiLine|textAutoCorrect").

The class and modifiers tailor the keyboard. So, a plain text-entry field results in a plain soft keyboard, as shown in Figure 10–2.

Figure 10–2. *A standard input method editor (a.k.a., soft keyboard)*

An e-mail address field puts the @ symbol on the soft keyboard, at the cost of a smaller spacebar, as shown in Figure 10–3.

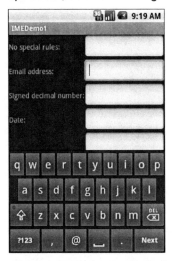

Figure 10–3. *The input method editor for e-mail addresses*

Number and date fields restrict the keys to numeric keys, plus a set of symbols that may or may not be valid on a given field, as shown in Figure 10–4.

Figure 10–4. *The input method editor for signed decimal numbers*

These are just a few examples. By choosing the appropriate android:inputType, you can give users a soft keyboard that best suits the data they should be entering.

Tell Android Where It Can Go

You may have noticed a subtle difference between the IME shown in Figure 10–2 and the one shown in Figure 10–4, beyond the addition of the @ key. If you look in the lower-right corner of the soft keyboard, the second field's editor has a Next button, while the first field's editor has a newline button. This points out two things:

■ EditText widgets are multiline by default if you do not specify android:inputType.

■ You can control what goes on with that lower-right button, called the *accessory button*.

By default, on an EditText widget where you have specified android:inputType, the accessory button will be Next, moving you to the next EditText in sequence, or Done, if you are on the last EditText on the screen. You can manually stipulate what the accessory button will be labeled via the android:imeOptions attribute. For example, in the res/layout/main.xml from InputMethod/IMEDemo2, you will see an augmented version of the previous example, where two input fields specify the appearance of the accessory button:

```xml
<?xml version="1.0" encoding="utf-8"?>
<ScrollView xmlns:android="http://schemas.android.com/apk/res/android"
  android:layout_width="fill_parent"
  android:layout_height="fill_parent"
>
  <TableLayout
    android:layout_width="fill_parent"
    android:layout_height="fill_parent"
    android:stretchColumns="1"
    >
    <TableRow>
      <TextView
        android:text="No special rules:"
      />
      <EditText
      />
    </TableRow>
    <TableRow>
      <TextView
        android:text="Email address:"
      />
      <EditText
        android:inputType="text|textEmailAddress"
        android:imeOptions="actionSend"
      />
    </TableRow>
    <TableRow>
      <TextView
        android:text="Signed decimal number:"
      />
      <EditText
        android:inputType="number|numberSigned|numberDecimal"
        android:imeOptions="actionDone"
      />
    </TableRow>
    <TableRow>
      <TextView
        android:text="Date:"
      />
      <EditText
        android:inputType="date"
      />
    </TableRow>
    <TableRow>
      <TextView
        android:text="Multi-line text:"
      />
      <EditText
        android:inputType="text|textMultiLine|textAutoCorrect"
        android:minLines="3"
        android:gravity="top"
      />
    </TableRow>
  </TableLayout>
</ScrollView>
```

Here, we attach a Send action to the accessory button for the e-mail address
(android:imeOptions = "actionSend"), and the Done action on the middle field
(android:imeOptions = "actionDone").

By default, Next will move the focus to the next EditText, and Done will close the IME.
However, for those actions, or for any other ones like Send, you can use
setOnEditorActionListener() on EditText (technically, on the TextView superclass) to
get control when the accessory button is clicked or the user presses the Enter key. You
are provided with a flag indicating the desired action (e.g., IME_ACTION_SEND), and you
can then do something to handle that request (e.g., send an e-mail to the supplied e-
mail address).

Fitting In

You will notice that the IMEDemo2 layout shown in the preceding section has another
difference from its IMEDemo1 predecessor: the use of a ScrollView container wrapping
the TableLayout. This ties into another level of control you have over IMEs: what
happens to your activity's own layout when the soft keyboard appears? There are three
possibilities, depending on the circumstances:

- Android can "pan" your activity, effectively sliding the whole layout up
  to accommodate the IME, or overlaying your layout, depending on
  whether the EditText being edited is at the top or bottom. This has the
  effect of hiding some portion of your UI.

- Android can resize your activity, effectively causing it to shrink to a
  smaller screen dimension, allowing the IME to sit below the activity
  itself. This is great when the layout can readily be shrunk (e.g., it is
  dominated by a list or multiline input field that does not need the whole
  screen to be functional).

- In landscape mode, Android may display the IME full-screen,
  obscuring your entire activity. This allows for a bigger keyboard and
  generally easier data entry.

Android controls the full-screen option purely on its own. And, by default, Android will
choose between pan and resize modes depending on what your layout looks like. If you
want to specifically choose between pan and resize, you can do so via an
android:windowSoftInputMode attribute on the <activity> element in your
AndroidManifest.xml file. For example, here is the manifest from IMEDemo2:

```
<?xml version="1.0" encoding="utf-8"?>
<manifest xmlns:android="http://schemas.android.com/apk/res/android"
      package="com.commonsware.android.imf.two"
      android:versionCode="1"
      android:versionName="1.0">
  <application android:label="@string/app_name"
      android:icon="@drawable/cw">
    <activity android:name=".IMEDemo2"
            android:label="@string/app_name"
            android:windowSoftInputMode="adjustResize">
```

```
    <intent-filter>
        <action android:name="android.intent.action.MAIN" />
        <category android:name="android.intent.category.LAUNCHER" />
    </intent-filter>
</activity>
</application>
</manifest>
```

Because we specified resize, Android will shrink our layout to accommodate the IME. With the ScrollView in place, this means the scroll bar will appear as needed, as shown in Figure 10–5.

Figure 10–5. *The shrunken, scrollable layout*

Unleash Your Inner Dvorak

You are also welcome to make and distribute your own IME. Perhaps you want to create a Dvorak soft keyboard, a keyboard for another language, or one that echoes pressed keys verbally.

An IME is packaged in the form of a service, an Android component described in Chapters 29 and 30. If you are interested in creating such an editor, you should take a look at the SoftKeyboard sample application distributed with the Android 1.5 SDK and, of course, the Android source code (search for the LatinIME class).

Chapter 11

Applying Menus

Like applications for the desktop and some mobile operating systems, such as Windows Mobile, Android supports activities with application menus. In Android, this is called an *options menu*. Some Android phones will have a dedicated key for popping up the options menu; others will offer alternate means for triggering the menu to appear, such as the on-screen button used by the Archos 5 Android tablet.

Also, as with many GUI toolkits, you can create context menus for your Android applications. On mobile devices, context menus typically appear when the user taps and holds over a particular widget. For example, if a TextView had a context menu, and the device was designed for finger-based touch input, you could push the TextView with your finger, hold it for a second or two, and a pop-up menu would appear.

This chapter describes how to work with Android options and context menus.

Menus of Options

The options menu is triggered by pressing the hardware Menu button on the device.

This menu operates in one of two modes: icon and expanded. When the user first presses the Menu button, the icon mode will appear, showing up to the first six menu choices as large, finger-friendly buttons in a grid at the bottom of the screen. If the menu has more than six choices, the sixth button will be labeled More. Choosing the More option will bring up the expanded mode, showing the remaining choices not visible in the regular menu. The menu is scrollable, so the user can get to any of the menu choices.

Creating an Options Menu

Rather than building your activity's options menu during onCreate(), the way you wire up the rest of your UI, you instead need to implement onCreateOptionsMenu(). This callback receives an instance of Menu.

The first thing you should do is chain upward to the superclass
(super.onCreateOptionsMenu(menu)), so the Android framework can add in any menu
choices it feels are necessary. Then you can go about adding your own options, as
described in the next section.

If you will need to adjust the menu during your activity's use (e.g., disable a now-invalid
menu choice), just hold onto the Menu instance you receive in onCreateOptionsMenu().
Alternatively, you can implement onPrepareOptionsMenu(), which is called just before
displaying the menu each time it is requested.

Adding Menu Choices and Submenus

Given that you have received a Menu object via onCreateOptionsMenu(), you add menu
choices by calling add(). There are many flavors of this method, which require some
combination of the following parameters:

- A group identifier (int), which should be NONE unless you are creating a
  specific grouped set of menu choices for use with
  setGroupCheckable() (described shortly)

- A choice identifier (also an int), for use in identifying this choice in the
  onOptionsItemSelected() callback when a menu choice is chosen

- An order identifier (yet another int), for indicating where this menu
  choice should be slotted if the menu has Android-supplied choices
  alongside your own; for now, just use NONE

- The text of the menu choice, as a String or a resource ID

The add() family of methods all return an instance of MenuItem, where you can adjust
any of the menu item settings you have already set (e.g., the text of the menu choice).

You can also set the shortcuts for the menu choice, which are single-character
mnemonics that choose that menu item when the menu is visible. Android supports both
an alphabetic (or QWERTY) set of shortcuts and a numeric set of shortcuts. These are
set individually by calling setAlphabeticShortcut() and setNumericShortcut(),
respectively. The menu is placed into alphabetic shortcut mode by calling
setQwertyMode() on the menu with a true parameter.

The choice and group identifiers are keys used to unlock additional menu features, such
as the following:

- Calling MenuItem#setCheckable() with a choice identifier, to control if
  the menu choice has a two-state check box alongside the title, where
  the check box value is toggled when the user chooses that item

- Calling Menu#setGroupCheckable() with a group identifier, to turn a set
  of menu choices into ones with a mutual-exclusion radio button
  between them, so only one choice in the group can be in the checked
  state at any time

Finally, you can create fly-out submenus by calling addSubMenu(), supplying the same parameters as addMenu(). Android will eventually call onCreatePanelMenu(), passing it the choice identifier of your submenu, along with another Menu instance representing the submenu itself. As with onCreateOptionsMenu(), you should chain upward to the superclass, and then add menu choices to the submenu. One limitation is that you cannot indefinitely nest submenus. A menu can have a submenu, but a submenu cannot have a sub-submenu.

If the user makes a menu choice, your activity will be notified that a menu choice was selected via the onOptionsItemSelected() callback. You are given the MenuItem object corresponding to the selected menu choice. A typical pattern is to switch() on the menu ID (item.getItemId()) and take appropriate behavior. Note that onOptionsItemSelected() is used regardless of whether the chosen menu item was in the base menu or a submenu.

Menus in Context

The context menu is raised by a tap-and-hold action on the widget sporting the menu.

By and large, context menus use the same guts as option menus. The two main differences are how you populate the menu and how you are informed of menu choices.

First, you need to indicate which widget(s) on your activity have context menus. To do this, call registerForContextMenu() from your activity, supplying the View that is the widget needing a context menu.

Next, you need to implement onCreateContextMenu(), which, among other things, is passed the View you supplied in registerForContextMenu(). You can use that to determine which menu to build, assuming your activity has more than one.

The onCreateContextMenu() method gets the ContextMenu itself, the View the context menu is associated with, and a ContextMenu.ContextMenuInfo, which tells you which item in the list the user did the tap-and-hold over, in case you want to customize the context menu based on that information. For example, you could toggle a checkable menu choice based on the current state of the item.

It is also important to note that onCreateContextMenu() is called for each time the context menu is requested. Unlike the options menu (which is built only once per activity), context menus are discarded after they are used or dismissed. Hence, you do not want to hold onto the supplied ContextMenu object; just rely on getting the chance to rebuild the menu to suit your activity's needs on an on-demand basis based on user actions.

To find out when a context menu choice was chosen, implement onContextItemSelected() on the activity. Note that you get only the MenuItem instance that was chosen in this callback. As a result, if your activity has two or more context menus, you may want to ensure they have unique menu item identifiers for all their choices, so you can distinguish between them in this callback. Also, you can call getMenuInfo() on the MenuItem to get the ContextMenu.ContextMenuInfo you received in

onCreateContextMenu(). Otherwise, this callback behaves the same as
onOptionsItemSelected(), as described in the previous section.

Taking a Peek

In the sample project Menus/Menus, you will find an amended version of the ListView
sample (List) from Chapter 7 with an associated menu. Since the menus are defined in
Java code, the XML layout does not need to change from the one shown in that chapter.
However, the Java code has a few new behaviors:

```java
public class MenuDemo extends ListActivity {
  TextView selection;
  String[] items={"lorem", "ipsum", "dolor", "sit", "amet",
          "consectetuer", "adipiscing", "elit", "morbi", "vel",
          "ligula", "vitae", "arcu", "aliquet", "mollis",
          "etiam", "vel", "erat", "placerat", "ante",
          "porttitor", "sodales", "pellentesque", "augue", "purus"};
  public static final int EIGHT_ID = Menu.FIRST+1;
  public static final int SIXTEEN_ID = Menu.FIRST+2;
  public static final int TWENTY_FOUR_ID = Menu.FIRST+3;
  public static final int TWO_ID = Menu.FIRST+4;
  public static final int THIRTY_TWO_ID = Menu.FIRST+5;
  public static final int FORTY_ID = Menu.FIRST+6;
  public static final int ONE_ID = Menu.FIRST+7;

  @Override
  public void onCreate(Bundle icicle) {
    super.onCreate(icicle);
    setContentView(R.layout.main);
    setListAdapter(new ArrayAdapter<String>(this,
              android.R.layout.simple_list_item_1, items));
    selection=(TextView)findViewById(R.id.selection);

    registerForContextMenu(getListView());
  }

  public void onListItemClick(ListView parent, View v,
                                int position, long id) {
   selection.setText(items[position]);
  }

  @Override
  public void onCreateContextMenu(ContextMenu menu, View v,
                                ContextMenu.ContextMenuInfo menuInfo) {
    populateMenu(menu);
  }

  @Override
  public boolean onCreateOptionsMenu(Menu menu) {
    populateMenu(menu);

    return(super.onCreateOptionsMenu(menu));
  }
```

```java
@Override
public boolean onOptionsItemSelected(MenuItem item) {
  return(applyMenuChoice(item) ||
          super.onOptionsItemSelected(item));
}

@Override
public boolean onContextItemSelected(MenuItem item) {
  return(applyMenuChoice(item) ||
          super.onContextItemSelected(item));
}

private void populateMenu(Menu menu) {
  menu.add(Menu.NONE, ONE_ID, Menu.NONE, "1 Pixel");
  menu.add(Menu.NONE, TWO_ID, Menu.NONE, "2 Pixels");
  menu.add(Menu.NONE, EIGHT_ID, Menu.NONE, "8 Pixels");
  menu.add(Menu.NONE, SIXTEEN_ID, Menu.NONE, "16 Pixels");
  menu.add(Menu.NONE, TWENTY_FOUR_ID, Menu.NONE, "24 Pixels");
  menu.add(Menu.NONE, THIRTY_TWO_ID, Menu.NONE, "32 Pixels");
  menu.add(Menu.NONE, FORTY_ID, Menu.NONE, "40 Pixels");
}

private boolean applyMenuChoice(MenuItem item) {
  switch (item.getItemId()) {
    case ONE_ID:
      getListView().setDividerHeight(1);
      return(true);

    case EIGHT_ID:
      getListView().setDividerHeight(8);
      return(true);

    case SIXTEEN_ID:
      getListView().setDividerHeight(16);
      return(true);

    case TWENTY_FOUR_ID:
      getListView().setDividerHeight(24);
      return(true);

    case TWO_ID:
      getListView().setDividerHeight(2);
      return(true);

    case THIRTY_TWO_ID:
      getListView().setDividerHeight(32);
      return(true);

    case FORTY_ID:
      getListView().setDividerHeight(40);
      return(true);
  }

  return(false);
}
}
```

In onCreate(), we register our list widget as having a context menu, which we fill in via our populateMenu() private method, by way of onCreateContextMenu().

We also implement the onCreateOptionsMenu() callback, indicating that our activity also has an options menu. Once again, we delegate to populateMenu() to fill in the menu.

Our implementations of onOptionsItemSelected() (for options menu selections) and onContextItemSelected() (for context menu selections) both delegate to a private applyMenuChoice() method, plus chaining upward to the superclass if none of our menu choices was the one selected by the user.

In populateMenu(), we add seven menu choices, each with a unique identifier. Being lazy, we eschew the icons.

In applyMenuChoice(), we see if any of our menu choices were chosen. If so, we set the list's divider size to be the user-selected width.

Initially, the activity looks the same in the emulator as it did for ListDemo, as shown in Figure 11–1.

Figure 11–1. *The MenuDemo sample application, as initially launched*

When you press the Menu button, you will get our options menu, as shown in Figure 11–2.

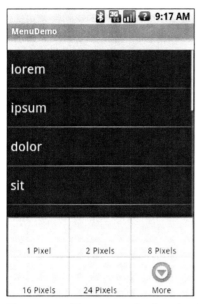

Figure 11–2. *The same application, showing the options menu*

Choosing the More button shows the remaining two menu choices, as shown in Figure 11–3.

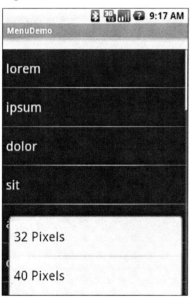

Figure 11–3. *The same application, showing the remaining menu choices*

Choosing a height (say, 16 pixels) from the menu changes the divider height of the list to something garish, as shown in Figure 11–4.

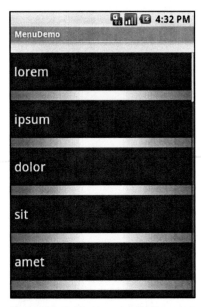

Figure 11–4. *The same application, made ugly*

You can trigger the context menu, shown in Figure 11–5, by tapping and holding on any item in the list. Once again, choosing an option sets the divider height.

Figure 11–5. *The same application, showing a context menu*

Yet More Inflation

Chapter 8 explained how you can describe Views via XML files and "inflate" them into actual View objects at runtime. Android also allows you to describe menus via XML files and inflate them when a menu is needed. This helps you keep your menu structure separate from the implementation of menu-handling logic, and it provides easier ways to develop menu-authoring tools.

Menu XML Structure

Menu XML goes in res/menu/ in your project tree, alongside the other types of resources that your project might employ. As with layouts, you can have several menu XML files in your project, each with its own filename and the .xml extension.

For example, from the Menus/Inflation sample project, here is a menu called sample.xml:

```xml
<?xml version="1.0" encoding="utf-8"?>
<menu xmlns:android="http://schemas.android.com/apk/res/android">
  <item android:id="@+id/close"
    android:title="Close"
    android:orderInCategory="3"
    android:icon="@drawable/eject" />
  <item android:id="@+id/no_icon"
    android:orderInCategory="2"
    android:title="Sans Icon" />
  <item android:id="@+id/disabled"
    android:orderInCategory="4"
    android:enabled="false"
    android:title="Disabled" />
  <group android:id="@+id/other_stuff"
    android:menuCategory="secondary"
    android:visible="false">
    <item android:id="@+id/later"
      android:orderInCategory="0"
      android:title="2nd-To-Last" />
    <item android:id="@+id/last"
      android:orderInCategory="1"
      android:title="Last" />
  </group>
  <item android:id="@+id/submenu"
    android:orderInCategory="3"
    android:title="A Submenu">
    <menu>
      <item android:id="@+id/non_ghost"
        android:title="Non-Ghost"
        android:visible="true"
        android:alphabeticShortcut="n" />
      <item android:id="@+id/ghost"
        android:title="A Ghost"
        android:visible="false"
        android:alphabeticShortcut="g" />
    </menu>
  </item>
</menu>
```

Note the following about the XML for menus:

- You must start with a menu root element.

- Inside a menu element are item elements and group elements. The latter represents a collection of menu items that can be operated upon as a group.

- Submenus are specified by adding a menu element as a child of an item element, using this new menu element to describe the contents of the submenu.

- If you want to detect when an item is chosen, or to reference an item or group from your Java code, be sure to apply an android:id, just as you do with View layout XML.

Menu Options and XML

Inside the item and group elements, you can specify various options, matching up with corresponding methods on Menu or MenuItem, as follows:

- *Title*: The title of a menu item is provided via the android:title attribute on an item element. This can be either a literal string or a reference to a string resource (e.g., @string/foo).

- *Icon*: Menu items optionally have icons. To provide an icon, in the form of a reference to a drawable resource (e.g., @drawable/eject), use the android:icon attribute on the item element.

- *Order*: By default, the order of the items in the menu is determined by the order in which they appear in the menu XML. You can change that by specifying the android:orderInCategory attribute on the item element. This is a 0-based index of the order for the items associated with the current category. There is an implicit default category. Groups can provide an android:menuCategory attribute to specify a different category to use for items in that group. Generally, it is simplest just to put the items in the XML in the order you want them to appear.

- *Enabled*: Items and groups can be enabled or disabled, controlled in the XML via the android:enabled attribute on the item or group element. By default, items and groups are enabled. Disabled items and groups appear in the menu but cannot be selected. You can change an item's status at runtime via the setEnabled() method on MenuItem, or change a group's status via setGroupEnabled() on Menu.

■ *Visible*: Items and groups can be visible or invisible, controlled in the XML via the android:visible attribute on the item or group element. By default, items and groups are visible. Invisible items and groups do not appear in the menu. You can change an item's status at runtime via the setVisible() method on MenuItem, or change a group's status via setGroupVisible() on Menu. In the layout XML shown in the previous section, the other_stuff group is initially invisible. If we make it visible in our Java code, the two menu items in the group will "magically" appear.

■ *Shortcut*: Items can have shortcuts—single letters (android:alphabeticShortcut) or numbers (android:numericShortcut) that can be pressed to choose the item without needing to use the touchscreen, D-pad, or trackball to navigate the full menu.

Inflating the Menu

Actually using the menu, once it's defined in XML, is easy. Just create a MenuInflater and tell it to inflate your menu:

```
@Override
public boolean onCreateOptionsMenu(Menu menu) {
  theMenu=menu;

  new MenuInflater(getApplication())
                          .inflate(R.menu.sample, menu);

  return(super.onCreateOptionsMenu(menu));
}
```

Chapter 12

Fonts

When you're developing any types of applications, inevitably, you'll get the question, "Hey, can we change this font?" The answer depends on which fonts come with the platform, whether you can add other fonts, and how to apply them to the widget or whatever needs the font change.

Fonts in Android applications are no different. Android comes with some fonts, plus a means for adding new fonts. But, as with any new environment, there are a few idiosyncrasies to deal with, as you'll learn in this chapter.

Love the One You're With

Android natively knows three fonts, by the shorthand names of "sans", "serif", and "monospace". These fonts are actually the Droid series of fonts, created for the Open Handset Alliance by Ascender (http://www.ascendercorp.com/oha.html). To use these fonts, you can just reference them in your layout XML, such as the following layout from the Fonts/FontSampler sample project:

```xml
<?xml version="1.0" encoding="utf-8"?>
<TableLayout
  xmlns:android="http://schemas.android.com/apk/res/android"
  android:layout_width="fill_parent"
  android:layout_height="fill_parent"
  android:stretchColumns="1">
  <TableRow>
    <TextView
      android:text="sans:"
      android:layout_marginRight="4px"
      android:textSize="20sp"
    />
    <TextView
      android:id="@+id/sans"
      android:text="Hello, world!"
      android:typeface="sans"
      android:textSize="20sp"
    />
  </TableRow>
  <TableRow>
```

```
    <TextView
      android:text="serif:"
      android:layout_marginRight="4px"
      android:textSize="20sp"
    />
    <TextView
      android:id="@+id/serif"
      android:text="Hello, world!"
      android:typeface="serif"
      android:textSize="20sp"
    />
  </TableRow>
  <TableRow>
    <TextView
      android:text="monospace:"
      android:layout_marginRight="4px"
      android:textSize="20sp"
    />
    <TextView
      android:id="@+id/monospace"
      android:text="Hello, world!"
      android:typeface="monospace"
      android:textSize="20sp"
    />
  </TableRow>
  <TableRow>
    <TextView
      android:text="Custom:"
      android:layout_marginRight="4px"
      android:textSize="20sp"
    />
    <TextView
      android:id="@+id/custom"
      android:text="Hello, world!"
      android:textSize="20sp"
    />
  </TableRow>
</TableLayout>
```

This layout builds a table showing short samples of the four fonts. Notice how the first three have the android:typeface attribute, whose value is one of the three built-in font faces (e.g., "sans").

More Fonts

The three built-in fonts are very nice. However, it may be that a designer, a manager, or a customer wants to use a different font, or perhaps you want to use a font for specialized purposes, such as a dingbats font instead of a series of PNG graphics. The easiest way to accomplish this is to package the desired font(s) with your application. Simply create an assets/ folder in the project root, and put your TrueType (TTF) fonts in that folder. You might, for example, create assets/fonts/ and put your TTF files there.

Then you need to tell your widgets to use that font. Unfortunately, you can no longer use layout XML for this, since the XML does not know about any fonts you may have tucked away as an application asset. Instead, you need to make the change in Java code:

```java
public class FontSampler extends Activity {
  @Override
  public void onCreate(Bundle icicle) {
    super.onCreate(icicle);
    setContentView(R.layout.main);

    TextView tv=(TextView)findViewById(R.id.custom);
    Typeface face=Typeface.createFromAsset(getAssets(),
                                "fonts/HandmadeTypewriter.ttf");

    tv.setTypeface(face);
  }
}
```

Here, we grab the TextView for our custom sample, and then create a Typeface object via the static createFromAsset() builder method. This takes the application's AssetManager (from getAssets()) and a path within your assets/ directory to the font you want.

Then it is just a matter of telling the TextView to setTypeface(), providing the Typeface you just created. In this case, we are using the Handmade Typewriter font (http://moorstation.org/typoasis/designers/klein07/text01/handmade.htm). Figure 12–1 shows the results.

Figure 12–1. *The FontSampler application*

Note that Android does not seem to like all TrueType fonts. When Android dislikes a custom font, rather than raise an Exception, it seems to substitute Droid Sans ("sans") quietly. So, if you try to use a different font and it does not appear to be working, the font in question may be incompatible with Android.

Also, you are probably best served by changing the case of your font filenames to be all lowercase, to match the naming convention used in the rest of your resources.

Android 1.6 added the ability to create `Typeface` objects based on TrueType files in the filesystem, such as on the user's SD card, via the `createFromFile()` static method on `Typeface`.

Here a Glyph, There a Glyph

TrueType fonts can be rather pudgy, particularly if they support an extensive subset of the available Unicode characters. The Handmade Typewriter font used in the previous example runs over 70KB. The DejaVu free fonts can run upwards of 500KB apiece. Even compressed, these add bulk to your application, so be careful not to go overboard with custom fonts, lest your application take up too much room on your users' phones.

Conversely, bear in mind that fonts may not have all of the glyphs that you need. As an example, let's talk about the ellipsis.

Android's `TextView` class has the built-in ability to "ellipsize" text, truncating it and adding an ellipsis if the text is longer than the available space. You can use this via the `android:ellipsize` attribute, for example. This works fairly well, at least for single-line text.

The ellipsis that Android uses is not three periods. Rather, it is an actual ellipsis character, where the three dots are contained in a single glyph. Hence, if you use the ellipsizing feature, any font that you display will need the ellipsis glyph.

Beyond that, though, Android pads out the string that is rendered on the screen, such that the length (in characters) is the same before and after ellipsizing. To make this work, Android replaces one character with the ellipsis, and replaces all other removed characters with the Unicode character 'ZERO WIDTH NO-BREAK SPACE' (U+FEFF). This way, the extra characters after the ellipsis do not take up any visible space on the screen, yet they can be part of the string. However, this means any custom fonts you use for `TextView` widgets that you use with `android:ellipsize` must also support this special Unicode character. Not all fonts do, and you will get artifacts in the on-screen representation of your shortened strings if your font lacks this character (e.g., rogue *X*s appear at the end of the line).

And, of course, Android's international deployment means your font must handle any language your users might want to enter, perhaps through a language-specific input method editor.

Hence, while using custom fonts in Android is very possible, there are many potential problems. For your applications, you should weigh carefully the benefits of the custom fonts versus their potential costs.

Chapter 13

Embedding the WebKit Browser

Other GUI toolkits let you use HTML for presenting information, from limited HTML renderers (e.g., Java/Swing and wxWidgets) to embedding Internet Explorer into .NET applications. Android is much the same, in that you can embed the built-in web browser as a widget in your own activities, for displaying HTML or full-fledged browsing. The Android browser is based on WebKit, the same engine that powers Apple's Safari web browser.

The Android browser is sufficiently complex that it gets its own Java package (android.webkit). Using the WebView widget itself can be simple or powerful, based on your requirements, as you'll learn in this chapter.

A Browser, Writ Small

For simple stuff, WebView is not significantly different than any other widget in Android. You pop it into a layout, tell it which URL to navigate to via Java code, and you're finished.

For example (WebKit/Browser1), here is a simple layout with a WebView:

```xml
<?xml version="1.0" encoding="utf-8"?>
<LinearLayout xmlns:android="http://schemas.android.com/apk/res/android"
  android:orientation="vertical"
  android:layout_width="fill_parent"
  android:layout_height="fill_parent"
  >
  <WebView android:id="@+id/webkit"
    android:layout_width="fill_parent"
    android:layout_height="fill_parent"
  />
</LinearLayout>
```

As with any other widget, you need to tell it how it should fill up the space in the layout. In this case, it fills all remaining space.

The Java code is equally simple:

```
package com.commonsware.android.browser1;

import android.app.Activity;
import android.os.Bundle;
import android.webkit.WebView;

public class BrowserDemo1 extends Activity {
  WebView browser;

  @Override
  public void onCreate(Bundle icicle) {
    super.onCreate(icicle);
    setContentView(R.layout.main);
    browser=(WebView)findViewById(R.id.webkit);

    browser.loadUrl("http://commonsware.com");
  }
}
```

The only unusual bit with this edition of onCreate() is that we invoke loadUrl() on the WebView widget, to tell it to load a web page (in this case, the home page of some random firm).

However, we also need to make one change to AndroidManifest.xml, requesting permission to access the Internet:

```
<manifest xmlns:android="http://schemas.android.com/apk/res/android"
  package="com.commonsware.android.browser1">
  <uses-permission android:name="android.permission.INTERNET" />
  <application android:icon="@drawable/cw">
    <activity android:name=".BrowserDemo1" android:label="BrowserDemo1">
      <intent-filter>
        <action android:name="android.intent.action.MAIN" />
        <category android:name="android.intent.category.LAUNCHER" />
      </intent-filter>
    </activity>
  </application>
</manifest>
```

If we fail to add this permission, the browser will refuse to load pages. Permissions are covered in greater detail in Chapter 28.

The resulting activity looks like a web browser, but with hidden scrollbars, as shown in Figure 13–1.

Figure 13–1. *The Browser1 sample application*

As with the regular Android browser, you can pan around the page by dragging it. The D-pad moves you around all the focusable elements on the page.

What is missing is all the extra stuff that makes up a web browser, such as a navigational toolbar.

Now, you may be tempted to replace the URL in that source code with something that relies on JavaScript, such as Google's home page. By default, JavaScript is turned off in WebView widgets. If you want to enable JavaScript, call getSettings().setJavaScriptEnabled(true); on the WebView instance.

Loading It Up

There are two main ways to get content into the WebView. One is to provide the browser with a URL and have the browser display that page via loadUrl(), as described in the previous section. The browser will access the Internet through whatever means are available to that specific device at the present time (Wi-Fi, cellular network, Bluetooth-tethered phone, well-trained tiny carrier pigeons, etc.).

The alternative is to use loadData(). Here, you supply the HTML for the browser to view. You might use this to do the following:

- Display a manual that was installed as a file with your application package.

- Display snippets of HTML you retrieved as part of other processing, such as the description of an entry in an Atom feed.

■ Generate a whole UI using HTML, instead of using the Android widget set.

There are two flavors of `loadData()`. The simpler one allows you to provide the content, the MIME type, and the encoding, all as strings. Typically, your MIME type will be `text/html` and your encoding will be `UTF-8` for ordinary HTML.

For example, you could replace the `loadUrl()` invocation in the previous example with the following:

```
browser.loadData("<html><body>Hello, world!</body></html>",
                 "text/html", "UTF-8");
```

The result would be as shown in Figure 13–2.

Figure 13–2. *The Browser2 sample application*

This is also available as a fully buildable sample, as `WebKit/Browser2`.

Navigating the Waters

As you've seen, the `WebView` widget doesn't come with a navigation toolbar. This allows you to use it in places where such a toolbar would be pointless and a waste of screen real estate. That being said, if you want to offer navigational capabilities, you can, but you need to supply the UI.

`WebView` offers ways to perform garden-variety browser navigation, including the following methods:

■ `reload()`: Refreshes the currently viewed web page.

■ `goBack()`: Goes back one step in the browser history.

- `canGoBack()`: Determines if there is any history to go back to.

- `goForward()`: Goes forward one step in the browser history.

- `canGoForward()`: Determines if there is any history to go forward to.

- `goBackOrForward()`: Goes backward or forward in the browser history. A negative number as an argument represents a count of steps to go backward. A positive number represents how many steps to go forward.

- `canGoBackOrForward()`: Determines if the browser can go backward or forward the stated number of steps (following the same positive/negative convention as `goBackOrForward()`).

- `clearCache()`: Clears the browser resource cache.

- `clearHistory()`: Clears the browsing history.

Entertaining the Client

If you are going to use the `WebView` as a local UI (versus browsing the Web), you will want to be able to get control at key times, particularly when users click links. You will want to make sure those links are handled properly, by loading your own content back into the `WebView`, by submitting an `Intent` to Android to open the URL in a full browser, or by some other means (see Chapter 18).

Your hook into the `WebView` activity is via `setWebViewClient()`, which takes an instance of a `WebViewClient` implementation as a parameter. The supplied callback object will be notified of a wide range of activities. For example, it will be notified when parts of a page have been retrieved (e.g., `onPageStarted()`), as well as when you, as the host application, need to handle certain user- or circumstance-initiated events (e.g., `onTooManyRedirects()` or `onReceivedHttpAuthRequest()`).

A common hook will be `shouldOverrideUrlLoading()`, where your callback is passed a URL (plus the `WebView` itself), and you return `true` if you will handle the request or `false` if you want default handling (e.g., actually fetch the web page referenced by the URL). In the case of a feed reader application, for example, you will probably not have a full browser with navigation built into your reader. In this case, if the user clicks a URL, you probably want to use an `Intent` to ask Android to load that page in a full browser. But if you have inserted a "fake" URL into the HTML, representing a link to some activity-provided content, you can update the `WebView` yourself.

As an example, let's amend the first browser demo to make it an application that, upon a click, shows the current time. From `WebKit/Browser3`, here is the revised Java:

```
public class BrowserDemo3 extends Activity {
  WebView browser;

  @Override
  public void onCreate(Bundle icicle) {
    super.onCreate(icicle);
```

```
        setContentView(R.layout.main);
        browser=(WebView)findViewById(R.id.webkit);
        browser.setWebViewClient(new Callback());

        loadTime();
    }

    void loadTime() {
        String page="<html><body><a href=\"clock\">"
                +new Date().toString()
                +"</a></body></html>";

                browser.loadDataWithBaseURL("x-data://base", page,
                                            "text/html", "UTF-8",
                                            null);
    }

    private class Callback extends WebViewClient {
        public boolean shouldOverrideUrlLoading(WebView view, String url) {
            loadTime();

            return(true);
        }
    }
}
```

Here, we load a simple web page into the browser (loadTime()) that consists of the current time, made into a hyperlink to the /clock URL. We also attach an instance of a WebViewClient subclass, providing our implementation of shouldOverrideUrlLoading(). In this case, no matter what the URL, we want to just reload the WebView via loadTime().

Running this activity gives the result shown in Figure 13–3.

Figure 13–3. *The Browser3 sample application*

Selecting the link and clicking the D-pad center button will select the link, causing the page to be rebuilt with the new time.

Settings, Preferences, and Options (Oh My!)

With your favorite desktop web browser, you have some sort of settings, preferences, or options window. Between that and the toolbar controls, you can tweak and twiddle the behavior of your browser, from preferred fonts to the behavior of JavaScript.

Similarly, you can adjust the settings of your WebView widget as you see fit, via the WebSettings instance returned from calling the widget's getSettings() method.

There are a lot of options on WebSettings to play with. Most appear fairly esoteric (e.g., setFantasyFontFamily()). However, here are some that you may find more useful:

- Control the font sizing via setDefaultFontSize() (to use a point size) or setTextSize() (to use constants indicating relative sizes like LARGER and SMALLEST).

- Control JavaScript via setJavaScriptEnabled() (to disable it outright) and setJavaScriptCanOpenWindowsAutomatically() (to merely stop it from opening pop-up windows).

- Control web site rendering via setUserAgent(). A value of 0 means the WebView gives the web site a user-agent string that indicates it is a mobile browser. A value of 1 results in a user-agent string that suggests it is a desktop browser.

The settings you change are not persistent, so you should store them somewhere (such as via the Android preferences engine, discussed in Chapter 21) if you are allowing your users to determine the settings, rather than hard-wiring the settings in your application.

Chapter 14

Showing Pop-Up Messages

Sometimes, your activity (or other piece of Android code) will need to speak up.

Not every interaction with Android users will be tidy and containable in activities composed of views. Errors will crop up. Background tasks may take much longer than expected. Something asynchronous may occur, such as an incoming message. In these and other cases, you may need to communicate with the user outside the bounds of the traditional UI.

Of course, this is nothing new. Error messages in the form of dialog boxes have been around for a very long time. More subtle indicators also exist—from task tray icons to bouncing dock icons to vibrating cell phones.

Android has quite a few systems for letting you alert your users outside the bounds of an `Activity`-based UI. One, notifications, is tied heavily into intents and services and, as such, is covered in Chapter 31. In this chapter, you will learn about two means of raising pop-up messages: toasts and alerts.

Raising Toasts

A `Toast` is a transient message, meaning that it displays and disappears on its own without user interaction. Moreover, it does not take focus away from the currently active `Activity`, so if the user is busy writing the next Great Programming Guide, his keystrokes will not be "eaten" by the message.

Since a `Toast` is transient, you have no way of knowing if the user even notices it. You get no acknowledgment, nor does the message stick around for a long time to pester the user. Hence, the `Toast` is mostly for advisory messages, such as indicating a long-running background task is completed, the battery has dropped to a low (but not too low) level, and so on.

Making a Toast is fairly easy. The Toast class offers a static makeText() that accepts a String (or string resource ID) and returns a Toast instance. The makeText() method also needs the Activity (or other Context) plus a duration. The duration is expressed in the form of the LENGTH_SHORT or LENGTH_LONG constants to indicate, on a relative basis, how long the message should remain visible.

If you would prefer your Toast be made out of some other View, rather than be a boring old piece of text, simply create a new Toast instance via the constructor (which takes a Context), and then call setView() to supply it with the view to use and setDuration() to set the duration.

Once your Toast is configured, call its show() method, and the message will be displayed.

Alert! Alert!

If you would prefer something in the more classic dialog box style, what you want is an AlertDialog. As with any other modal dialog box, an AlertDialog pops up, grabs the focus, and stays there until closed by the user. You might use this for a critical error, a validation message that cannot be effectively displayed in the base activity UI, or some other situation where you are sure that the user needs to see the message and needs to see it now.

The simplest way to construct an AlertDialog is to use the Builder class. Following in true builder style, Builder offers a series of methods to configure an AlertDialog, each method returning the Builder for easy chaining. At the end, you call show() on the builder to display the dialog.

Commonly used configuration methods on Builder include the following:

- setMessage(): Sets the "body" of the dialog to be a simple textual message, from either a supplied String or a supplied string resource ID.

- setTitle() and setIcon(): Configure the text and/or icon to appear in the title bar of the dialog.

- setPositiveButton(), setNeutralButton(), and setNegativeButton(): Indicate which button(s) should appear across the bottom of the dialog, where they should be positioned (left, center, or right, respectively), what their captions should be, and what logic should be invoked when the button is clicked (besides dismissing the dialog).

If you need to configure the AlertDialog beyond what the builder allows, instead of calling show(), call create() to get the partially built AlertDialog instance, configure it the rest of the way, and then call one of the flavors of show() on the AlertDialog itself.

Once show() is called, the dialog will appear and await user input.

Checking Them Out

To see how these work in practice, take a peek at Messages/Message, containing the following layout:

```xml
<?xml version="1.0" encoding="utf-8"?>
<LinearLayout xmlns:android="http://schemas.android.com/apk/res/android"
  android:orientation="vertical"
  android:layout_width="fill_parent"
  android:layout_height="fill_parent" >
  <Button
    android:id="@+id/alert"
    android:text="Raise an alert"
    android:layout_width="fill_parent"
    android:layout_height="wrap_content"/>
  <Button
    android:id="@+id/toast"
    android:text="Make a toast"
    android:layout_width="fill_parent"
    android:layout_height="wrap_content"/>
</LinearLayout>
```

Here's the Java code:

```java
public class MessageDemo extends Activity implements View.OnClickListener {
  Button alert;
  Button toast;

  @Override
  public void onCreate(Bundle icicle) {
    super.onCreate(icicle);

    setContentView(R.layout.main);

    alert=(Button)findViewById(R.id.alert);
    alert.setOnClickListener(this);
    toast=(Button)findViewById(R.id.toast);
    toast.setOnClickListener(this);
  }

  public void onClick(View view) {
    if (view==alert) {
      new AlertDialog.Builder(this)
        .setTitle("MessageDemo")
        .setMessage("eek!")
        .setNeutralButton("Close", new DialogInterface.OnClickListener() {
          public void onClick(DialogInterface dlg, int sumthin) {
            // do nothing - it will close on its own
          }
        })
        .show();
    }
    else {
      Toast
        .makeText(this, "<clink, clink>", Toast.LENGTH_SHORT)
```

```
            .show();
        }
    }
}
```

The layout is unremarkable—just a pair of buttons to trigger the alert and the toast.

When the Raise an alert button is clicked, we use a builder (new Builder(this)) to set the title (setTitle("MessageDemo")), message (setMessage("eek!")), and neutral button (setNeutralButton("Close", new OnClickListener() ...) before showing the dialog. When the Close button is clicked, the OnClickListener callback does nothing; the mere fact that the button was pressed causes the dialog to be dismissed. However, you could update information in your activity based on the user action, particularly if you have multiple buttons for the user to choose from. The result is a typical dialog, as shown in Figure 14–1.

Figure 14–1. *The MessageDemo sample application, after clicking the Raise an alert button*

When the Make a toast button is clicked, the Toast class makes us a text-based toast (makeText(this, "<clink, clink>", LENGTH_SHORT)), which we then show(). The result is a short-lived, noninterrupting message, as shown in Figure 14–2.

Figure 14–2. *The same application, after clicking the Make a toast button*

Chapter **15**

Dealing with Threads

Ideally, you want your activities to be downright snappy, so your users don't feel that your application is sluggish. Responding to user input quickly (e.g., within in 200 milliseconds) is a fine goal. At minimum, though, you need to make sure you respond within 5 seconds, lest the ActivityManager decide to play the role of the Grim Reaper and kill off your activity as being nonresponsive.

Of course, your activity might have real work to do, which takes nonnegligible amount of time. This invariably involves the use of a background thread. Android provides a veritable cornucopia of means to set up background threads, yet allow them to safely interact with the UI on the UI thread.

The "safely interact" concept is crucial. You cannot modify any part of the UI from a background thread. That must be done on the UI thread. This generally means that there will need to be some coordination between background threads doing the work and the UI thread showing the results of that work.

This chapter covers how to work with background and UI threads in your Android applications.

Getting Through the Handlers

The most flexible means of making an Android-friendly background thread is to create an instance of a Handler subclass. You need only one Handler object per activity, and you do not need to manually register it. Merely creating the instance is sufficient to register it with the Android threading subsystem.

Your background thread can communicate with the Handler, which will do all of its work on the activity's UI thread. This is important, as UI changes, such as updating widgets, should occur only on the activity's UI thread.

You have two options for communicating with the Handler: messages and Runnable objects.

Messages

To send a Message to a Handler, first invoke obtainMessage() to get the Message object out of the pool. There are a few flavors of obtainMessage(), allowing you to create empty Message objects or ones populated with message identifiers and arguments. The more complicated your Handler processing needs to be, the more likely it is you will need to put data into the Message to help the Handler distinguish different events.

Then you send the Message to the Handler via its message queue, using one of the sendMessage...() family of methods, such as the following:

- sendMessage(): Puts the message on the queue immediately.

- sendMessageAtFrontOfQueue(): Puts the message on the queue immediately, placing it at the front of the message queue, so your message takes priority over all others.

- sendMessageAtTime(): Puts the message on the queue at the stated time, expressed in the form of milliseconds based on system uptime (SystemClock.uptimeMillis()).

- sendMessageDelayed(): Puts the message on the queue after a delay, expressed in milliseconds.

To process these messages, your Handler needs to implement handleMessage(), which will be called with each message that appears on the message queue. There, the handler can update the UI as needed. However, it should still do that work quickly, as other UI work is suspended until the Handler is finished.

For example, let's create a ProgressBar and update it via a Handler. Here is the layout from the Threads/Handler sample project:

```xml
<?xml version="1.0" encoding="utf-8"?>
<LinearLayout xmlns:android="http://schemas.android.com/apk/res/android"
  android:orientation="vertical"
  android:layout_width="fill_parent"
  android:layout_height="fill_parent"
  >
  <ProgressBar android:id="@+id/progress"
    style="?android:attr/progressBarStyleHorizontal"
    android:layout_width="fill_parent"
    android:layout_height="wrap_content" />
</LinearLayout>
```

The ProgressBar, in addition to setting the width and height as normal, also employs the style property. This particular style indicates the ProgressBar should be drawn as the traditional horizontal bar showing the amount of work that has been completed.

And here is the Java:

```java
package com.commonsware.android.threads;

import android.app.Activity;
import android.os.Bundle;
import android.os.Handler;
```

```java
import android.os.Message;
import android.widget.ProgressBar;

public class HandlerDemo extends Activity {
  ProgressBar bar;
  Handler handler=new Handler() {
    @Override
    public void handleMessage(Message msg) {
      bar.incrementProgressBy(5);
    }
  };
  boolean isRunning=false;

  @Override
  public void onCreate(Bundle icicle) {
    super.onCreate(icicle);
    setContentView(R.layout.main);
    bar=(ProgressBar)findViewById(R.id.progress);
  }

  public void onStart() {
    super.onStart();
    bar.setProgress(0);

    Thread background=new Thread(new Runnable() {
      public void run() {
        try {
          for (int i=0;i<20 && isRunning;i++) {
            Thread.sleep(1000);
            handler.sendMessage(handler.obtainMessage());
          }
        }
        catch (Throwable t) {
          // just end the background thread
        }
      }
    });

    isRunning=true;
    background.start();
  }

  public void onStop() {
    super.onStop();
    isRunning=false;
  }
}
```

As part of constructing the Activity, we create an instance of Handler, with our implementation of handleMessage(). Basically, for any message received, we update the ProgressBar by 5 points, and then exit the message handler.

In onStart(), we set up a background thread. In a real system, this thread would do something meaningful. Here, we just sleep 1 second, post a Message to the Handler, and repeat for a total of 20 passes. This, combined with the 5-point increase in the

ProgressBar position, will march the bar clear across the screen, as the default maximum value for ProgressBar is 100. You can adjust that maximum via setMax(). For example, you might set the maximum to be the number of database rows you are processing, and update once per row.

Note that we then *leave* onStart(). This is crucial. The onStart() method is invoked on the activity UI thread, so it can update widgets and such. However, that means we need to get out of onStart(), both to let the Handler get its work done and also so Android does not think our activity is stuck.

The resulting activity is simply a horizontal progress bar, as shown in Figure 15–1.

Figure 15–1. *The HandlerDemo sample application*

Note, though, that while ProgressBar samples like this one show your code arranging to update the progress on the UI thread, for this specific widget, that is not necessary. At least as of Android 1.5, ProgressBar is now UI thread-safe, in that you can update it from any thread, and it will handle the details of performing the actual UI update on the UI thread.

Runnables

If you would rather not fuss with Message objects, you can also pass Runnable objects to the Handler, which will run those Runnable objects on the activity UI thread. Handler offers a set of post...() methods for passing Runnable objects in for eventual processing.

Running in Place

Just as Handler supports post() and postDelayed() to add Runnable objects to the event queue, you can use those same methods on View. This slightly simplifies your code, in that you can then skip the Handler object. However, you lose a bit of flexibility. Also, the Handler has been in the Android toolkit longer, and it may be more tested.

Where Oh Where Has My UI Thread Gone?

Sometimes, you may not know if you are currently executing on the UI thread of your application. For example, if you package some of your code in a JAR file for others to reuse, you might not know whether your code is being executed on the UI thread or from a background thread.

To help combat this problem, Activity offers runOnUiThread(). This works similar to the post() methods on Handler and View, in that it queues up a Runnable to run on the UI thread, if you are not on the UI thread right now. If you are already on the UI thread, it invokes the Runnable immediately. This gives you the best of both worlds: no delay if you are on the UI thread, yet safety in case you are not.

Asyncing Feeling

Android 1.5 introduced a new way of thinking about background operations: AsyncTask. In one (reasonably) convenient class, Android will handle all of the chores of doing work on the UI thread versus on a background thread. Moreover, Android itself allocates and removes that background thread. And it maintains a small work queue, further accentuating the fire-and-forget feel to AsyncTask.

The Theory

There is a saying, popular in marketing circles: "When a man buys a 1/4-inch drill bit at a hardware store, he does not want a 1/4-inch drill bit—he wants 1/4-inch holes." Hardware stores cannot sell holes, so they sell the next-best thing: devices (drills and drill bits) that make creating holes easy.

Similarly, Android developers who have struggled with background thread management do not strictly want background threads. Rather, they want work to be done off the UI thread, so users are not stuck waiting and activities do not get the dreaded "application not responding" (ANR) error. And while Android cannot magically cause work to not consume UI thread time, it can offer things that make such background operations easier and more transparent. AsyncTask is one such example.

To use AsyncTask, you must:

- Create a subclass of AsyncTask, commonly as a private inner class of something that uses the task (e.g., an activity).

- Override one or more AsyncTask methods to accomplish the background work, plus whatever work associated with the task that needs to be done on the UI thread (e.g., update progress).

- When needed, create an instance of the AsyncTask subclass and call execute() to have it begin doing its work.

What you do *not* need to do is:

- Create your own background thread.

- Terminate that background thread at an appropriate time.

- Call all sorts of methods to arrange for bits of processing to be done on the UI thread.

AsyncTask, Generics, and Varargs

Creating a subclass of AsyncTask is not quite as easy as, say, implementing the Runnable interface. AsyncTask uses generics, and so you need to specify three data types:

- The type of information that is needed to process the task (e.g., URLs to download)

- The type of information that is passed within the task to indicate progress

- The type of information that is passed when the task is completed to the post-task code

What makes this all the more confusing is that the first two data types are actually used as varargs, meaning that an array of these types is used within your AsyncTask subclass.

This should become clearer as we work our way toward an example.

The Stages of AsyncTask

There are four methods you can override in AsyncTask to accomplish your ends.

The one you must override, for the task class to be useful, is doInBackground(). This will be called by AsyncTask on a background thread. It can run as long as necessary in order to accomplish whatever work needs to be done for this specific task. Note, though, that tasks are meant to be finite; using AsyncTask for an infinite loop is not recommended.

The doInBackground() method will receive, as parameters, a varargs array of the first of the three data types listed in the preceding section—the data needed to process the task. So, if your task's mission is to download a collection of URLs, doInBackground() will receive those URLs to process. The doInBackground() method must return a value of the third data type listed—the result of the background work.

You may wish to override onPreExecute(). This method is called, from the UI thread, before the background thread executes doInBackground(). Here, you might initialize a ProgressBar or otherwise indicate that background work is commencing.

Also, you may wish to override onPostExecute(). This method is called, from the UI thread, after doInBackground() completes. It receives, as a parameter, the value returned by doInBackground() (e.g., success or failure flag). Here, you might dismiss the ProgressBar and make use of the work done in the background, such as updating the contents of a list.

In addition, you may wish to override onProgressUpdate(). If doInBackground() calls the task's publishProgress() method, the object(s) passed to that method are provided to onProgressUpdate(), but in the UI thread. That way, onProgressUpdate() can alert the user as to the progress that has been made on the background work, such as updating a ProgressBar or continuing an animation. The onProgressUpdate() method will receive a varargs of the second data type from the list in the preceding section—the data published by doInBackground() via publishProgress().

A Sample Task

As mentioned earlier, implementing an AsyncTask is not quite as easy as implementing a Runnable. However, once you get past the generics and varargs, it is not too bad.

For example, the following is an implementation of a ListActivity that uses an AsyncTask, from the Threads/Asyncer sample project:

```
package com.commonsware.android.async;

import android.app.ListActivity;
import android.os.AsyncTask;
import android.os.Bundle;
import android.os.SystemClock;
import android.widget.ArrayAdapter;
import android.widget.Toast;
import java.util.ArrayList;

public class AsyncDemo extends ListActivity {
  private static String[] items={"lorem", "ipsum", "dolor",
                                 "sit", "amet", "consectetuer",
                                 "adipiscing", "elit", "morbi",
                                 "vel", "ligula", "vitae",
                                 "arcu", "aliquet", "mollis",
                                 "etiam", "vel", "erat",
                                 "placerat", "ante",
                                 "porttitor", "sodales",
                                 "pellentesque", "augue",
                                 "purus"};
  @Override
  public void onCreate(Bundle savedInstanceState) {
    super.onCreate(savedInstanceState);
    setContentView(R.layout.main);

    setListAdapter(new ArrayAdapter<String>(this,
                   android.R.layout.simple_list_item_1,
```

```
                               new ArrayList()));

           new AddStringTask().execute();
    }

    class AddStringTask extends AsyncTask<Void, String, Void> {
      @Override
      protected Void doInBackground(Void... unused) {
        for (String item : items) {
          publishProgress(item);
          SystemClock.sleep(200);
        }

        return(null);
      }

      @Override
      protected void onProgressUpdate(String... item) {
        ((ArrayAdapter)getListAdapter()).add(item[0]);
      }

      @Override
      protected void onPostExecute(Void unused) {
        Toast
          .makeText(AsyncDemo.this, "Done!", Toast.LENGTH_SHORT)
          .show();
      }
    }
  }
}
```

This is another variation on the *lorem ipsum* list of words, used frequently throughout this book. This time, rather than simply hand the list of words to an ArrayAdapter, we simulate needing to work to create these words in the background using AddStringTask, our AsyncTask implementation.

If you build, install, and run this project, you will see the list being populated in real time over a few seconds, followed by a Toast indicating completion, as shown in Figure 15–2.

Figure 15–2. *The AsyncDemo, partway through loading the list of words*

Let's examine this project's code piece by piece.

The AddStringTask Declaration

First, let's look at the AddStringTask declaration:

```
class AddStringTask extends AsyncTask<Void, String, Void> {
```

Here, we use the generics to set up the specific types of data we are going to leverage in AddStringTask, as follows:

- We do not need any configuration information in this case, so our first type is Void.

- We want to pass each string generated by our background task to onProgressUpdate(), to allow us to add it to our list, so our second type is String.

- We do not have any results, strictly speaking (beyond the updates), so our third type is Void.

The doInBackground() Method

Next up is the doInBackground() method:

```
@Override
protected Void doInBackground(Void... unused) {
  for (String item : items) {
    publishProgress(item);
    SystemClock.sleep(200);
  }

  return(null);
}
```

The doInBackground() method is invoked in a background thread. Hence, we can take as long as we like. In a production application, we might be doing something like iterating over a list of URLs and downloading each. Here, we iterate over our static list of *lorem ipsum* words, call publishProgress() for each, and then sleep 1/4 second to simulate real work being done.

Since we elected to have no configuration information, we should not need parameters to doInBackground(). However, the contract with AsyncTask says we need to accept a varargs of the first data type, which is why our method parameter is Void... unused.

Since we elected to have no results, we should not need to return anything. Again, though, the contract with AsyncTask says we must return an object of the third data type. Since that data type is Void, our returned object is null.

The onProgressUpdate() Method

The onProgressUpdate() method looks like this:

```
@Override
protected void onProgressUpdate(String... item) {
  ((ArrayAdapter)getListAdapter()).add(item[0]);
}
```

The onProgressUpdate() method is called on the UI thread, and we want to do something to let the user know we are making progress on loading these strings. In this case, we simply add the string to the ArrayAdapter, so it is appended to the end of the list.

The onProgressUpdate() method receives a String... varargs because that is the second data type in our class declaration. Since we are passing only one string per call to publishProgress(), we need to examine just the first entry in the varargs array.

The onPostExecute() Method

Here's the onPostExecute() method:

```
@Override
protected void onPostExecute(Void unused) {
  Toast
    .makeText(AsyncDemo.this, "Done!", Toast.LENGTH_SHORT)
    .show();
}
```

The onPostExecute() method is called on the UI thread, and we want to do something to indicate that the background work is complete. In a real system, there may be some ProgressBar to dismiss or some animation to stop. Here, we simply raise a Toast.

Since we elected to have no results, we should not need any parameters. The contract with AsyncTask says we must accept a parameter of the third data type. Since that data type is Void, our method parameter is Void unused.

The Activity

Finally, let's look at the activity:

```
new AddStringTask().execute();
```

To use AddStringsTask, we simply create an instance and call execute() on it. That starts the chain of events eventually leading to the background thread doing its work.

If AddStringsTask required configuration parameters, we would not have used Void as our first data type, and the constructor would accept zero or more parameters of the defined type. Those values would eventually be passed to doInBackground().

And Now, the Caveats

Background threads, while eminently possible using the Android Handler system, are not all happiness and warm puppies. Background threads not only add complexity, but they also have real-world costs in terms of available memory, CPU, and battery life.

Hence, there are a wide range of scenarios you need to account for with your background thread, including the following:

- The possibility that users will interact with your activity's UI while the background thread is chugging along. If the work that the background thread is doing is altered or invalidated by the user input, you will need to communicate this to the background thread. Android includes many classes in the `java.util.concurrent` package that will help you communicate safely with your background thread.

- The possibility that the activity will be killed off while background work is occurring. For example, after starting your activity, the user might have a call come in, followed by a text message, followed by a need to look up a contact—all of which might be sufficient to kick your activity out of memory. Chapter 16 will cover the various events Android will take your activity through. Hook to the proper ones, and be sure to shut down your background thread cleanly when you have the chance.

- The possibility that your user will get irritated if you chew up a lot of CPU time and battery life without giving any payback. Tactically, this means using `ProgressBar` or other means of letting the user know that something is happening. Strategically, this means you still need to be efficient at what you do—background threads are no panacea for sluggish or pointless code.

- The possibility that you will encounter an error during background processing. For example, if you are gathering information from the Internet, the device might lose connectivity. Alerting the user of the problem via a notification (discussed in Chapter 31) and shutting down the background thread may be your best option.

Chapter 16

Handling Activity Life Cycle Events

As you know, Android devices, by and large, are phones. As such, some activities are more important that others—taking a call is probably more important to users than playing Sudoku. And, since it is a phone, it probably has less RAM than your current desktop or notebook possesses.

As a result of the device's limited RAM, your activity may find itself being killed off because other activities are going on and the system needs your activity's memory. Think of it as the Android equivalent of the circle of life: Your activity dies so others may live, and so on.

You cannot assume that your activity will run until you think it is complete, or even until the user thinks it is complete. This is one example—perhaps the most important example—of how an activity's life cycle will affect your own application logic.

This chapter covers the various states and callbacks that make up an activity's life cycle, and how you can hook into them appropriately.

Schroedinger's Activity

An activity, generally speaking, is in one of four states at any point in time:

- *Active*: The activity was started by the user, is running, and is in the foreground. This is what you're used to thinking of in terms of your activity's operation.

- *Paused*: The activity was started by the user, is running, and is visible, but a notification or something is overlaying part of the screen. During this time, the user can see your activity but may not be able to interact with it. For example, if a call comes in, the user will get the opportunity to take the call or ignore it.

- *Stopped*: The activity was started by the user, is running, but is hidden by other activities that have been launched or switched to. Your application will not be able to present anything meaningful to the user directly, but may communicate by way of a notification (discussed in Chapter 31).

- *Dead*: Either the activity was never started (e.g., just after a phone reset) or the activity was terminated, perhaps due to lack of available memory.

Life, Death, and Your Activity

Android will call into your activity as the activity transitions between the four states listed in the previous section, using the methods described in this section. Some transitions may result in multiple calls to your activity, and sometimes Android will kill your application without calling it. This whole area is rather murky and probably subject to change, so pay close attention to the official Android documentation as well as the information here when deciding which events deserve attention and which you can safely ignore.

Note that for all of these methods, you should chain upward and invoke the superclass's edition of the method, or Android may raise an exception.

onCreate() and onDestroy()

We have been implementing onCreate() in all of our Activity subclasses in all the examples. This method will be called in three situations:

- When the activity is first started (e.g., since a system restart), onCreate() will be invoked with a null parameter.

- If the activity had been running, then sometime later was killed off, onCreate() will be invoked with the Bundle from onSaveInstanceState() as a parameter.

- If the activity had been running and you have set up your activity to have different resources based on different device states (e.g., landscape versus portrait), your activity will be re-created and onCreate() will be called. Resources are covered in Chapter 20.

Here is where you initialize your UI and set up anything that needs to be done once, regardless of how the activity is used.

On the other end of the life cycle, onDestroy() may be called when the activity is shutting down, either because the activity called finish() (which "finishes" the activity) or because Android needs RAM and is closing the activity prematurely. Note that onDestroy() may not be called if the need for RAM is urgent (e.g., an incoming phone call), and that the activity will still be shut down. Hence, onDestroy() is mostly for cleanly releasing resources you obtained in onCreate() (if any).

onStart(), onRestart(), and onStop()

An activity can come to the foreground because it is first being launched, or because it is being brought back to the foreground after having been hidden (e.g., by another activity or by an incoming phone call). The onStart() method is called in either of those cases.

The onRestart() method is called in the case where the activity had been stopped and is now restarting.

Conversely, onStop() is called when the activity is about to be stopped.

onPause() and onResume()

The onResume() method is called just before your activity comes to the foreground, after being initially launched, being restarted from a stopped state, or a pop-up dialog (e.g., an incoming call) is cleared. This is a great place to refresh the UI based on things that may have occurred since the user was last looking at your activity. For example, if you are polling a service for changes to some information (e.g., new entries for a feed), onResume() is a fine time to both refresh the current view and, if applicable, kick off a background thread to update the view (e.g., via a Handler).

Conversely, anything that steals your user away from your activity—usually, the activation of another activity—will result in your onPause() being called. Here, you should undo anything you did in onResume(), such as stopping background threads, releasing any exclusive-access resources you may have acquired (e.g., a camera), and the like.

Once onPause() is called, Android reserves the right to kill off your activity's process at any point. Hence, you should not be relying on receiving any further events.

The Grace of State

Mostly, the aforementioned methods are for dealing with things at the application-general level (e.g., wiring together the last pieces of your UI in onCreate() or closing down background threads in onPause()).

However, a large part of the goal of Android is to have a patina of seamlessness. Activities may come and go as dictated by memory requirements, but ideally, users are unaware that this is occurring. If, for example, a user was working with a calculator, and came back to that calculator after an absence, he should see whatever number he was working on originally, unless he actually took some action to close down the calculator.

To make all this work, activities need to be able to save their application-instance state, and to do so quickly and cheaply. Since activities could be killed off at any time, activities may need to save their state more frequently than you might expect. Then, when the activity restarts, the activity should get its former state back, so it can restore the activity to the way it appeared previously.

Saving instance state is handled by onSaveInstanceState(). This supplies a Bundle, into which activities can pour whatever data they need (e.g., the number showing on the calculator's display). This method implementation needs to be speedy, so do not try to be fancy—just put your data in the Bundle and exit the method.

That instance state is provided to you again in two places: in onCreate() and in onRestoreInstanceState(). It is your choice when you wish to reapply the state data to your activity; either callback is a reasonable option.

Chapter 17

Creating Intent Filters

Up to now, the focus of this book has been on activities opened directly by the user from the device's launcher. This is the most obvious case for getting your activity up and visible to the user. And, in many cases, it is the primary way the user will start using your application.

However, the Android system is based on many loosely coupled components. The things that you might accomplish in a desktop GUI via dialog boxes, child windows, and the like are mostly supposed to be independent activities. While one activity will be "special," in that it shows up in the launcher, the other activities all need to be reached somehow.

The "somehow" is via intents.

An intent is basically a message that you pass to Android saying, "Yo! I want to do...er...something! Yeah!" How specific the "something" is depends on the situation. Sometimes you know exactly what you want to do (e.g., open one of your other activities), and sometimes you don't.

In the abstract, Android is all about intents and receivers of those intents. So, now let's dive into intents, so we can create more complex applications while simultaneously being "good Android citizens."

What's Your Intent?

When Sir Tim Berners-Lee cooked up the Hypertext Transfer Protocol (HTTP), he set up a system of verbs plus addresses in the form of URLs. The address indicates a resource, such as a web page, graphic, or server-side program. The verb indicates what should be done: GET to retrieve it, POST to send form data to it for processing, and so on.

Intents are similar, in that they represent an action plus context. There are more actions and more components to the context with Android intents than there are with HTTP verbs and resources, but the concept is the same. Just as a web browser knows how to process a verb+URL pair, Android knows how to find activities or other application logic that will handle a given intent.

Pieces of Intents

The two most important pieces of an intent are the action and what Android refers to as the *data*. These are almost exactly analogous to HTTP verbs and URLs: the action is the verb, and the data is a Uri, such as content://contacts/people/1, representing a contact in the contacts database. Actions are constants, such as ACTION_VIEW (to bring up a viewer for the resource), ACTION_EDIT (to edit the resource), or ACTION_PICK (to choose an available item given a Uri representing a collection, such as content://contacts/people).

If you were to create an intent combining ACTION_VIEW with a content Uri of content://contacts/people/1, and pass that intent to Android, Android would know to find and open an activity capable of viewing that resource.

You can place other criteria inside an intent (represented as an Intent object), besides the action and data Uri, such as the following:

- *Category*: Your "main" activity will be in the LAUNCHER category, indicating it should show up on the launcher menu. Other activities will probably be in the DEFAULT or ALTERNATIVE categories.

- *MIME type*: This indicates the type of resource on which you want to operate, if you don't know a collection Uri.

- *Component*: This is the class of the activity that is supposed to receive this intent. Using components this way obviates the need for the other properties of the intent. However, it does make the intent more fragile, as it assumes specific implementations.

- *Extras*: A Bundle of other information you want to pass along to the receiver with the intent, that the receiver might want to take advantage of. Which pieces of information a given receiver can use is up to the receiver and (hopefully) is well-documented.

You will find rosters of the standard actions and categories in the Android SDK documentation for the Intent class.

Intent Routing

As noted in the previous section, if you specify the target component in your intent, Android has no doubt where the intent is supposed to be routed to, and it will launch the named activity. This might be appropriate if the target intent is in your application. It definitely is not recommended for sending intents to other applications.

Component names, by and large, are considered private to the application and are subject to change. Content Uri templates and MIME types are the preferred ways of identifying services you wish third-party code to supply.

If you do not specify the target component, Android must figure out which activities (or other intent receivers) are eligible to receive the intent. Note the use of the plural *activities*, as a broadly written intent might well resolve to several activities. That is the...ummm...intent (pardon the pun), as you will see later in this chapter. This routing approach is referred to as *implicit routing*.

Basically, there are three rules, all of which must be true for a given activity to be eligible for a given intent:

- The activity must support the specified action.
- The activity must support the stated MIME type (if supplied).
- The activity must support all of the categories named in the intent.

The upshot is that you want to make your intents specific enough to find the correct receiver(s), and no more specific than that. This will become clearer as we work through some examples later in this chapter.

Stating Your Intent(ions)

All Android components that wish to be notified via intents must declare intent filters, so Android knows which intents should go to that component. To do this, you need to add `intent-filter` elements to your `AndroidManifest.xml` file.

All of the example projects have intent filters defined, courtesy of the Android application-building script (`activityCreator` or the IDE equivalent). They look something like this:

```
<manifest xmlns:android="http://schemas.android.com/apk/res/android"
    package="com.commonsware.android.skeleton">
    <application>
        <activity android:name=".Now" android:label="Now">
            <intent-filter>
                <action android:name="android.intent.action.MAIN" />
                <category android:name="android.intent.category.LAUNCHER" />
            </intent-filter>
        </activity>
    </application>
</manifest>
```

Note the `intent-filter` element under the `activity` element. Here, we declare that this activity:

- Is the main activity for this application
- Is in the `LAUNCHER` category, meaning it gets an icon in the Android main menu

Because this activity is the main one for the application, Android knows this is the component it should launch when someone chooses the application from the main menu.

You are welcome to have more than one action or more than one category in your intent filters. That indicates that the associated component (e.g., activity) handles multiple different sorts of intents.

More than likely, you will also want to have your secondary (non-MAIN) activities specify the MIME type of data on which they work. Then, if an intent is targeted for that MIME type—either directly, or indirectly by the Uri referencing something of that type—Android will know that the component handles such data.

For example, you could have an activity declared like this:

```
<activity android:name=".TourViewActivity">
  <intent-filter>
    <action android:name="android.intent.action.VIEW" />
    <category android:name="android.intent.category.DEFAULT" />
    <data android:mimeType="vnd.android.cursor.item/vnd.commonsware.tour" />
  </intent-filter>
</activity>
```

This activity will be launched by an intent requesting to view a Uri representing a vnd.android.cursor.item/vnd.commonsware.tour piece of content. That Intent could come from another activity in the same application (e.g., the MAIN activity for this application) or from another activity in another Android application that happens to know a Uri that this activity handles.

Narrow Receivers

In the preceding examples, the intent filters were set up on activities. Sometimes, tying intents to activities is not exactly what you want, as in these cases:

- Some system events might cause you to want to trigger something in a service rather than an activity.

- Some events might need to launch different activities in different circumstances, where the criteria are not solely based on the intent itself, but some other state (e.g., if you get intent X and the database has a Y, then launch activity M; if the database does not have a Y, then launch activity N).

For these cases, Android offers the intent receiver, defined as a class implementing the BroadcastReceiver interface. Intent receivers are disposable objects designed to receive intents—particularly broadcast intents—and take action. The action typically involves launching other intents to trigger logic in an activity, service, or other component.

The BroadcastReceiver interface has only one method: onReceive(). Intent receivers implement that method, where they do whatever it is they wish to do upon an incoming intent. To declare an intent receiver, add a receiver element to your AndroidManifest.xml file:

```
<receiver android:name=".MyIntentReceiverClassName" />
```

An intent receiver is alive for only as long as it takes to process onReceive(). As soon as that method returns, the receiver instance is subject to garbage collection and will not be reused. This means intent receivers are somewhat limited in what they can do, mostly to avoid anything that involves any sort of callback. For example, they cannot bind to a service, and they cannot open a dialog.

The exception is if the `BroadcastReceiver` is implemented on some longer-lived component, such as an activity or service. In that case, the intent receiver lives as long as its "host" does (e.g., until the activity is frozen). However, in this case, you cannot declare the intent receiver via `AndroidManifest.xml`. Instead, you need to call `registerReceiver()` on your `Activity`'s `onResume()` callback to declare interest in an intent, and then call `unregisterReceiver()` from your `Activity`'s `onPause()` when you no longer need those intents.

The Pause Caveat

There is one hiccup with using `Intent` objects to pass arbitrary messages around: It works only when the receiver is active. To quote from the documentation for `BroadcastReceiver`:

> *If registering a receiver in your Activity.onResume() implementation, you should unregister it in Activity.onPause(). (You won't receive intents when paused, and this will cut down on unnecessary system overhead). Do not unregister in Activity.onSaveInstanceState(), because this won't be called if the user moves back in the history stack.*

Hence, you can use the `Intent` framework as an arbitrary message bus only in the following situations:

- Your receiver does not care if it misses messages because it was not active.
- You provide some means of getting the receiver "caught up" on messages it missed while it was inactive.

In Chapters 29 and 30, you will see an example of the former condition, where the receiver (service client) will use `Intent`-based messages when they are available, but does not need them if the client is not active.

Chapter 18

Launching Activities and Subactivities

As you've learned, the theory behind the Android UI architecture is that developers should decompose their application into distinct activities Each activity is implemented as an `Activity`, and each is reachable via intents, with a "main" activity being the one launched by the Android launcher. For example, a calendar application could have activities for viewing the calendar, viewing a single event, editing an event (including adding a new one), and so forth.

This implies that one of your activities has the means to start up another activity. For example, if someone selects an event from the view-calendar activity, you might want to show the view-event activity for that event. So, you need to be able to cause the view-event activity to launch and show a specific event (the one the user chose). This chapter describes how to do that.

> **NOTE:** This chapter assumes that you know which activity you want to launch, probably because it is another activity in your own application. It's also possible that you have a content `Uri` to do something, and you want your users to be able to do something with it, but you do not know up front what the options are. This situation requires more advanced handling, which I cover in my book *The Busy Coders Guide to Advanced Android Development* (CommonsWare, 2009).

Peers and Subs

One key question you need to answer when you decide to launch an activity is this: Does your activity need to know when the launched activity ends?

For example, suppose you want to spawn an activity to collect authentication information for some web service you are connecting to—maybe you need to authenticate with OpenID (`http://openid.net/`) in order to use an OAuth service (http://oauth.net/). In this case, your main activity will need to know when the authentication is complete so it can start to use the web service.

On the other hand, imagine an e-mail application in Android. When the user elects to view an attachment, neither you nor the user necessarily expect the main activity to know when the user is finished viewing that attachment.

In the first scenario, the launched activity is clearly subordinate to the launching activity. In that case, you probably want to launch the child as a subactivity, which means your activity will be notified when the child activity is complete.

In the second scenario, the launched activity is more a peer of your activity, so you probably want to launch the child just as a regular activity. Your activity will not be informed when the child is done, but, then again, your activity really doesn't need to know.

Start 'Em Up

The two pieces for starting an activity are an intent and your choice of how to start it up.

Make an Intent

As discussed in the previous chapter, intents encapsulate a request, made to Android, for some activity or other intent receiver to do something.

If the activity you intend to launch is one of your own, you may find it simplest to create an explicit intent, naming the component you wish to launch. For example, from within your activity, you could create an intent like this:

```
new Intent(this, HelpActivity.class);
```

This stipulates that you want to launch the HelpActivity. This activity would need to be named in your AndroidManifest.xml file, though not necessarily with any intent filter, since you are trying to request it directly.

Or you could put together an intent for some Uri, requesting a particular action:

```
Uri uri=Uri.parse("geo:"+lat.toString()+","+lon.toString());
Intent i=new Intent(Intent.ACTION_VIEW, uri);
```

Here, given that you have the latitude and longitude of some position (lat and lon, respectively) of type Double, you construct a geo scheme Uri and create an intent requesting to view this Uri (ACTION_VIEW).

Make the Call

Once you have your intent, you need to pass it to Android and get the child activity to launch. You have two choices:

- The simplest option is to call startActivity() with the Intent. This will cause Android to find the best-match activity and pass the intent to it for handling. Your activity will not be informed when the child activity is complete.

- You can call startActivityForResult(), passing it the Intent and a number (unique to the calling activity). Android will find the best-match activity and pass the intent over to it. Your activity will be notified when the child activity is complete via the onActivityResult() callback.

With startActivityForResult(), as noted, you can implement the onActivityResult() callback to be notified when the child activity has completed its work. The callback receives the unique number supplied to startActivityForResult(), so you can determine which child activity is the one that has completed. You also get the following:

- A result code, from the child activity calling setResult(). Typically, this is RESULT_OK or RESULT_CANCELLED, though you can create your own return codes (pick a number starting with RESULT_FIRST_USER).

- An optional String containing some result data, possibly a URL to some internal or external resource. For example, an ACTION_PICK intent typically returns the selected bit of content via this data string.

- An optional Bundle containing additional information beyond the result code and data string.

To demonstrate launching a peer activity, take a peek at the Activities/Launch sample application. The XML layout is fairly straightforward: two fields for the latitude and longitude, plus a button.

```xml
<?xml version="1.0" encoding="utf-8"?>
<LinearLayout xmlns:android="http://schemas.android.com/apk/res/android"
  android:orientation="vertical"
  android:layout_width="fill_parent"
  android:layout_height="fill_parent"
  >
  <TableLayout
    android:layout_width="fill_parent"
    android:layout_height="wrap_content"
    android:stretchColumns="1,2"
  >
    <TableRow>
      <TextView
        android:layout_width="wrap_content"
        android:layout_height="wrap_content"
        android:paddingLeft="2dip"
        android:paddingRight="4dip"
        android:text="Location:"
      />
      <EditText android:id="@+id/lat"
        android:layout_width="fill_parent"
        android:layout_height="wrap_content"
        android:cursorVisible="true"
        android:editable="true"
        android:singleLine="true"
```

```
          android:layout_weight="1"
        />
        <EditText android:id="@+id/lon"
          android:layout_width="fill_parent"
          android:layout_height="wrap_content"
          android:cursorVisible="true"
          android:editable="true"
          android:singleLine="true"
          android:layout_weight="1"
        />
      </TableRow>
    </TableLayout>
    <Button android:id="@+id/map"
      android:layout_width="fill_parent"
      android:layout_height="wrap_content"
      android:text="Show Me!"
    />
</LinearLayout>
```

The button's OnClickListener simply takes the latitude and longitude, pours them into a geo scheme Uri, and then starts the activity.

```
package com.commonsware.android.activities;

import android.app.Activity;
import android.content.Intent;
import android.net.Uri;
import android.os.Bundle;
import android.view.View;
import android.widget.Button;
import android.widget.EditText;

public class LaunchDemo extends Activity {
  private EditText lat;
  private EditText lon;

  @Override
  public void onCreate(Bundle icicle) {
    super.onCreate(icicle);
    setContentView(R.layout.main);

    Button btn=(Button)findViewById(R.id.map);
    lat=(EditText)findViewById(R.id.lat);
    lon=(EditText)findViewById(R.id.lon);

    btn.setOnClickListener(new View.OnClickListener() {
      public void onClick(View view) {
        String _lat=lat.getText().toString();
        String _lon=lon.getText().toString();
        Uri uri=Uri.parse("geo:"+_lat+","+_lon);

        startActivity(new Intent(Intent.ACTION_VIEW, uri));
      }
    });
  }
}
```

The activity is not much to look at, as you can see in Figure 18–1.

Figure 18–1. *The LaunchDemo sample application, with a location filled in*

If you fill in a location (e.g., 38.8891 latitude and -77.0492 longitude) and click the button, the resulting map is more interesting, as shown in Figure 18–2.

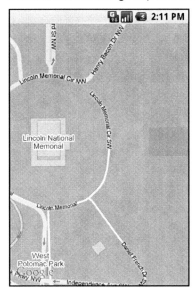

Figure 18–2. *The map launched by LaunchDemo, showing the Lincoln Memorial in Washington DC*

Note that this is the built-in Android map activity; we did not create our own activity to display this map. In Chapter 33, you will see how you can create maps in your own activities, in case you need greater control over how the map is displayed.

NOTE: This sample application may not work on an Android 2.0 AVD in the emulator, as the AVD appears to lack the Maps application.

Tabbed Browsing, Sort Of

One of the main features of the modern desktop web browser is tabbed browsing, where a single browser window can show several pages split across a series of tabs. On a mobile device, this may not make a lot of sense, given that you lose screen real estate for the tabs themselves. In this book, however, we do not let little things like sensibility stop us, so let's demonstrate a tabbed browser, using TabActivity and Intent objects.

As you may recall from Chapter 9, a tab can have either a View or an Activity as its contents. If you want to use an Activity as the content of a tab, you provide an Intent that will launch the desired Activity; Android's tab-management framework will then pour the Activity's UI into the tab.

Your natural instinct might be to use an http: Uri the way we used a geo: Uri in the previous example:

```
Intent i=new Intent(Intent.ACTION_VIEW);
i.setData(Uri.parse("http://commonsware.com"));
```

That way, you could use the built-in browser application and get all of the features that it offers.

Alas, this does not work. You cannot host other applications' activities in your tabs; only your own activities are allowed, for security reasons.

So, we dust off our WebView demos from Chapter 13 and use those instead, repackaged as Activities/IntentTab.

Here is the source to the main activity, the one hosting the TabView:

```
public class IntentTabDemo extends TabActivity {
  @Override
  public void onCreate(Bundle savedInstanceState) {
    super.onCreate(savedInstanceState);

    TabHost host=getTabHost();

    host.addTab(host.newTabSpec("one")
            .setIndicator("CW")
            .setContent(new Intent(this, CWBrowser.class)));
    host.addTab(host.newTabSpec("two")
            .setIndicator("Android")
            .setContent(new Intent(this, AndroidBrowser.class)));
  }
}
```

As you can see, we are using TabActivity as the base class, and so we do not need our own layout XML, since TabActivity supplies it for us. All we do is get access to the TabHost and add two tabs, each specifying an Intent that directly refers to another class. In this case, our two tabs will host a CWBrowser and an AndroidBrowser, respectively.

Those activities are simple modifications to the earlier browser demos:

```
public class CWBrowser extends Activity {
  WebView browser;

  @Override
  public void onCreate(Bundle icicle) {
    super.onCreate(icicle);

    browser=new WebView(this);
    setContentView(browser);
    browser.loadUrl("http://commonsware.com");
  }
}
public class AndroidBrowser extends Activity {
  WebView browser;

  @Override
  public void onCreate(Bundle icicle) {
    super.onCreate(icicle);

    browser=new WebView(this);
    setContentView(browser);
    browser.loadUrl("http://www.android.com/");
  }
}
```

They simply load a different URL into the browser: the CommonsWare home page in one and the Android home page in the other.

TIP: Using distinct subclasses for each targeted page is rather wasteful. Instead, you could package the URL to open as an "extra" in an Intent and used that Intent to spawn a general-purpose BrowserTab activity, which would read the URL out of the Intent extra and use that.

The resulting UI shows what tabbed browsing could look like on Android, as shown in Figures 18–3 and 18–4.

Figure 18–3. *The IntentTabDemo sample application, showing the first tab*

Figure 18–4. *The IntentTabDemo sample application, showing the second tab*

Chapter 19

Handling Rotation

Some Android handsets, like the T-Mobile G1, offer a slide-out keyboard that triggers rotating the screen from portrait to landscape orientation. Other handsets might use accelerometers to determine screen rotation, as the iPhone does. As a result, it is reasonable to assume that switching from portrait to landscape orientation and back again may be something your users will want to do.

As you'll learn in this chapter, Android has a number of ways for you to handle screen rotation, so your application can properly handle either orientation. But realize that these facilities just help you detect and manage the rotation process. You are still required to make sure you have layouts that look decent in each orientation.

A Philosophy of Destruction

By default, when there is a change in the phone configuration that might affect resource selection, Android will destroy and re-create any running or paused activities the next time they are to be viewed. While this could happen for a variety of different configuration changes (e.g., change of language selection), it is most likely to trip you up for rotations, since a change in orientation can cause you to load a different set of resources (e.g., layouts).

The key here is that this is the default behavior. It may even be the behavior that is best for one or more of your activities. You do have some control over the matter, though, and can tailor how your activities respond to orientation changes or similar configuration switches.

It's All the Same, Just Different

Since, by default, Android destroys and re-creates your activity on a rotation, you may only need to hook into the same onSaveInstanceState() that you would if your activity were destroyed for any other reason (e.g., low memory). Implement that method in your activity and fill in the supplied Bundle with enough information to get you back to your current state. Then, in onCreate() (or onRestoreInstanceState(), if you prefer), pick the data out of the Bundle and use it to bring your activity back to the way it was.

To demonstrate this, let's take a look at the `Rotation/RotationOne` project. This and the other sample projects in this chapter use a pair of `main.xml` layouts: one in `res/layout/` and one in `res/layout-land/` for use in landscape mode. Here is the portrait layout:

```xml
<?xml version="1.0" encoding="utf-8"?>
<LinearLayout xmlns:android="http://schemas.android.com/apk/res/android"
  android:orientation="vertical"
  android:layout_width="fill_parent"
  android:layout_height="fill_parent"
  >
  <Button android:id="@+id/pick"
    android:layout_width="fill_parent"
    android:layout_height="fill_parent"
    android:layout_weight="1"
    android:text="Pick"
    android:enabled="true"
  />
  <Button android:id="@+id/view"
    android:layout_width="fill_parent"
    android:layout_height="fill_parent"
    android:layout_weight="1"
    android:text="View"
    android:enabled="false"
  />
</LinearLayout>
```

Here is the similar landscape layout:

```xml
<?xml version="1.0" encoding="utf-8"?>
<LinearLayout xmlns:android="http://schemas.android.com/apk/res/android"
  android:orientation="horizontal"
  android:layout_width="fill_parent"
  android:layout_height="fill_parent"
  >
  <Button android:id="@+id/pick"
    android:layout_width="fill_parent"
    android:layout_height="fill_parent"
    android:layout_weight="1"
    android:text="Pick"
    android:enabled="true"
  />
  <Button android:id="@+id/view"
    android:layout_width="fill_parent"
    android:layout_height="fill_parent"
    android:layout_weight="1"
    android:text="View"
    android:enabled="false"
  />
</LinearLayout>
```

Basically, the layout contains a pair of buttons, each taking up half the screen. In portrait mode, the buttons are stacked; in landscape mode, they are side by side.

If you were to simply create a project, put in those two layouts, and compile it, the application would appear to work just fine—a rotation (pressing Ctrl+F12 in the emulator) will cause the layout to change. And while buttons lack state, if you were using other widgets (e.g., EditText), you would even find that Android hangs onto some of the widget state for you (e.g., the text entered in the EditText).

What Android cannot help you with automatically is anything held outside the widgets.

This application lets you pick a contact, and then view the contact, via separate buttons. The View button is enabled only after a contact has been selected.

Let's see how we handle this, using onSaveInstanceState():

```
public class RotationOneDemo extends Activity {
  static final int PICK_REQUEST=1337;
  Button viewButton=null;
  Uri contact=null;

  @Override
  public void onCreate(Bundle savedInstanceState) {
    super.onCreate(savedInstanceState);
    setContentView(R.layout.main);

    Button btn=(Button)findViewById(R.id.pick);

    btn.setOnClickListener(new View.OnClickListener() {
      public void onClick(View view) {
        Intent i=new Intent(Intent.ACTION_PICK,
                            Contacts.CONTENT_URI);

        startActivityForResult(i, PICK_REQUEST);
      }
    });

    viewButton=(Button)findViewById(R.id.view);

    viewButton.setOnClickListener(new View.OnClickListener() {
      public void onClick(View view) {
        startActivity(new Intent(Intent.ACTION_VIEW, contact));
      }
    });

    restoreMe(savedInstanceState);

    viewButton.setEnabled(contact!=null);
  }

  @Override
  protected void onActivityResult(int requestCode, int resultCode,
                                  Intent data) {
    if (requestCode==PICK_REQUEST) {
      if (resultCode==RESULT_OK) {
        contact=data.getData();
        viewButton.setEnabled(true);
      }
    }
  }

  @Override
```

```
protected void onSaveInstanceState(Bundle outState) {
  super.onSaveInstanceState(outState);

  if (contact!=null) {
    outState.putString("contact", contact.toString());
  }
}

private void restoreMe(Bundle state) {
  contact=null;

  if (state!=null) {
    String contactUri=state.getString("contact");

    if (contactUri!=null) {
      contact=Uri.parse(contactUri);
    }
  }
}
}
```

By and large, it looks like a normal activity (because it is). Initially, the "model"—a Uri named contact—is null. It is set as the result of spawning the ACTION_PICK subactivity. Its string representation is saved in onSaveInstanceState() and restored in restoreMe() (called from onCreate()). If the contact is not null, the View button is enabled and can be used to view the chosen contact.

Visually, it looks pretty much as you would expect, as shown in Figures 19–1 and 19–2.

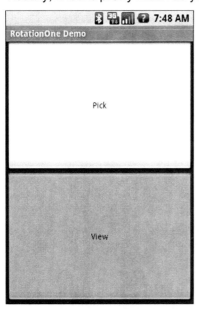

Figure 19–1. *The RotationOne application, in portrait mode*

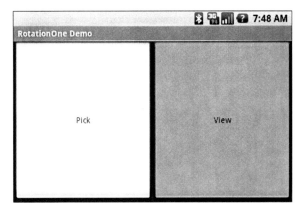

Figure 19–2. *The RotationOne application, in landscape mode*

The benefit to this implementation is that it handles a number of system events beyond mere rotation, such as being closed by Android due to low memory.

For fun, comment out the `restoreMe()` call in `onCreate()` and try running the application. You will see that the application "forgets" a contact selected in one orientation when you rotate the emulator or device.

NOTE: All the samples for this chapter work only on Android 2.0 and higher, as they use the newer means of picking a contact from the Contacts content provider (discussed in Chapter 26).

Now with More Savings!

The problem with `onSaveInstanceState()` is that you are limited to a `Bundle`. That's because this callback is also used in cases where your whole process might be terminated (e.g., low memory), so the data to be saved must be something that can be serialized and does not have any dependencies on your running process.

For some activities, that limitation is not a problem. For others, it is more annoying. Take an online chat, for example. You have no means of storing a socket in a `Bundle`, so by default, you will need to drop your connection to the chat server and reestablish it. That not only may be a performance hit, but it might also affect the chat itself, such as appearing in the chat logs as disconnecting and reconnecting.

One way to get past this is to use `onRetainNonConfigurationInstance()` instead of `onSaveInstanceState()` for "light" changes like a rotation. Your activity's `onRetainNonConfigurationInstance()` callback can return an `Object`, which you can retrieve later via `getLastNonConfigurationInstance()`. The `Object` can be just about anything you want. Typically, it will be some kind of "context" object holding activity state, such as running threads, open sockets, and the like. Your activity's `onCreate()` can call `getLastNonConfigurationInstance()`. Then if you get a non-null response, you now have your sockets and threads and whatnot. The biggest limitation is that you do not want to put in the saved context anything that might reference a resource that will get swapped out, such as a `Drawable` loaded from a resource.

Let's take a look at the Rotation/RotationTwo sample project, which uses this approach to handling rotations. The layouts, and hence the visual appearance, is the same as with Rotation/RotationOne. Where things differ slightly is in the Java code:

```java
public class RotationTwoDemo extends Activity {
  static final int PICK_REQUEST=1337;
  Button viewButton=null;
  Uri contact=null;

  @Override
  public void onCreate(Bundle savedInstanceState) {
    super.onCreate(savedInstanceState);
    setContentView(R.layout.main);

    Button btn=(Button)findViewById(R.id.pick);

    btn.setOnClickListener(new View.OnClickListener() {
      public void onClick(View view) {
        Intent i=new Intent(Intent.ACTION_PICK,
                            Contacts.CONTENT_URI);

        startActivityForResult(i, PICK_REQUEST);
      }
    });

    viewButton=(Button)findViewById(R.id.view);

    viewButton.setOnClickListener(new View.OnClickListener() {
      public void onClick(View view) {
        startActivity(new Intent(Intent.ACTION_VIEW, contact));
      }
    });

    restoreMe();

    viewButton.setEnabled(contact!=null);
  }

  @Override
  protected void onActivityResult(int requestCode, int resultCode,
                                  Intent data) {
    if (requestCode==PICK_REQUEST) {
      if (resultCode==RESULT_OK) {
        contact=data.getData();
        viewButton.setEnabled(true);
      }
    }
  }

  @Override
  public Object onRetainNonConfigurationInstance() {
    return(contact);
```

```
    }

    private void restoreMe() {
      contact=null;

      if (getLastNonConfigurationInstance()!=null) {
        contact=(Uri)getLastNonConfigurationInstance();
      }
    }
}
```

In this case, we override onRetainNonConfigurationInstance(), returning the actual Uri for our contact, rather than a string representation of it. In turn, restoreMe() calls getLastNonConfigurationInstance(), and if it is not null, we hold onto it as our contact and enable the View button.

The advantage here is that we are passing around the Uri rather than a string representation. In this case, that is not a big saving. But our state could be much more complicated, including threads, sockets, and other things we cannot pack into a Bundle.

However, even this approach may be too intrusive to your application. Suppose, for example, you are creating a real-time game, such as a first-person shooter. The "hiccup" your users experience as your activity is destroyed and re-created might be enough to get them shot, which they may not appreciate. While this would be less of an issue on the T-Mobile G1, since a rotation requires sliding open the keyboard and therefore is unlikely to be done mid-game, other devices might rotate based solely on the device's position as determined by accelerometers. For these situations, you may want to tell Android that you will rotations yourself, and you do not want any assistance from the framework, as described next.

DIY Rotation

To handle rotations on your own, do this:

1. Put an android:configChanges entry in your AndroidManifest.xml file, listing the configuration changes you want to handle yourself versus allowing Android to handle for you.

2. Implement onConfigurationChanged() in your Activity, which will be called when one of the configuration changes you listed in android:configChanges occurs.

Now, for any configuration change you want, you can bypass the whole activity-destruction process and simply get a callback letting you know of the change.

To see this in action, turn to the Rotation/RotationThree sample application. Once again, our layouts are the same, so the application looks just like the preceding two samples. However, the Java code is significantly different, because we are no longer concerned with saving our state, but rather with updating our UI to deal with the layout.

But first, we need to make a small change to our manifest:

```xml
<?xml version="1.0" encoding="utf-8"?>
<manifest xmlns:android="http://schemas.android.com/apk/res/android"
        package="com.commonsware.android.rotation.three"
        android:versionCode="1"
        android:versionName="1.0.0">
    <uses-sdk
        android:minSdkVersion="5"
        android:targetSdkVersion="6"
    />
    <application android:label="@string/app_name"
        android:icon="@drawable/cw">
        <activity android:name=".RotationThreeDemo"
                android:label="@string/app_name"
                android:configChanges="keyboardHidden|orientation">
            <intent-filter>
                <action android:name="android.intent.action.MAIN" />
                <category android:name="android.intent.category.LAUNCHER" />
            </intent-filter>
        </activity>
    </application>
</manifest>
```

Here, we state that we will handle keyboardHidden and orientation configuration
changes ourselves. This covers us for any cause of the rotation, whether it is a sliding
keyboard or a physical rotation. Note that this is set on the activity, not the application. If
you have several activities, you will need to decide for each which of the tactics outlined
in this chapter you wish to use.

The Java code for this project is as follows:

```java
public class RotationThreeDemo extends Activity {
  static final int PICK_REQUEST=1337;
  Button viewButton=null;
  Uri contact=null;

  @Override
  public void onCreate(Bundle savedInstanceState) {
    super.onCreate(savedInstanceState);

    setupViews();
  }

  @Override
  protected void onActivityResult(int requestCode, int resultCode,
                                  Intent data) {
    if (requestCode==PICK_REQUEST) {
      if (resultCode==RESULT_OK) {
        contact=data.getData();
        viewButton.setEnabled(true);
      }
    }
  }

  public void onConfigurationChanged(Configuration newConfig) {
```

```
    super.onConfigurationChanged(newConfig);

    setupViews();
  }

  private void setupViews() {
    setContentView(R.layout.main);

    Button btn=(Button)findViewById(R.id.pick);

    btn.setOnClickListener(new View.OnClickListener() {
      public void onClick(View view) {
        Intent i=new Intent(Intent.ACTION_PICK,
                            Contacts.CONTENT_URI);

        startActivityForResult(i, PICK_REQUEST);
      }
    });

    viewButton=(Button)findViewById(R.id.view);

    viewButton.setOnClickListener(new View.OnClickListener() {
      public void onClick(View view) {
        startActivity(new Intent(Intent.ACTION_VIEW, contact));
      }
    });

    viewButton.setEnabled(contact!=null);
  }
}
```

The onCreate() implementation delegates most of its logic to a setupViews() method, which loads the layout and sets up the buttons. This logic was broken out into its own method because it is also called from onConfigurationChanged().

Forcing the Issue

In the previous three sections, we covered ways to deal with rotational events. There is, of course, a radical alternative: tell Android not to rotate your activity at all. If the activity does not rotate, you do not need to worry about writing code to deal with rotations.

To block Android from rotating your activity, all you need to do is add android:screenOrientation = "portrait" (or "landscape", as you prefer) to your AndroidManifest.xml file, as follows (from the Rotation/RotationFour sample project):

```
<?xml version="1.0" encoding="utf-8"?>
<manifest xmlns:android="http://schemas.android.com/apk/res/android"
      package="com.commonsware.android.rotation.four"
      android:versionCode="1"
      android:versionName="1.0.0">
  <uses-sdk
      android:minSdkVersion="5"
      android:targetSdkVersion="6"
```

```
    />
    <application android:label="@string/app_name"
        android:icon="@drawable/cw">
        <activity android:name=".RotationFourDemo"
                android:screenOrientation="portrait"
                android:label="@string/app_name">
            <intent-filter>
                <action android:name="android.intent.action.MAIN" />
                <category android:name="android.intent.category.LAUNCHER" />
            </intent-filter>
        </activity>
    </application>
</manifest>
```

Since this is applied on a per-activity basis, you will need to decide which of your activities may need it turned on.

At this point, your activity is locked into whatever orientation you specified, regardless of what you do. Figures 19–3 and 19–4 show the same activity as in the previous three sections, but using the preceding manifest and with the emulator set for both portrait and landscape orientation. Notice that the UI does not move a bit, but remains in portrait mode.

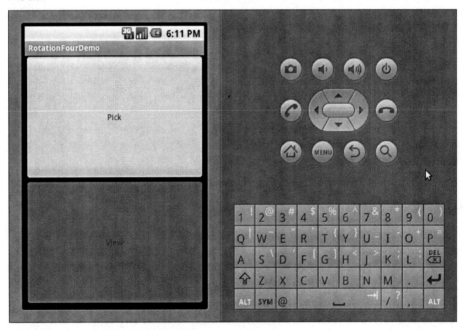

Figure 19–3. *The RotationFour application, in portrait mode*

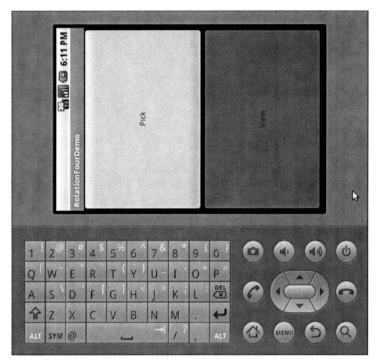

Figure 19–4. *The RotationFour application, in landscape mode*

Note that Android will still destroy and re-create your activity, even if you have the orientation set to a specific value as shown here. If you wish to avoid that, you will also need to set android:configChanges in the manifest, as described earlier in this chapter.

Making Sense of It All

All of the scenarios presented in this chapter assume that you rotate the screen by opening the keyboard on the device (or by pressing Ctrl+F12 in the emulator). Certainly, this is the norm for Android applications. However, we haven't covered the iPhone scenario.

You may have seen one (or several) commercials for the iPhone, showing how the screen rotates just by turning the device. Some Android devices, such as the HTC Magic, will behave the same way. With other devices, though, you do not get this behavior; instead, the screen rotates based on whether the keyboard is open or closed.

However, even for those devices, it is easy for you to change this behavior, so your screen will rotate based on the position of the phone. Just add android:screenOrientation = "sensor" to your AndroidManifest.xml file (from the Rotation/RotationFive sample project):

```
<?xml version="1.0" encoding="utf-8"?>
<manifest xmlns:android="http://schemas.android.com/apk/res/android"
      package="com.commonsware.android.rotation.five"
```

```
            android:versionCode="1"
            android:versionName="1.0.0">
    <uses-sdk
            android:minSdkVersion="5"
            android:targetSdkVersion="6"
    />
    <application android:label="@string/app_name"
            android:icon="@drawable/cw">
            <activity android:name=".RotationFiveDemo"
                    android:screenOrientation="sensor"
                    android:label="@string/app_name">
                <intent-filter>
                    <action android:name="android.intent.action.MAIN" />
                    <category android:name="android.intent.category.LAUNCHER" />
                </intent-filter>
            </activity>
    </application>
</manifest>
```

The sensor, in this case, tells Android you want the accelerometers to control the screen orientation, so the physical shift in the device orientation controls the screen orientation.

At least on the T-Mobile G1, this appears to work only when going from the traditional upright portrait position to the traditional landscape position—rotating 90 degrees counterclockwise. Rotating the device 90 degrees clockwise results in no change in the screen.

Also note that this setting disables having the keyboard trigger a rotation event. Leaving the device in the portrait position, if you slide out the keyboard, in a normal Android activity, the screen will rotate; in an android:screenOrientation = "sensor" activity, the screen will not rotate.

Chapter 20

Working with Resources

Resources are static bits of information held outside the Java source code. You have seen one type of resource—the layout—frequently in the examples in this book. As you'll learn in this chapter, there are many other types of resources, such as images and strings, that you can take advantage of in your Android applications.

The Resource Lineup

Resources are stored as files under the res/ directory in your Android project layout. With the exception of raw resources (res/raw/), all the other types of resources are parsed for you, either by the Android packaging system or by the Android system on the device or emulator. So, for example, when you lay out an activity's UI via a layout resource (res/layout/), you do not need to parse the layout XML yourself; Android handles that for you.

In addition to layout resources (introduced in Chapter 4) and animation resources (introduced in Chapter 9), several other types of resources are available, including the following:

- Images (res/drawable/), for putting static icons or other pictures in a user interface

- Raw (res/raw/), for arbitrary files that have meaning to your application but not necessarily to Android frameworks

- Strings, colors, arrays, and dimensions (res/values/), to both give these sorts of constants symbolic names and to keep them separate from the rest of the code (e.g., for internationalization and localization)

- XML (res/xml/), for static XML files containing your own data and structure

String Theory

Keeping your labels and other bits of text outside the main source code of your application is generally considered to be a very good idea. In particular, it helps with internationalization and localization, covered in the "Different Strokes for Different Folks" section later in this chapter. Even if you are not going to translate your strings to other languages, it is easier to make corrections if all the strings are in one spot, instead of scattered throughout your source code.

Android supports regular externalized strings, along with string formats, where the string has placeholders for dynamically inserted information. On top of that, Android supports simple text formatting, called *styled text*, so you can make your words be bold or italic intermingled with normal text.

Plain Strings

Generally speaking, all you need for plain strings is an XML file in the res/values directory (typically named res/values/strings.xml), with a resources root element, and one child string element for each string you wish to encode as a resource. The string element takes a name attribute, which is the unique name for this string, and a single text element containing the text of the string.

```
<resources>
  <string name="quick">The quick brown fox...</string>
  <string name="laughs">He who laughs last...</string>
</resources>
```

The only tricky part is if the string value contains a quotation mark (") or an apostrophe ('). In those cases, you will want to escape those values, by preceding them with a backslash (e.g., These are the times that try men\'s souls). Or, if it is just an apostrophe, you could enclose the value in quotation marks (e.g., "These are the times that try men's souls.").

You can then reference this string from a layout file (as @string/..., where the ellipsis is the unique name, such as @string/laughs). Or you can get the string from your Java code by calling getString() with the resource ID of the string resource, which is the unique name prefixed with R.string. (e.g., getString(R.string.quick)).

String Formats

As with other implementations of the Java language, Android's Dalvik virtual machine supports string formats. Here, the string contains placeholders representing data to be replaced at runtime by variable information (e.g., My name is %1$s). Plain strings stored as resources can be used as string formats:

```
String strFormat=getString(R.string.my_name);
String strResult=String.format(strFormat, "Tim");
((TextView)findViewById(R.id.some_label)).setText(strResult);
```

Styled Text

If you want really rich text, you should have raw resources containing HTML, and then pour those into a WebKit widget. However, for light HTML formatting, using <b>, <i>, and <u>, you can just use a string resource. The catch is that you must escape the HTML tags, rather than treating them normally:

```
<resources>
  <string name="b">This has &lt;b&gt;bold&lt;/b&gt; in it.</string>
  <string name="i">Whereas this has &lt;i&gt;italics&lt;/i&gt;!</string>
</resources>
```

You can access these the same way as you get plain strings, with the exception that the result of the getString() call is really an object supporting the android.text.Spanned interface:

```
((TextView)findViewById(R.id.another_label))
          .setText(getString(R.string.b));
```

Styled String Formats

Where styled text gets tricky is with styled string formats, as String.format() works on String objects, not Spanned objects with formatting instructions. If you really want to have styled string formats, here is the work-around:

1. Entity-escape the angle brackets in the string resource (e.g., this is <b>%1$s</b>).

2. Retrieve the string resource as normal, though it will not be styled at this point (e.g., getString(R.string.funky_format)).

3. Generate the format results, being sure to escape any string values you substitute, in case they contain angle brackets or ampersands.

```
String.format(getString(R.string.funky_format),
              TextUtils.htmlEncode(strName));
```

4. Convert the entity-escaped HTML into a Spanned object via Html.fromHtml().

```
someTextView.setText(Html
              .fromHtml(resultFromStringFormat));
```

To see this in action, let's look at the Resources/Strings demo. Here is the layout file:

```
<?xml version="1.0" encoding="utf-8"?>
<LinearLayout xmlns:android="http://schemas.android.com/apk/res/android"
  android:orientation="vertical"
  android:layout_width="fill_parent"
  android:layout_height="fill_parent"
  >
  <LinearLayout
    android:orientation="horizontal"
    android:layout_width="fill_parent"
```

```
    android:layout_height="wrap_content"
    >
    <Button android:id="@+id/format"
      android:layout_width="wrap_content"
      android:layout_height="wrap_content"
      android:text="@string/btn_name"
      />
    <EditText android:id="@+id/name"
      android:layout_width="fill_parent"
      android:layout_height="wrap_content"
      />
  </LinearLayout>
  <TextView android:id="@+id/result"
    android:layout_width="fill_parent"
    android:layout_height="wrap_content"
    />
</LinearLayout>
```

As you can see, it is just a button, a field, and a label. The idea is for users to enter their name in the field, and then click the button to cause the label to be updated with a formatted message containing their name.

The Button in the layout file references a string resource (@string/btn_name), so we need a string resource file (res/values/strings.xml):

```
<?xml version="1.0" encoding="utf-8"?>
<resources>
  <string name="app_name">StringsDemo</string>
  <string name="btn_name">Name:</string>
  <string name="funky_format">My name is &lt;b&gt;%1$s&lt;/b&gt;</string>
</resources>
```

The app_name resource is automatically created by the activityCreator script. The btn_name string is the caption of the Button, while our styled string format is in funky_format.

Finally, to hook all this together, we need a pinch of Java:

```
package com.commonsware.android.strings;

import android.app.Activity;
import android.os.Bundle;
import android.text.TextUtils;
import android.text.Html;
import android.view.View;
import android.widget.Button;
import android.widget.EditText;
import android.widget.TextView;

public class StringsDemo extends Activity {
  EditText name;
  TextView result;

  @Override
  public void onCreate(Bundle icicle) {
    super.onCreate(icicle);
    setContentView(R.layout.main);
```

```
name=(EditText)findViewById(R.id.name);
result=(TextView)findViewById(R.id.result);

Button btn=(Button)findViewById(R.id.format);

btn.setOnClickListener(new Button.OnClickListener() {
  public void onClick(View v) {
    applyFormat();
  }
});
}

private void applyFormat() {
  String format=getString(R.string.funky_format);
  String simpleResult=String.format(format,
                TextUtils.htmlEncode(name.getText().toString()));
  result.setText(Html.fromHtml(simpleResult));
}
}
```

The string resource manipulation can be found in `applyFormat()`, which is called when the button is clicked. First, we get our format via `getString()` (something we could have done at `onCreate()` time for efficiency). Next, we format the value in the field using this format, getting a `String` back, since the string resource is in entity-encoded HTML. Note the use of `TextUtils.htmlEncode()` to entity-encode the entered name, in case someone decides to use an ampersand or something. Finally, we convert the simple HTML into a styled text object via `Html.fromHtml()` and update our label.

When the activity is first launched, we have an empty label, as shown in Figure 20–1.

Figure 20–1. *The StringsDemo sample application, as initially launched*

When you fill in a name and click the button, you get the result shown in Figure 20–2.

Figure 20–2. *The same application, after filling in some heroic figure's name*

Got the Picture?

Android supports images in the PNG, JPEG, and GIF formats. GIF is officially discouraged, however. PNG is the overall preferred format. Images can be used anywhere you require a Drawable, such as the image and background of an ImageView.

Using images is simply a matter of putting your image files in res/drawable/ and then referencing them as a resource. Within layout files, images are referenced as @drawable/... where the ellipsis is the base name of the file (e.g., for res/drawable/foo.png, the resource name is @drawable/foo). In Java, where you need an image resource ID, use R.drawable. plus the base name (e.g., R.drawable.foo).

To demonstrate, let's update the previous example to use an icon for the button instead of the string resource. This can be found as Resources/Images. First, we slightly adjust the layout file, using an ImageButton and referencing a Drawable named @drawable/icon:

```xml
<?xml version="1.0" encoding="utf-8"?>
<LinearLayout xmlns:android="http://schemas.android.com/apk/res/android"
  android:orientation="vertical"
  android:layout_width="fill_parent"
  android:layout_height="fill_parent"
  >
  <LinearLayout
    android:orientation="horizontal"
    android:layout_width="fill_parent"
    android:layout_height="wrap_content"
    >
    <ImageButton android:id="@+id/format"
```

```
      android:layout_width="wrap_content"
      android:layout_height="wrap_content"
      android:src="@drawable/icon"
      />
    <EditText android:id="@+id/name"
      android:layout_width="fill_parent"
      android:layout_height="wrap_content"
      />
  </LinearLayout>
  <TextView android:id="@+id/result"
    android:layout_width="fill_parent"
    android:layout_height="wrap_content"
    />
</LinearLayout>
```

Next, we need to put an image file in res/drawable with a base name of icon. In this case, we use a 32-by-32 PNG file from the Nuvola icon set (http://www.icon-king.com/projects/nuvola/). Finally, we twiddle the Java source, replacing our Button with an ImageButton:

```
package com.commonsware.android.images;

import android.app.Activity;
import android.os.Bundle;
import android.text.TextUtils;
import android.text.Html;
import android.view.View;
import android.widget.Button;
import android.widget.ImageButton;
import android.widget.EditText;
import android.widget.TextView;

public class ImagesDemo extends Activity {
  EditText name;
  TextView result;

  @Override
  public void onCreate(Bundle icicle) {
    super.onCreate(icicle);
    setContentView(R.layout.main);

    name=(EditText)findViewById(R.id.name);
    result=(TextView)findViewById(R.id.result);

    ImageButton btn=(ImageButton)findViewById(R.id.format);

    btn.setOnClickListener(new Button.OnClickListener() {
      public void onClick(View v) {
        applyFormat();
      }
    });
  }

  private void applyFormat() {
    String format=getString(R.string.funky_format);
    String simpleResult=String.format(format,
```

```
                         TextUtils.htmlEncode(name.getText().toString()));
       result.setText(Html.fromHtml(simpleResult));
     }
}
```

Now, our button has the desired icon, as shown in Figure 20–3.

Figure 20–3. *The ImagesDemo sample application*

XML: The Resource Way

If you wish to package static XML with your application, you can use an XML resource.
Simply put the XML file in res/xml/. Then you can access it by getXml() on a Resources
object, supplying it a resource ID of R.xml. plus the base name of your XML file. For
example, in an activity, with an XML file of words.xml, you could call
getResources().getXml(R.xml.words).

This returns an instance of an XmlPullParser, found in the org.xmlpull.v1 Java
namespace. An XML pull parser is event-driven: you keep calling next() on the parser to
get the next event, which could be START_TAG, END_TAG, END_DOCUMENT, and so on. On a
START_TAG event, you can access the tag's name and attributes; a single TEXT event
represents the concatenation of all text nodes that are direct children of this element. By
looping, testing, and invoking per-element logic, you parse the file.

To see this in action, let's rewrite the Java code for the Files/Static sample project to
use an XML resource. This new project, Resources/XML, requires that you place the
words.xml file from Static not in res/raw/, but in res/xml/. The layout stays the same,
so all that needs to be replaced is the Java source:

```java
package com.commonsware.android.resources;

import android.app.Activity;
import android.os.Bundle;
import android.app.ListActivity;
import android.view.View;
import android.widget.AdapterView;
import android.widget.ArrayAdapter;
import android.widget.ListView;
import android.widget.TextView;
import android.widget.Toast;
import java.io.InputStream;
import java.util.ArrayList;
import org.xmlpull.v1.XmlPullParser;
import org.xmlpull.v1.XmlPullParserException;

public class XMLResourceDemo extends ListActivity {
  TextView selection;
  ArrayList<String> items=new ArrayList<String>();

  @Override
  public void onCreate(Bundle icicle) {
    super.onCreate(icicle);
    setContentView(R.layout.main);
    selection=(TextView)findViewById(R.id.selection);

    try {
      XmlPullParser xpp=getResources().getXml(R.xml.words);

      while (xpp.getEventType()!=XmlPullParser.END_DOCUMENT) {
        if (xpp.getEventType()==XmlPullParser.START_TAG) {
          if (xpp.getName().equals("word")) {
            items.add(xpp.getAttributeValue(0));
          }
        }

        xpp.next();
      }
    }
    catch (Throwable t) {
      Toast
        .makeText(this, "Request failed: "+t.toString(), 4000)
        .show();
    }

    setListAdapter(new ArrayAdapter<String>(this,
                        android.R.layout.simple_list_item_1,
                        items));
  }

  public void onListItemClick(ListView parent, View v, int position,
                  long id) {
    selection.setText(items.get(position).toString());
  }
}
```

Now, inside our try...catch block, we get our XmlPullParser and loop until the end of the document. If the current event is START_TAG and the name of the element is word (xpp.getName().equals("word")), then we get the one and only attribute, and pop that into our list of items for the selection widget. Since we have complete control over the XML file, it is safe enough to assume there is exactly one attribute. If you are not sure that the XML is properly defined, you might consider checking the attribute count (getAttributeCount()) and the name of the attribute (getAttributeName()) before blindly assuming the 0-index attribute is what you think it is.

The result looks the same as before, albeit with a different name in the title bar, as shown in Figure 20–4.

Figure 20–4. *The XMLResourceDemo sample application*

Miscellaneous Values

In the res/values/ directory, in addition to string resources, you can place one (or more) XML files describing other simple resources, such as dimensions, colors, and arrays. You have already seen uses of dimensions and colors in previous examples, where they were passed as simple strings (e.g., "10px") as parameters to calls. You could set these up as Java static final objects and use their symbolic names, but that works only inside Java source, not in layout XML files. By putting these values in resource XML files, you can reference them from both Java and layouts, plus have them centrally located for easy editing.

Resource XML files have a root element of resources; everything else is a child of that root.

Dimensions

Dimensions are used in several places in Android to describe distances, such a widget's padding. Most of this book's examples use pixels (e.g., 10px for 10 pixels). Several different units of measurement are also available:

- in and mm for inches and millimeters, respectively. These are based on the actual size of the screen.

- pt for points. In publishing terms, a point is 1/72 inch (again, based on the actual physical size of the screen).

- dip and sp for device-independent pixels and scale-independent pixels, respectively. One pixel equals one dip for a 160-dpi resolution screen, with the ratio scaling based on the actual screen pixel density. Scale-independent pixels also take into account the user's preferred font size.

To encode a dimension as a resource, add a dimen element, with a name attribute for your unique name for this resource, and a single child text element representing the value:

```
<resources>
  <dimen name="thin">10px</dimen>
  <dimen name="fat">1in</dimen>
</resources>
```

In a layout, you can reference dimensions as @dimen/..., where the ellipsis is a placeholder for your unique name for the resource (e.g., thin and fat from the preceding sample). In Java, you reference dimension resources by the unique name prefixed with R.dimen. (e.g., Resources.getDimen(R.dimen.thin)).

Colors

Colors in Android are hexadecimal RGB values, also optionally specifying an alpha channel. You have your choice of single-character hex values or double-character hex values, providing four styles:

- #RGB

- #ARGB

- #RRGGBB

- #AARRGGBB

These work similarly to their counterparts in Cascading Style Sheets (CSS).

You can, of course, put these RGB values as string literals in Java source or layout resources. If you wish to turn them into resources, though, all you need to do is add color elements to the resource file, with a name attribute for your unique name for this color, and a single text element containing the RGB value itself:

```
<resources>
```

```
    <color name="yellow_orange">#FFD555</color>
    <color name="forest_green">#005500</color>
    <color name="burnt_umber">#8A3324</color>
</resources>
```

In a layout, you can reference colors as @color/..., replacing the ellipsis with your unique name for the color (e.g., burnt_umber). In Java, you reference color resources by the unique name prefixed with R.color. (e.g., Resources.getColor(R.color.forest_green)).

Arrays

Array resources are designed to hold lists of simple strings, such as a list of honorifics (Mr., Mrs., Ms., Dr., etc.).

In the resource file, you need one string-array element per array, with a name attribute for the unique name you are giving the array. Then add one or more child item elements, each with a single text element containing the value for that entry in the array:

```
<?xml version="1.0" encoding="utf-8"?>
<resources>
  <string-array name="cities">
    <item>Philadelphia</item>
    <item>Pittsburgh</item>
    <item>Allentown/Bethlehem</item>
    <item>Erie</item>
    <item>Reading</item>
    <item>Scranton</item>
    <item>Lancaster</item>
    <item>Altoona</item>
    <item>Harrisburg</item>
  </string-array>
  <string-array name="airport_codes">
    <item>PHL</item>
    <item>PIT</item>
    <item>ABE</item>
    <item>ERI</item>
    <item>RDG</item>
    <item>AVP</item>
    <item>LNS</item>
    <item>AOO</item>
    <item>MDT</item>
  </string-array>
</resources>
```

From your Java code, you can then use Resources.getStringArray() to get a String[] of the items in the list. The parameter to getStringArray() is your unique name for the array, prefixed with R.array. (e.g., Resources.getStringArray(R.array.honorifics)).

Different Strokes for Different Folks

One set of resources may not fit all situations where your application may be used. One obvious area comes with string resources and dealing with internationalization (I18N) and localization (L10N). Putting strings all in one language works fine—at least, for the developer—but covers only one language.

That is not the only scenario where resources might need to differ, though. Here are others:

■ *Screen orientation*: Is the screen in a portrait or landscape orientation? Or is the screen square and, therefore, without an orientation?

■ *Screen size*: How many pixels does the screen have, so you can size your resources accordingly (e.g., large versus small icons)?

■ *Touchscreen*: does the device have a touchscreen? If so, is the touchscreen set up to be used with a stylus or a finger?

■ *Keyboard*: Which keyboard does the user have (QWERTY, numeric, neither), either now or as an option?

■ *Other input*: Does the device have some other form of input, like a D-pad or click-wheel?

The way Android currently handles this is by having multiple resource directories, with the criteria for each embedded in their names.

Suppose, for example, you want to support strings in both English and Spanish. Normally, for a single-language setup, you would put your strings in a file named res/values/strings.xml. To support both English and Spanish, you would create two folders, named res/values-en/ and res/values-es/, where the value after the hyphen is the ISO 639-1 two-letter code for the language. Your English strings would go in res/values-en/strings.xml, and the Spanish ones would go in res/values-es/strings.xml. Android will choose the proper file based on the user's device settings.

An even better approach is for you to consider some language to be your default, and put those strings in res/values/strings.xml. Then create other resource directories for your translations (e.g., res/values-es/strings.xml for Spanish). Android will try to match a specific language set of resources; failing that, it will fall back to the default of res/values/strings.xml.

Seems easy, right?

Where things start to get complicated is when you need to use multiple disparate criteria for your resources. For example, suppose you want to develop both for the T-Mobile G1 and two currently fictitious devices. One device (Fictional One) has a VGA ("large") screen normally in a landscape orientation, an always-open QWERTY keyboard, a D-pad, but no touchscreen. The other device (Fictional Two) has a G1-sized screen (normal), a numeric keyboard but no QWERTY, a D-pad, and no touchscreen.

You may want to have somewhat different layouts for these devices, to take advantage of different screen real estate and different input options, as follows:

■ For each combination of resolution and orientation

■ For touchscreen devices versus ones without touchscreens

■ For QWERTY versus non-QWERTY devices

Once you get into these sorts of situations, all sorts of rules come into play, such as these:

- The configuration options (e.g., -en) have a particular order of precedence, and they must appear in the directory name in that order. The Android documentation outlines the specific order in which these options can appear. For the purposes of this example, screen orientation must precede touchscreen type, which must precede screen size.

- There can be only one value of each configuration option category per directory.

- Options are case-sensitive.

So, for the sample scenario, in theory, we would need the following directories:

- `res/layout-large-port-notouch-qwerty`
- `res/layout-normal-port-notouch-qwerty`
- `res/layout-large-port-notouch-12key`
- `res/layout-normal-port-notouch-12key`
- `res/layout-large-port-notouch-nokeys`
- `res/layout-normal-port-notouch-nokeys`
- `res/layout-large-port-stylus-qwerty`
- `res/layout-normal-port-stylus-qwerty`
- `res/layout-large-port-stylus-12key`
- `res/layout-normal-port-stylus-12key`
- `res/layout-large-port-stylus-nokeys`
- `res/layout-normal-port-stylus-nokeys`
- `res/layout-large-port-finger-qwerty`
- `res/layout-normal-port-finger-qwerty`
- `res/layout-large-port-finger-12key`
- `res/layout-normal-port-finger-12key`
- `res/layout-large-port-finger-nokeys`
- `res/layout-normal-port-finger-nokeys`
- `res/layout-large-land-notouch-qwerty`
- `res/layout-normal-land-notouch-qwerty`
- `res/layout-large-land-notouch-12key`
- `res/layout-normal-land-notouch-12key`
- `res/layout-large-land-notouch-nokeys`

- ▧ `res/layout-normal-land-notouch-nokeys`
- ▧ `res/layout-large-land-stylus-qwerty`
- ▧ `res/layout-normal-land-stylus-qwerty`
- ▧ `res/layout-large-land-stylus-12key`
- ▧ `res/layout-normal-land-stylus-12key`
- ▧ `res/layout-large-land-stylus-nokeys`
- ▧ `res/layout-normal-land-stylus-nokeys`
- ▧ `res/layout-large-land-finger-qwerty`
- ▧ `res/layout-normal-land-finger-qwerty`
- ▧ `res/layout-large-land-finger-12key`
- ▧ `res/layout-normal-land-finger-12key`
- ▧ `res/layout-large-land-finger-nokeys`
- ▧ `res/layout-normal-land-finger-nokeys`

Don't panic! We will shorten this list in just a moment.

Note that for many of these, the actual layout files will be identical. For example, we only care about touchscreen layouts being different from the other two layouts, but since we cannot combine those two, we would theoretically need separate directories with identical contents for `finger` and `stylus`.

Also note that there is nothing preventing you from having another directory with the unadorned base name (`res/layout`). In fact, this is probably a good idea, in case future editions of the Android runtime introduce other configuration options you did not consider. Having a default layout might make the difference between your application working or failing on that new device.

Now, we can cheat a bit, by decoding the rules Android uses for determining which, among a set of candidates, is the correct resource directory to use:

- ▧ First up, Android tosses out ones that are specifically invalid. So, for example, if the screen size of the device is normal, the `-large` directories would be dropped as candidates, since they call for some other size.
- ▧ Next, Android counts the number of matches for each folder, and pays attention to only those with the most matches.
- ▧ Finally, Android goes in the order of precedence of the options; in other words, it goes from left to right in the directory name.

So, we could skate by with only the following configurations:

- ▧ `res/layout-large-port-notouch-qwerty`
- ▧ `res/layout-port-notouch-qwerty`

- res/layout-large-port-notouch
- res/layout-port-notouch
- res/layout-large-port-qwerty
- res/layout-port-qwerty
- res/layout-large-port
- res/layout-port
- res/layout-large-land-notouch-qwerty
- res/layout-land-notouch-qwerty
- res/layout-large-land-notouch
- res/layout-land-notouch
- res/layout-large-land-qwerty
- res/layout-land-qwerty
- res/layout-large-land
- res/layout-land

Here, we take advantage of the fact that specific matches take precedence over unspecified values. So, a device with a QWERTY keyboard will choose a resource with qwerty in the directory over a resource that does not specify its keyboard type. Combining that with the "most matches wins" rule, we see that res/layout-port will match only devices with normal-sized screens, no QWERTY keyboard, and a touchscreen in portrait orientation.

We could refine this even further, to cover only the specific devices we are targeting (T-Mobile G1, Fictional One, and Fictional Two), plus take advantage of res/layout being the overall default:

- res/layout-large-port-notouch
- res/layout-port-notouch
- res/layout-large-land-notouch
- res/layout-land-notouch
- res/layout-large-land
- res/layout

Here, -large differentiates Fictional One from the other two devices, while notouch differentiates Fictional Two from the T-Mobile G1.

You will see these resource sets again in Chapter 36, which describes how to support multiple screen sizes.

Chapter 21

Using Preferences

Android has many different ways for you to store data for long-term use by your activity. The simplest to use is the preferences system, which is the topic of this chapter.

Android allows activities and applications to keep preferences, in the form of key/value pairs (akin to a Map), which will hang around between invocations of an activity. As the name suggests, the primary purpose is for you to store user-specified configuration details, such as the last feed the user looked at in your feed reader, the sort order to use by default on a list, or whatever. Of course, you can store in the preferences whatever you like, as long as it is keyed by a String and has a primitive value (boolean, String, etc.)

Preferences can be for a single activity or shared among all activities in an application. (Eventually, preferences might be shareable across applications, but that is not supported as of the time of this writing.)

Getting What You Want

To get access to the preferences, you can use the following APIs:

- getPreferences() from within your Activity, to access activity-specific preferences

- getSharedPreferences() from within your Activity (or other application Context), to access application-level preferences

- getDefaultSharedPreferences(), on PreferencesManager, to get the shared preferences that work in concert with Android's overall preference framework

The first two take a security mode parameter; for now, pass in 0. The getSharedPreferences() method also takes a name of a set of preferences. getPreferences() effectively calls getSharedPreferences() with the activity's class name as the preference set name. The getDefaultSharedPreferences() method takes the Context for the preferences (e.g., your Activity).

All of these methods return an instance of SharedPreferences, which offers a series of getters to access named preferences, returning a suitably typed result (e.g., getBoolean() to return a Boolean preference). The getters also take a default value, which is returned if there is no preference set under the specified key.

Stating Your Preference

Given the appropriate SharedPreferences object, you can use edit() to get an editor for the preferences. This object has a set of setters that mirror the getters on the parent SharedPreferences object. It also has the following methods:

- remove(): Deletes a single named preference.
- clear(): Deletes all preferences.
- commit(): Persists your changes made via the editor.

The commit() method is important. If you modify preferences via the editor and fail to commit() the changes, those changes will evaporate once the editor goes out of scope.

Conversely, since the preferences object supports live changes, if one part of your application (say, an activity) modifies shared preferences, another part of your application (say, a service) will have access to the changed value immediately.

And Now, a Word from Our Framework

Beginning with the 0.9 SDK, Android has introduced a framework for managing preferences. Ironically, this framework does not change anything shown so far. Instead, the framework is more for presenting a consistent set of preference-setting options for users, so different applications do not need to reinvent the wheel.

The linchpin to the preferences framework is yet another XML data structure. You can describe your application's preferences in an XML file stored in your project's res/xml/ directory. Given that, Android can present a pleasant UI for manipulating those preferences, which are then stored in the SharedPreferences you get back from getDefaultSharedPreferences().

The following is the preference XML for the Prefs/Simple preferences sample project:

```
<PreferenceScreen
  xmlns:android="http://schemas.android.com/apk/res/android">
  <CheckBoxPreference
    android:key="checkbox"
    android:title="Checkbox Preference"
    android:summary="Check it on, check it off" />
  <RingtonePreference
    android:key="ringtone"
    android:title="Ringtone Preference"
    android:showDefault="true"
    android:showSilent="true"
```

```
        android:summary="Pick a tone, any tone" />
</PreferenceScreen>
```

The root of the preference XML is a `PreferenceScreen` element. You will see why it is named that later in this chapter. For now, take it on faith that it is a sensible name.

Some of the things you can have inside a `PreferenceScreen` element, not surprisingly, are preference definitions. These are subclasses of `Preference`, such as `CheckBoxPreference` or `RingtonePreference`, as shown in the preceding XML. As you might expect, these allow you to check a check box or choose a ringtone, respectively. In the case of `RingtonePreference`, you have the option of allowing users to choose the system default ringtone or to choose "silence" as a ringtone.

Letting Users Have Their Say

Given that you have set up the preference XML, you can use a nearly built-in activity for allowing your users to set their preferences. The activity is "nearly built-in" because you merely need to subclass it and point it to your preference XML, plus hook the activity into the rest of your application.

For example, here is the `EditPreferences` activity of the `Prefs/Simple` project:

```
package com.commonsware.android.simple;

import android.app.Activity;
import android.os.Bundle;
import android.preference.PreferenceActivity;


public class EditPreferences extends PreferenceActivity {
  @Override
  public void onCreate(Bundle savedInstanceState) {
    super.onCreate(savedInstanceState);

    addPreferencesFromResource(R.xml.preferences);
  }
}
```

As you can see, there is not much *to* see. All you need to do is call `addPreferencesFromResource()` and specify the XML resource containing your preferences.

You will also need to add this as an activity to your `AndroidManifest.xml` file:

```
<?xml version="1.0" encoding="utf-8"?>
<manifest xmlns:android="http://schemas.android.com/apk/res/android"
    package="com.commonsware.android.simple">
    <application android:label="@string/app_name"
        android:icon="@drawable/cw">
        <activity
            android:name=".SimplePrefsDemo"
            android:label="@string/app_name">
            <intent-filter>
                <action android:name="android.intent.action.MAIN" />
```

```
            <category android:name="android.intent.category.LAUNCHER" />
        </intent-filter>
      </activity>
      <activity
          android:name=".EditPreferences"
          android:label="@string/app_name">
      </activity>
    </application>
</manifest>
```

And you will need to arrange to invoke the activity, such as from a menu option, here pulled from SimplePrefsDemo:

```
public boolean onCreateOptionsMenu(Menu menu) {
  menu.add(Menu.NONE, EDIT_ID, Menu.NONE, "Edit Prefs")
      .setIcon(R.drawable.misc)
      .setAlphabeticShortcut('e');

  return(super.onCreateOptionsMenu(menu));
}

@Override
public boolean onOptionsItemSelected(MenuItem item) {
  switch (item.getItemId()) {
    case EDIT_ID:
      startActivity(new Intent(this, EditPreferences.class));
      return(true);
  }

  return(super.onOptionsItemSelected(item));
}
}
```

That is all that is required, and it really is not that much code outside the preferences XML. What you get for your effort is an Android-supplied preference UI, as shown in Figure 21–1.

The check box can be directly checked or unchecked. To change the ringtone preference, just select the entry in the preference list to bring up a selection dialog, as shown in Figure 21–2.

Figure 21–1. *The Simple project's preference UI*

Figure 21–2. *Choosing a ringtone preference*

Notice that there is no explicit save or commit button or menu. Any changes are persisted as soon as they are made.

The SimplePrefsDemo activity, beyond having the aforementioned menu, also displays the current preferences via a TableLayout:

```
<?xml version="1.0" encoding="utf-8"?>
<TableLayout
  xmlns:android="http://schemas.android.com/apk/res/android"
  android:layout_width="fill_parent"
  android:layout_height="fill_parent"
>
  <TableRow>
    <TextView
        android:text="Checkbox:"
        android:paddingRight="5px"
    />
    <TextView android:id="@+id/checkbox"
    />
  </TableRow>
  <TableRow>
    <TextView
        android:text="Ringtone:"
        android:paddingRight="5px"
    />
    <TextView android:id="@+id/ringtone"
    />
  </TableRow>
</TableLayout>
```

The fields for the table are found in onCreate():

```
public void onCreate(Bundle savedInstanceState) {
  super.onCreate(savedInstanceState);
  setContentView(R.layout.main);

  checkbox=(TextView)findViewById(R.id.checkbox);
  ringtone=(TextView)findViewById(R.id.ringtone);
}
```

The fields are updated on each onResume():

```
public void onResume() {
  super.onResume();

  SharedPreferences prefs=PreferenceManager
                    .getDefaultSharedPreferences(this);

  checkbox.setText(new Boolean(prefs
                        .getBoolean("checkbox", false))
                .toString());
  ringtone.setText(prefs.getString("ringtone", "<unset>"));
}
```

This means that the fields will be updated when the activity is opened and after the preferences activity is left (e.g., via the back button), as shown in Figure 21–3.

Figure 21–3. *The Simple project's list of saved preferences*

Adding a Wee Bit o' Structure

If you have a lot of preferences for users to set, putting them all in one big list may not be the best idea. Android's preference framework gives you a few ways to impose a bit of structure on your bag of preferences, including categories and screens.

Categories are added via a PreferenceCategory element in your preference XML and are used to group together related preferences. Rather than have your preferences all as children of the root PreferenceScreen, you can place a few PreferenceCategory elements in the PreferenceScreen, and then put your preferences in their appropriate categories. Visually, this adds a divider with the category title between groups of preferences.

If you have a whole lot of preferences—more than are convenient for users to scroll through—you can also put them on separate "screens" by introducing the PreferenceScreen element. Yes, *that* PreferenceScreen element.

Any children of PreferenceScreen go on their own screen. If you nest PreferenceScreens, the parent screen displays the screen as a placeholder entry, and tapping that entry brings up the child screen.

For example, from the Prefs/Structured sample project, here is a preference XML file that contains both PreferenceCategory and nested PreferenceScreen elements:

```
<PreferenceScreen
  xmlns:android="http://schemas.android.com/apk/res/android">
  <PreferenceCategory android:title="Simple Preferences">
    <CheckBoxPreference
      android:key="checkbox"
```

```
      android:title="Checkbox Preference"
      android:summary="Check it on, check it off"
  />
  <RingtonePreference
    android:key="ringtone"
    android:title="Ringtone Preference"
    android:showDefault="true"
    android:showSilent="true"
    android:summary="Pick a tone, any tone"
  />
</PreferenceCategory>
<PreferenceCategory android:title="Detail Screens">
  <PreferenceScreen
    android:key="detail"
    android:title="Detail Screen"
    android:summary="Additional preferences held in another page">
    <CheckBoxPreference
      android:key="checkbox2"
      android:title="Another Checkbox"
      android:summary="On. Off. It really doesn't matter."
    />
  </PreferenceScreen>
</PreferenceCategory>
</PreferenceScreen>
```

The result, when you use this preference XML with your PreferenceActivity implementation, is a categorized list of elements, as shown in Figure 21–4.

Figure 21–4. *The Structured project's preference UI, showing categories and a screen placeholder*

If you tap the Detail Screen entry, you are taken to the child preference screen, as shown in Figure 21–5.

Figure 21–5. *The child preference screen of the Structured project's preference UI*

The Kind of Pop-Ups You Like

Of course, not all preferences are check boxes and ringtones. For others, like entry fields and lists, Android uses pop-up dialogs. Users do not enter their preference directly in the preference UI activity, but rather tap a preference, fill in a value, and click OK to commit the change.

Structurally, in the preference XML, fields and lists are not significantly different from other preference types, as seen in this preference XML from the Prefs/Dialogs sample project:

```
<PreferenceScreen
  xmlns:android="http://schemas.android.com/apk/res/android">
  <PreferenceCategory android:title="Simple Preferences">
    <CheckBoxPreference
      android:key="checkbox"
      android:title="Checkbox Preference"
      android:summary="Check it on, check it off"
    />
    <RingtonePreference
      android:key="ringtone"
      android:title="Ringtone Preference"
      android:showDefault="true"
      android:showSilent="true"
      android:summary="Pick a tone, any tone"
    />
  </PreferenceCategory>
  <PreferenceCategory android:title="Detail Screens">
    <PreferenceScreen
      android:key="detail"
```

```
          android:title="Detail Screen"
          android:summary="Additional preferences held in another page">
          <CheckBoxPreference
            android:key="checkbox2"
            android:title="Another Checkbox"
            android:summary="On. Off. It really doesn't matter."
          />
        </PreferenceScreen>
      </PreferenceCategory>
      <PreferenceCategory android:title="Simple Preferences">
        <EditTextPreference
          android:key="text"
          android:title="Text Entry Dialog"
          android:summary="Click to pop up a field for entry"
          android:dialogTitle="Enter something useful"
        />
        <ListPreference
          android:key="list"
          android:title="Selection Dialog"
          android:summary="Click to pop up a list to choose from"
          android:entries="@array/cities"
          android:entryValues="@array/airport_codes"
          android:dialogTitle="Choose a Pennsylvania city" />
      </PreferenceCategory>
    </PreferenceScreen>
```

With the field (EditTextPreference), in addition to the title and summary you put on the preference itself, you can also supply the title to use for the dialog.

With the list (ListPreference), you supply both a dialog title and two string-array resources: one for the display names and one for the values. These need to be in the same order, because the index of the chosen display name determines which value is stored as the preference in the SharedPreferences. For example, here are the arrays for use by the ListPreference shown in the preceding example:

```
<?xml version="1.0" encoding="utf-8"?>
<resources>
  <string-array name="cities">
    <item>Philadelphia</item>
    <item>Pittsburgh</item>
    <item>Allentown/Bethlehem</item>
    <item>Erie</item>
    <item>Reading</item>
    <item>Scranton</item>
    <item>Lancaster</item>
    <item>Altoona</item>
    <item>Harrisburg</item>
  </string-array>
  <string-array name="airport_codes">
    <item>PHL</item>
    <item>PIT</item>
    <item>ABE</item>
    <item>ERI</item>
    <item>RDG</item>
    <item>AVP</item>
    <item>LNS</item>
    <item>AOO</item>
```

```
    <item>MDT</item>
  </string-array>
</resources>
```

When you bring up the preference UI, you start with another category with another pair of preference entries, as shown in Figure 21–6.

Figure 21–6. *The preference screen of the Dialogs project's preference UI*

Tapping the Text Entry Dialog entry brings up a text-entry dialog with the prior preference entry already filled in, as shown in Figure 21–7.

Figure 21–7. *Editing a text preference*

Tapping Selection Dialog brings up a selection dialog showing the display names from the one array, as shown in Figure 21–8.

Figure 21–8. *Editing a list preference*

Chapter 22

Managing and Accessing Local Databases

SQLite is a very popular embedded database, as it combines a clean SQL interface with a very small memory footprint and decent speed. Moreover, it is public domain, so everyone can use it. Many firms (e.g., Adobe, Apple, Google, Sun, and Symbian) and open source projects (e.g., Mozilla, PHP, and Python) ship products with SQLite.

For Android, SQLite is "baked into" the Android runtime, so every Android application can create SQLite databases. Since SQLite uses a SQL interface, it is fairly straightforward to use for people with experience in other SQL-based databases. However, its native API is not JDBC, and JDBC might be too much overhead for a memory-limited device like a phone, anyway. Hence, Android programmers have a different API to learn. The good news is that it is not that difficult.

This chapter will cover the basics of SQLite use in the context of working on Android. It by no means is a thorough coverage of SQLite as a whole. If you want to learn more about SQLite and how to use it in environments other than Android, a fine book is *The Definitive Guide to SQLite* by Michael Owens (Apress, 2006).

The Database Example

Much of the sample code shown in this chapter comes from the Database/Constants application. This application presents a list of physical constants, with names and values culled from Android's SensorManager, as shown in Figure 22–1.

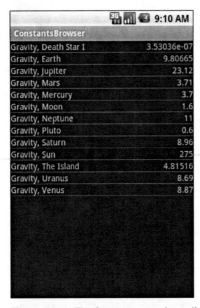

Figure 22–1. *The Constants sample application, as initially launched*

You can pop up a menu to add a new constant, which brings up a dialog to fill in the name and value of the constant, as shown in Figure 22–2.

Figure 22–2. *The Constants sample application's Add Constant dialog*

The constant is then added to the list. A long-tap on an existing constant will bring up a context menu with a Delete option, which, after confirmation, will delete the constant.

And, of course, all of this is stored in a SQLite database.

A Quick SQLite Primer

SQLite, as the name suggests, uses a dialect of SQL for queries (SELECT), data manipulation (INSERT, et. al.), and data definition (CREATE TABLE, et. al.). SQLite has a few places where it deviates from the SQL-92 standard, as is common for most SQL databases. The good news is that SQLite is so space-efficient that the Android runtime can include all of SQLite, not some arbitrary subset to trim it down to size.

A big difference between SQLite and other SQL databases is the data typing. While you can specify the data types for columns in a CREATE TABLE statement, and SQLite will use those as a hint, that is as far as it goes. You can put whatever data you want in whatever column you want. Put a string in an INTEGER column? Sure, no problem! Vice versa? That works, too! SQLite refers to this as *manifest typing*, as described in the documentation:

> *In manifest typing, the datatype is a property of the value itself, not of the column in which the value is stored. SQLite thus allows the user to store any value of any datatype into any column regardless of the declared type of that column.*

In addition, a handful of standard SQL features are not supported in SQLite, notably FOREIGN KEY constraints, nested transactions, RIGHT OUTER JOIN, FULL OUTER JOIN, and some flavors of ALTER TABLE.

Beyond that, though, you get a full SQL system, complete with triggers, transactions, and the like. Stock SQL statements, like SELECT, work pretty much as you might expect.

> **NOTE:** If you are used to working with a major database, like Oracle, you may look upon SQLite as being a "toy" database. Please bear in mind that Oracle and SQLite are meant to solve different problems, and that you will not be seeing a full copy of Oracle on a phone any time soon, in all likelihood.

Start at the Beginning

No databases are automatically supplied to you by Android. If you want to use SQLite, you will need to create your own database, and then populate it with your own tables, indexes, and data.

To create and open a database, your best option is to craft a subclass of SQLiteOpenHelper. This class wraps up the logic to create and upgrade a database, per your specifications, as needed by your application. Your subclass of SQLiteOpenHelper will need three methods:

- The constructor, chaining upward to the SQLiteOpenHelper constructor. This takes the Context (e.g., an Activity), the name of the database, an optional cursor factory (typically, just pass null), and an integer representing the version of the database schema you are using.

- onCreate(), which passes you a SQLiteDatabase object that you need to populate with tables and initial data, as appropriate.

- onUpgrade(), which passes you a SQLiteDatabase object and the old and new version numbers, so you can figure out how best to convert the database from the old schema to the new one. The simplest, albeit least friendly, approach is to drop the old tables and create new ones.

For example, here is a DatabaseHelper class from Database/Constants that, in onCreate(), creates a table and adds a number of rows, and in onUpgrade() cheats by dropping the existing table and executing onCreate():

```
package com.commonsware.android.constants;

import android.content.ContentValues;
import android.content.Context;
import android.database.Cursor;
import android.database.SQLException;
import android.database.sqlite.SQLiteOpenHelper;
import android.database.sqlite.SQLiteDatabase;
import android.hardware.SensorManager;

public class DatabaseHelper extends SQLiteOpenHelper {
  private static final String DATABASE_NAME="db";
  public static final String TITLE="title";
  public static final String VALUE="value";

  public DatabaseHelper(Context context) {
    super(context, DATABASE_NAME, null, 1);
  }

  @Override
  public void onCreate(SQLiteDatabase db) {
    db.execSQL("CREATE TABLE constants (_id INTEGER PRIMARY KEY AUTOINCREMENT,↵
title TEXT, value REAL);");

    ContentValues cv=new ContentValues();

    cv.put(TITLE, "Gravity, Death Star I");
    cv.put(VALUE, SensorManager.GRAVITY_DEATH_STAR_I);
    db.insert("constants", TITLE, cv);

    cv.put(TITLE, "Gravity, Earth");
    cv.put(VALUE, SensorManager.GRAVITY_EARTH);
    db.insert("constants", TITLE, cv);

    cv.put(TITLE, "Gravity, Jupiter");
    cv.put(VALUE, SensorManager.GRAVITY_JUPITER);
```

```
      db.insert("constants", TITLE, cv);

      cv.put(TITLE, "Gravity, Mars");
      cv.put(VALUE, SensorManager.GRAVITY_MARS);
      db.insert("constants", TITLE, cv);

      cv.put(TITLE, "Gravity, Mercury");
      cv.put(VALUE, SensorManager.GRAVITY_MERCURY);
      db.insert("constants", TITLE, cv);

      cv.put(TITLE, "Gravity, Moon");
      cv.put(VALUE, SensorManager.GRAVITY_MOON);
      db.insert("constants", TITLE, cv);

      cv.put(TITLE, "Gravity, Neptune");
      cv.put(VALUE, SensorManager.GRAVITY_NEPTUNE);
      db.insert("constants", TITLE, cv);

      cv.put(TITLE, "Gravity, Pluto");
      cv.put(VALUE, SensorManager.GRAVITY_PLUTO);
      db.insert("constants", TITLE, cv);

      cv.put(TITLE, "Gravity, Saturn");
      cv.put(VALUE, SensorManager.GRAVITY_SATURN);
      db.insert("constants", TITLE, cv);

      cv.put(TITLE, "Gravity, Sun");
      cv.put(VALUE, SensorManager.GRAVITY_SUN);
      db.insert("constants", TITLE, cv);

      cv.put(TITLE, "Gravity, The Island");
      cv.put(VALUE, SensorManager.GRAVITY_THE_ISLAND);
      db.insert("constants", TITLE, cv);

      cv.put(TITLE, "Gravity, Uranus");
      cv.put(VALUE, SensorManager.GRAVITY_URANUS);
      db.insert("constants", TITLE, cv);

      cv.put(TITLE, "Gravity, Venus");
      cv.put(VALUE, SensorManager.GRAVITY_VENUS);
      db.insert("constants", TITLE, cv);
   }

   @Override
   public void onUpgrade(SQLiteDatabase db, int oldVersion, int newVersion) {
      android.util.Log.w("Constants", "Upgrading database, which will destroy all old
data");
      db.execSQL("DROP TABLE IF EXISTS constants");
      onCreate(db);
   }
}
```

To use your `SQLiteOpenHelper` subclass, create an instance and ask it to `getReadableDatabase()` or `getWriteableDatabase()`, depending on whether or not you will be changing its contents. For example, our `ConstantsBrowser` activity opens the database in `onCreate()`:

```
db=(new DatabaseHelper(this)).getWritableDatabase();
```

This will return a `SQLiteDatabase` instance, which you can then use to query the database or modify its data.

When you are finished with the database (e.g., your activity is being closed), simply call `close()` on the `SQLiteDatabase` to release your connection.

Setting the Table

For creating your tables and indexes, you will need to call `execSQL()` on your `SQLiteDatabase`, providing the Data Definition Language (DDL) statement you wish to apply against the database. Barring a database error, this method returns nothing.

So, for example, you can call `execSQL()` to create the `constants` table, as shown in the `DatabaseHelper` `onCreate()` method:

```
db.execSQL("CREATE TABLE constants (_id INTEGER PRIMARY KEY AUTOINCREMENT, title
TEXT,⏎
 value REAL);");
```

This will create a table, named `constants`, with a primary key column named `_id` that is an autoincremented integer (i.e., SQLite will assign the value for you when you insert rows), plus two data columns: `title` (text) and `value` (a float, or *real* in SQLite terms). SQLite will automatically create an index for you on your primary key column. You could add other indexes here via some `CREATE INDEX` statements.

Most likely, you will create tables and indexes when you first create the database, or possibly when the database needs upgrading to accommodate a new release of your application. If you do not change your table schemas, you might never drop your tables or indexes, but if you do, just use `execSQL()` to invoke `DROP INDEX` and `DROP TABLE` statements as needed.

Makin' Data

Given that you have a database and one or more tables, you probably want to put some data in them. You have two major approaches for doing this.

 - Use `execSQL()`, just as you did for creating the tables. The `execSQL()` method works for any SQL that does not return results, so it can handle `INSERT`, `UPDATE`, `DELETE`, and so on just fine.

- Use the insert(), update(), and delete() methods on the SQLiteDatabase object. These are "builder" sorts of methods, in that they break down the SQL statements into discrete chunks, then take those chunks as parameters.

For example, here we insert() a new row into our constants table:

```
private void processAdd(DialogWrapper wrapper) {
  ContentValues values=new ContentValues(2);

  values.put("title", wrapper.getTitle());
  values.put("value", wrapper.getValue());

  db.insert("constants", "title", values);
  constantsCursor.requery();
}
```

These methods make use of ContentValues objects, which implement a Map-esque interface, albeit one that has additional methods for working with SQLite types. For example, in addition to get() to retrieve a value by its key, you have getAsInteger(), getAsString(), and so forth.

The insert() method takes the name of the table, the name of one column as the "null column hack," and a ContentValues with the initial values you want put into this row. The null column hack is for the case where the ContentValues instance is empty. The column named as the null column hack will be explicitly assigned the value NULL in the SQL INSERT statement generated by insert().

The update() method takes the name of the table, a ContentValues representing the columns and replacement values to use, an optional WHERE clause, and an optional list of parameters to fill into the WHERE clause, to replace any embedded question marks (?). Since update() replaces only columns with fixed values, versus ones computed based on other information, you may need to use execSQL() to accomplish some ends. The WHERE clause and parameter list work akin to the positional SQL parameters you may be used to from other SQL APIs.

The delete() method works similar to update(), taking the name of the table, the optional WHERE clause, and the corresponding parameters to fill into the WHERE clause. For example, here we delete a row from our constants table, given its _ID:

```
private void processDelete(long rowId) {
  String[] args={String.valueOf(rowId)};

  db.delete("constants", "_ID=?", args);
  constantsCursor.requery();
}
```

What Goes Around Comes Around

As with INSERT, UPDATE, and DELETE, you have two main options for retrieving data from a SQLite database using SELECT:

- Use rawQuery() to invoke a SELECT statement directly.
- Use query() to build up a query from its component parts.

Confounding matters further is the SQLiteQueryBuilder class and the issue of cursors and cursor factories. Let's take this one piece at a time.

Raw Queries

The simplest solution, at least in terms of the API, is rawQuery(). Just call it with your SQL SELECT statement. The SELECT statement can include positional parameters; the array of these forms your second parameter to rawQuery(). So, we wind up with this:

```
constantsCursor=db.rawQuery("SELECT _ID, title, value "+
                            "FROM constants ORDER BY title",
                            null);
```

The return value is a Cursor, which contains methods for iterating over results (discussed in the "Using Cursors" section a little later in the chapter).

If your queries are pretty much baked into your application, this is a very straightforward way to use them. However, it gets complicated if parts of the query are dynamic, beyond what positional parameters can really handle. For example, if the set of columns you need to retrieve is not known at compile time, puttering around concatenating column names into a comma-delimited list can be annoying, which is where query() comes in.

Regular Queries

The query() method takes the discrete pieces of a SELECT statement and builds the query from them. The pieces, in the order they appear as parameters to query(), are as follows:

- The name of the table to query against
- The list of columns to retrieve
- The WHERE clause, optionally including positional parameters
- The list of values to substitute in for those positional parameters
- The GROUP BY clause, if any
- The ORDER BY clause, if any
- The HAVING clause, if any

These can be null when they are not needed (except the table name, of course):

```
String[] columns={"ID", "inventory"};
String[] parms={"snicklefritz"};
Cursor result=db.query("widgets", columns, "name=?",
                       parms, null, null, null);
```

Building with Builders

Yet another option is to use SQLiteQueryBuilder, which offers much richer query-building options, particularly for nasty queries involving things like the union of multiple subquery results.

The SQLiteQueryBuilder interface dovetails nicely with the ContentProvider interface for executing queries. Hence, a common pattern for your content provider's query() implementation is to create a SQLiteQueryBuilder, fill in some defaults, and then allow it to build up (and optionally execute) the full query combining the defaults with what is provided to the content provider on the query request.

For example, here is a snippet of code from a content provider using SQLiteQueryBuilder:

```
@Override
public Cursor query(Uri url, String[] projection, String selection,
                    String[] selectionArgs, String sort) {
  SQLiteQueryBuilder qb=new SQLiteQueryBuilder();

  qb.setTables(getTableName());

  if (isCollectionUri(url)) {
    qb.setProjectionMap(getDefaultProjection());
  }
  else {
    qb.appendWhere(getIdColumnName()+"="+url.getPathSegments().get(1));
  }

  String orderBy;

  if (TextUtils.isEmpty(sort)) {
    orderBy=getDefaultSortOrder();
  } else {
    orderBy=sort;
  }

  Cursor c=qb.query(db, projection, selection, selectionArgs,
                    null, null, orderBy);
  c.setNotificationUri(getContext().getContentResolver(), url);
  return c;
}
```

Content providers are explained in greater detail in Chapters 26 and 27, so some of this you will have to take on faith until then. Here, you see the following:

- A SQLiteQueryBuilder is constructed.

- It is told the table to use for the query (setTables(getTableName())).

- It is told the default set of columns to return (setProjectionMap()), or it is given a piece of a WHERE clause to identify a particular row in the table by an identifier extracted from the Uri supplied to the query() call (appendWhere()).

- Finally, it is told to execute the query, blending the preset values with those supplied on the call to query() (qb.query(db, projection, selection, selectionArgs, null, null, orderBy)).

Instead of having the SQLiteQueryBuilder execute the query directly, we could have called buildQuery() to have it generate and return the SQL SELECT statement we needed, which we could then execute ourselves.

Using Cursors

No matter how you execute the query, you get a Cursor back. This is the Android/SQLite edition of the database cursor, a concept used in many database systems. With the cursor, you can do the following:

- Find out how many rows are in the result set via getCount().

- Iterate over the rows via moveToFirst(), moveToNext(), and isAfterLast().

- Find out the names of the columns via getColumnNames(), convert those into column numbers via getColumnIndex(), and get values for the current row for a given column via methods like getString(), getInt(), and so on.

- Reexecute the query that created the cursor via requery().

- Release the cursor's resources via close().

For example, here we iterate over a widgets table entries:

```
Cursor result=
  db.rawQuery("SELECT ID, name, inventory FROM widgets");

result.moveToFirst();

while (!result.isAfterLast()) {
 int id=result.getInt(0);
 String name=result.getString(1);
 int inventory=result.getInt(2);

 // do something useful with these
```

```
 result.moveToNext();
}

result.close();
```

You can also wrap a `Cursor` in a `SimpleCursorAdapter` or other implementation, and then hand the resulting adapter to a `ListView` or other selection widget. For example, after retrieving the sorted list of constants, we pop those into the `ListView` for the `ConstantsBrowser` activity in just a few lines of code:

```
ListAdapter adapter=new SimpleCursorAdapter(this,
                    R.layout.row, constantsCursor,
                    new String[] {"title", "value"},
                    new int[] {R.id.title, R.id.value});

setListAdapter(adapter);
```

> **TIP:** There may be circumstances in which you want to use your own `Cursor` subclass, rather than the stock implementation provided by Android. In those cases, you can use `queryWithFactory()` and `rawQueryWithFactory()`, which take a `SQLiteDatabase.CursorFactory` instance as a parameter. The factory is responsible for creating new cursors via its `newCursor()` implementation.

Data, Data, Everywhere

If you are used to developing for other databases, you are also probably used to having tools to inspect and manipulate the contents of the database, beyond merely the database's API. With Android's emulator, you have two main options for this.

First, the emulator is supposed to bundle in the `sqlite3` console program and make it available from the `adb shell` command. Once you are in the emulator's shell, just execute `sqlite3`, providing it the path to your database file. Your database file can be found at the following location:

`/data/data/your.app.package/databases/your-db-name`

Here, `your.app.package` is the Java package for your application (e.g., `com.commonsware.android`), and `your-db-name` is the name of your database, as supplied to `createDatabase()`.

The `sqlite3` program works, and if you are used to poking around your tables using a console interface, you are welcome to use it. If you prefer something a little friendlier, you can always copy the SQLite database off the device onto your development machine, and then use a SQLite-aware client program to putter around. Note, though, that you are working off a copy of the database; if you want your changes to go back to the device, you will need to transfer the database back over.

To get the database off the device, you can use the `adb pull` command (or the equivalent in your IDE, or File Manager in the Dalvik Debug Monitor Service, discussed in Chapter 35), which takes the path to the on-device database and the local destination as parameters. To store a modified database on the device, use adb push, which takes the local path to the database and the on-device destination as parameters.

One of the most accessible SQLite clients is the SQLite Manager extension for Firefox, shown in Figure 22–2, as it works across all platforms.

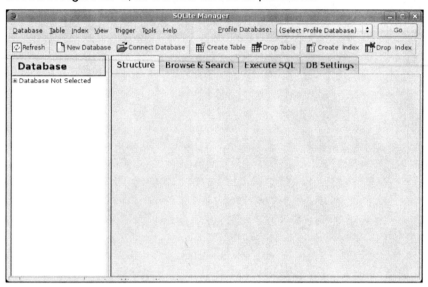

Figure 22–3. *SQLite Manager Firefox extension*

You can find other client tools on the SQLite web site.

Chapter **23**

Accessing Files

While Android offers structured storage, via preferences and databases, sometimes a simple file will suffice. Android offers two models for accessing files: one for files prepackaged with your application and one for files created on-device by your application. Both of these models are covered in this chapter.

You and the Horse You Rode in On

Let's suppose you have some static data you want to ship with the application, such as a list of words for a spell checker. The easiest way to deploy that is to place the file in the res/raw directory, so it will be put in the Android application APK file as part of the packaging process as a raw resource.

To access this file, you need to get yourself a Resources object. From an activity, that is as simple as calling getResources(). A Resources object offers openRawResource() to get an InputStream on the file you specify. Rather than a path, openRawResource() expects an integer identifier for the file as packaged. This works just like accessing widgets via findViewById(). For example, if you put a file named words.xml in res/raw, the identifier is accessible in Java as R.raw.words.

Since you can get only an InputStream, you have no means of modifying this file. Hence, it is really useful just for static reference data. Moreover, since it is unchanging until the user installs an updated version of your application package, either the reference data must be valid for the foreseeable future or you will need to provide some means of updating the data. The simplest way to handle that is to use the reference data to bootstrap some other modifiable form of storage (e.g., a database), but you end up with two copies of the data in storage.

An alternative is to keep the reference data as is but keep modifications in a file or database, and merge them together when you need a complete picture of the information. For example, if your application ships a file of URLs, you could have a second file that tracks URLs added by the user or reference URLs that were deleted by the user.

In the Files/Static sample project, you will find a reworking of the list box example from Chapter 7, this time using a static XML file instead of a hardwired array in Java. The layout is the same:

```xml
<?xml version="1.0" encoding="utf-8"?>
<LinearLayout xmlns:android="http://schemas.android.com/apk/res/android"
  android:orientation="vertical"
  android:layout_width="fill_parent"
  android:layout_height="fill_parent" >
  <TextView
    android:id="@+id/selection"
    android:layout_width="fill_parent"
    android:layout_height="wrap_content"
  />
  <ListView
    android:id="@android:id/list"
    android:layout_width="fill_parent"
    android:layout_height="fill_parent"
    android:drawSelectorOnTop="false"
  />
</LinearLayout>
```

In addition to that XML file, you also need an XML file with the words to show in the list:

```xml
<words>
  <word value="lorem" />
  <word value="ipsum" />
  <word value="dolor" />
  <word value="sit" />
  <word value="amet" />
  <word value="consectetuer" />
  <word value="adipiscing" />
  <word value="elit" />
  <word value="morbi" />
  <word value="vel" />
  <word value="ligula" />
  <word value="vitae" />
  <word value="arcu" />
  <word value="aliquet" />
  <word value="mollis" />
  <word value="etiam" />
  <word value="vel" />
  <word value="erat" />
  <word value="placerat" />
  <word value="ante" />
  <word value="porttitor" />
  <word value="sodales" />
  <word value="pellentesque" />
  <word value="augue" />
  <word value="purus" />
</words>
```

While this XML structure is not exactly a model of space efficiency, it will suffice for a demo.

The Java code now must read in that XML file, parse out the words, and put them someplace for the list to pick up:

```java
public class StaticFileDemo extends ListActivity {
  TextView selection;
  ArrayList<String> items=new ArrayList<String>();

  @Override
  public void onCreate(Bundle icicle) {
    super.onCreate(icicle);
    setContentView(R.layout.main);
    selection=(TextView)findViewById(R.id.selection);

    try {
      InputStream in=getResources().openRawResource(R.raw.words);
      DocumentBuilder builder=DocumentBuilderFactory
                          .newInstance()
                          .newDocumentBuilder();
      Document doc=builder.parse(in, null);
      NodeList words=doc.getElementsByTagName("word");

      for (int i=0;i<words.getLength();i++) {
        items.add(((Element)words.item(i)).getAttribute("value"));
      }

      in.close();
    }
    catch (Throwable t) {
      Toast
        .makeText(this, "Exception: "+t.toString(), 2000)
        .show();
    }

    setListAdapter(new ArrayAdapter<String>(this,
                              android.R.layout.simple_list_item_1,
                              items));
  }

  public void onListItemClick(ListView parent, View v, int position,
                  long id) {
    selection.setText(items.get(position).toString());
  }
}
```

The differences mostly lie within onCreate(). We get an InputStream for the XML file
(getResources().openRawResource(R.raw.words)), then use the built-in XML parsing
logic to parse the file into a DOM Document, pick out the word elements, and then pour
the value attributes into an ArrayList for use by the ArrayAdapter.

The resulting activity looks the same as before, as shown in Figure 23–1, since the list of
words is the same, just relocated.

Figure 23–1. *The StaticFileDemo sample application*

Of course, there are even easier ways to have XML files available to you as prepackaged files, such as by using an XML resource, as discussed in Chapter 20. However, while this example used XML, the file could just as easily have been a simple one-word-per-line list or in some other format not handled natively by the Android resource system.

Readin' 'n Writin'

Reading or writing your own, application-specific data files is nearly identical to what you might do in a desktop Java application. The key is to use openFileInput() or openFileOutput() on your Activity or other Context to get an InputStream or OutputStream, respectively. From that point forward, it is not much different from regular Java I/O logic:

- Wrap those streams as needed, such as using an InputStreamReader or OutputStreamWriter for text-based I/O.
- Read or write the data.
- Use close() to release the stream when done.

If two applications both try reading a notes.txt file via openFileInput(), each will access its own edition of the file. If you need to have one file accessible from many places, you probably want to create a content provider, as described in Chapter 27.

Note that openFileInput() and openFileOutput() do not accept file paths (e.g., path/to/file.txt), just simple filenames.

Here is the layout for the world's most trivial text editor, pulled from the `Files/ReadWrite` sample application:

```xml
<?xml version="1.0" encoding="utf-8"?>
<LinearLayout xmlns:android="http://schemas.android.com/apk/res/android"
  android:layout_width="fill_parent"
  android:layout_height="fill_parent"
  android:orientation="vertical">
  <Button android:id="@+id/close"
    android:layout_width="wrap_content"
    android:layout_height="wrap_content"
    android:text="Close" />
  <EditText
    android:id="@+id/editor"
    android:layout_width="fill_parent"
    android:layout_height="fill_parent"
    android:singleLine="false"
    android:gravity="top"
    />
</LinearLayout>
```

All we have here is a large text-editing widget, with a Close button above it.

The Java is only slightly more complicated:

```java
package com.commonsware.android.readwrite;

import android.app.Activity;
import android.os.Bundle;
import android.view.View;
import android.widget.Button;
import android.widget.EditText;
import android.widget.Toast;
import java.io.BufferedReader;
import java.io.File;
import java.io.InputStream;
import java.io.InputStreamReader;
import java.io.OutputStream;
import java.io.OutputStreamWriter;

public class ReadWriteFileDemo extends Activity {
  private final static String NOTES="notes.txt";
  private EditText editor;

  @Override
  public void onCreate(Bundle icicle) {
    super.onCreate(icicle);
    setContentView(R.layout.main);
    editor=(EditText)findViewById(R.id.editor);

    Button btn=(Button)findViewById(R.id.close);

    btn.setOnClickListener(new Button.OnClickListener() {
      public void onClick(View v) {
        finish();
      }
    });
```

```
      }

    public void onResume() {
      super.onResume();

      try {
        InputStream in=openFileInput(NOTES);

        if (in!=null) {
          InputStreamReader tmp=new InputStreamReader(in);
          BufferedReader reader=new BufferedReader(tmp);
          String str;
          StringBuffer buf=new StringBuffer();

          while ((str = reader.readLine()) != null) {
            buf.append(str+"\n");
          }

          in.close();
          editor.setText(buf.toString());
        }
      }
      catch (java.io.FileNotFoundException e) {
        // that's OK, we probably haven't created it yet
      }
      catch (Throwable t) {
        Toast
          .makeText(this, "Exception: "+t.toString(), 2000)
          .show();
      }
    }

    public void onPause() {
      super.onPause();

      try {
        OutputStreamWriter out=
            new OutputStreamWriter(openFileOutput(NOTES, 0));

        out.write(editor.getText().toString());
        out.close();
      }
      catch (Throwable t) {
        Toast
          .makeText(this, "Exception: "+t.toString(), 2000)
          .show();
      }
    }
  }
```

First, we wire up the button to close our activity when clicked by using setOnClickListener() to invoke finish() on the activity.

Next, we hook into onResume(), so we get control when our editor is coming back to life, from a fresh launch or after having been frozen. We use openFileInput() to read in notes.txt and pour the contents into the text editor. If the file is not found, we assume this is the first time the activity was run (or the file was deleted by other means), and we just leave the editor empty.

Finally, we hook into onPause(), so we get control as our activity is hidden by another activity or closed, such as via our Close button. Here, we use openFileOutput() to open notes.txt, into which we pour the contents of the text editor.

The net result is that we have a persistent notepad, as shown in Figures 23–2 and 23–3. Whatever is typed in will remain until deleted, surviving our activity being closed, the phone being turned off, or similar situations.

Figure 23–2. *The ReadWriteFileDemo sample application, as initially launched*

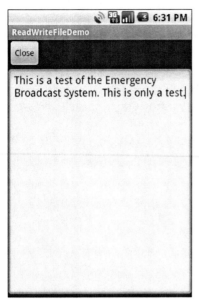

Figure 23–3. *The same application, after entering some text*

You are also welcome to read and write files on external storage (a.k.a., the SD card). Use Environment.getExternalStorageDirectory() to obtain a File object at the root of the SD card. Starting with Android 1.6, you will also need to hold permissions to work with external storage (e.g., WRITE_EXTERNAL_STORAGE). Permissions are covered in Chapter 28.

Bear in mind that external storage is accessible by all applications, whereas openFileInput() and openFileOutput() are in an application-private area.

Chapter 24

Leveraging Java Libraries

Java has as many, if not more, third-party libraries than any other modern programming language. The third-party libraries I'm referring to here are the innumerable JAR files that you can include in a server or desktop Java application—the things that the Java SDKs themselves do not provide.

In the case of Android, the Dalvik virtual machine (VM) at its heart is not precisely Java, and what it provides in its SDK is not precisely the same as any traditional Java SDK. That being said, many Java third-party libraries still provide capabilities that Android lacks natively, and therefore may be of use to you in your project (if you can get them to work with Android's flavor of Java).

This chapter explains what it will take for you to leverage such libraries and the limitations on Android's support for arbitrary third-party code.

The Outer Limits

Not all available Java code will work well with Android. There are a number of factors to consider, including the following:

- *Expected platform APIs*: Does the code assume a newer Java Virtual Machine (JVM) than the one Android is based on? Or, does the code assume the existence of Java APIs that ship with Java SE but not with Android, such as Swing?

- *Size*: Existing Java code designed for use on desktops or servers does not need to be concerned much with on-disk size, or, to some extent, even in-RAM size. Android, of course, is short on both. Using third-party Java code, particularly when prepackaged as JARs, may balloon the size of your application.

- *Performance*: Does the Java code effectively assume a much more powerful CPU than what you may find on many Android devices? Just because a desktop can run it without issue doesn't mean your average mobile phone will handle it well.

■   *Interface*: Does the Java code assume a console interface? Or is it a
    pure API that you can wrap your own interface around?

One trick for addressing some of these concerns is to use open source Java code, and
actually work with the code to make it more Android-friendly. For example, if you're using
just 10% of the third-party library, maybe it's worthwhile to recompile the subset of the
project to be only what you need, or at least to remove the unnecessary classes from the
JAR. The former approach is safer, in that you get compiler help to make sure you're not
discarding some essential piece of code, although it may be quite tedious to do.

Ants and JARs

You have two choices for integrating third-party code into your project: use source code
or use prepackaged JARs.

If you choose to use source code, all you need to do is copy it into your own source tree
(under `src/` in your project), so it can sit alongside your existing code, and then let the
compiler perform its magic.

If you choose to use an existing JAR, perhaps one for which you do not have the source
code, you will need to teach your build chain how to use the JAR. First, place the JAR in
the `libs/` directory in your Android project. Then, if you are using an IDE, you probably
need to add the JAR to your build path. (Ant will automatically pick up all JARs found in
`libs/`.)

Following the Script

Unlike other mobile device operating systems, Android has no restrictions on what you
can run on it, so long as you can do it in Java using the Dalvik VM. This includes
incorporating your own scripting language into your application, something that is
expressly prohibited on some other devices.

One possible Java scripting language is BeanShell (`http://beanshell.org`). BeanShell
gives you Java-compatible syntax with implicit typing and no compilation required.

To add BeanShell scripting, you need to put the BeanShell interpreter's JAR file in your
`libs/` directory. Unfortunately, the 2.0b4 JAR available for download from the BeanShell
site does not work out of the box with the Android 0.9 and newer SDKs (perhaps due to
the compiler that was used to build it). Instead, you should probably check out the
source code from Subversion and execute `ant jarcore` to build it, and then copy the
resulting JAR (in BeanShell's `dist/` directory) to your own project's `libs/`. Or, just use
the BeanShell JAR that accompanies the source code for this book, up in the
`Java/AndShell` project.

From there, using BeanShell on Android is no different than using BeanShell in any other Java environment:

1. Create an instance of the BeanShell Interpreter class.

2. Set any globals for the script's use via Interpreter#set().

3. Call Interpreter#eval() to run the script and, optionally, get the result of the last statement of the script.

For example, here is the XML layout for the world's smallest BeanShell IDE:

```
<?xml version="1.0" encoding="utf-8"?>
<LinearLayout xmlns:android="http://schemas.android.com/apk/res/android"
    android:orientation="vertical"
    android:layout_width="fill_parent"
    android:layout_height="fill_parent"
    >
<Button
    android:id="@+id/eval"
    android:layout_width="fill_parent"
    android:layout_height="wrap_content"
    android:text="Go!"
    />
<EditText
    android:id="@+id/script"
    android:layout_width="fill_parent"
    android:layout_height="fill_parent"
    android:singleLine="false"
    android:gravity="top"
    />
</LinearLayout>
```

Couple that with the following activity implementation:

```
package com.commonsware.android.andshell;

import android.app.Activity;
import android.app.AlertDialog;
import android.os.Bundle;
import android.view.View;
import android.widget.Button;
import android.widget.EditText;
import android.widget.Toast;
import bsh.Interpreter;

public class MainActivity extends Activity {
  private Interpreter i=new Interpreter();

  @Override
  public void onCreate(Bundle icicle) {
    super.onCreate(icicle);
    setContentView(R.layout.main);

    Button btn=(Button)findViewById(R.id.eval);
    final EditText script=(EditText)findViewById(R.id.script);
```

```
btn.setOnClickListener(new View.OnClickListener() {
  public void onClick(View view) {
    String src=script.getText().toString();

    try {
      i.set("context", MainActivity.this);
      i.eval(src);
    }
    catch (bsh.EvalError e) {
      AlertDialog.Builder builder=
              new AlertDialog.Builder(MainActivity.this);

      builder
        .setTitle("Exception!")
        .setMessage(e.toString())
        .setPositiveButton("OK", null)
        .show();
    }
  }
});
  }
}
```

Compile and run it (including incorporating the BeanShell JAR as mentioned earlier), and install it on the emulator. Fire it up, and you get a trivial IDE, with a large text area for your script and a big Go! button to execute it, as shown in Figure 24–1.

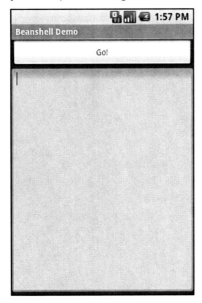

Figure 24–1. *The AndShell BeanShell IDE*

```
import android.widget.Toast;
```

```
Toast.makeText(context, "Hello, world!", 5000).show();
```

Note the use of `context` to refer to the activity when making the `Toast`. That is the global set by the activity to reference back to itself. You could call this global variable anything you want, as long as the `set()` call and the script code use the same name.

Click the Go! button, and you get the result shown in Figure 24–2.

Figure 24–2. *The AndShell BeanShell IDE, executing some code*

And now, some caveats:

- Not all scripting languages will work. For example, those that implement their own form of just-in-time (JIT) compilation, generating Java bytecodes on the fly, would probably need to be augmented to generate Dalvik VM bytecodes instead of those for stock Java implementations. Simpler languages that execute from parsed scripts, calling Java reflection APIs to call back into compiled classes, will likely work better. Even there, though, not every feature of the language may work, if it relies on some facility in a traditional Java API that does not exist in Dalvik. For example, there could be stuff hidden inside BeanShell or the add-on JARs that does not work on today's Android.

- Scripting languages without JIT will inevitably be slower than compiled Dalvik applications. Slower may mean users experience sluggishness. Slower definitely means more battery life is consumed for the same amount of work. So, building a whole Android application in BeanShell, simply because you feel it is easier to program in, may cause your users to be unhappy.

- Scripting languages that expose the whole Java API, like BeanShell, can pretty much do anything the underlying Android security model allows. So, if your application has the READ_CONTACTS permission, expect any BeanShell scripts your application runs to have the same permission. (Permissions are covered in Chapter 28.)

- Last, but certainly not least, is that language interpreter JARs tend to be rather portly. The BeanShell JAR used in this example is 200KB. That is not ridiculous, considering what it does, but it will make applications that use BeanShell that much bigger to download, take up that much more space on the device, and so on.

...And Not a Drop to Drink

As noted earlier, not all Java code will work on Android and Dalvik. Here are some examples:

- If the Java code assumes it runs on Java SE, Java ME, or Java EE, it may be missing some APIs that Android does not provide. For example, some charting libraries assume the existence of Swing or AWT drawing primitives, which are generally unavailable on Android.

- The Java code might have a dependency on other Java code that, in turn, might have problems running on Android. For example, you might want to use a JAR that relies on an earlier (or newer) version of the Apache HttpComponents than the one that is bundled with Android.

- The Java code may use language capabilities beyond what the Dalvik engine is capable of using.

In all these cases, if you have a compiled JAR to work with, you may not encounter problems at compile time, but only when running the application. Hence, where possible, it is best to use open source code with Android, so you can build the third-party code alongside your own and find out about difficulties sooner.

Reviewing the Script

Since this chapter covers scripting in Android, you may be interested to know that you have options beyond embedding BeanShell directly in your project.

Some experiments have been conducted with other JVM-based programming languages, such as JRuby and Jython. At present, their support for Android is incomplete, but progress is being made.

Additionally, the Android Scripting Environment (ASE), available from the Android Market, allows you to write scripts in Python and Lua, to go along with BeanShell. These scripts are not full-fledged applications and, at the time of this writing, are not really distributable to others. Also note that ASE is not precisely designed to extend other applications, though it can be used that way. But if you want to do on-device programming, ASE is probably the best answer. For more information about ASE, see its project page at http://code.google.com/p/android-scripting/.

Chapter 25

Communicating via the Internet

The expectation is that most, if not all, Android devices will have built-in Internet access. That could be Wi-Fi, cellular data services (EDGE, 3G, etc.), or possibly something else entirely. Regardless, most people—or at least those with a data plan or Wi-Fi access—will be able to get to the Internet from their Android phone.

Not surprisingly, the Android platform gives developers a wide range of ways to make use of this Internet access. Some offer high-level access, such as the integrated WebKit browser component. If you want, you can drop all the way down to using raw sockets. In between, you can leverage APIs—both on-device and from third-party JARs—that give you access to specific protocols: HTTP, XMPP, SMTP, and so on.

The emphasis of this book is on the higher-level forms of access: the WebKit component (discussed in Chapter 13) and Internet-access APIs (discussed in this chapter). As busy coders, we should be trying to reuse existing components versus rolling our own on-the-wire protocol wherever possible.

REST and Relaxation

Android does not have built-in SOAP or XML-RPC client APIs. However, it does have the Apache HttpComponents library baked in. You can either layer a SOAP/XML-RPC layer atop this library or use it "straight" for accessing REST-style web services. For the purposes of this book, REST-style web services are considered simple HTTP requests for ordinary URLs over the full range of HTTP verbs, with formatted payloads (XML, JSON, etc.) as responses.

More expansive tutorials, FAQs, and HOWTOs can be found at the HttpClient web site (http://hc.apache.org/). Here, we'll cover the basics, while checking the weather.

HTTP Operations via Apache HttpClient

The HttpClient component of HttpComponents handles all HTTP requests on your behalf. The first step to using HttpClient is, not surprisingly, to create an HttpClient object. Since HttpClient is an interface, you will need to actually instantiate some implementation of that interface, such as DefaultHttpClient.

Those requests are bundled up into HttpRequest instances, with different HttpRequest implementations for each different HTTP verb (e.g., HttpGet for HTTP GET requests). You create an HttpRequest implementation instance, fill in the URL to retrieve and other configuration data (e.g., form values if you are doing an HTTP POST via HttpPost), and then pass the method to the client to actually make the HTTP request via execute().

What happens at this point can be as simple or as complicated as you want. You can get an HttpResponse object back, with a response code (e.g., 200 for OK), HTTP headers, and the like. Or, you can use a flavor of execute() that takes a ResponseHandler<String> as a parameter, with the net result being that execute() returns just the String representation of the response body. In practice, this is not a recommended approach, because you really should be checking your HTTP response codes for errors. However, for trivial applications, like book examples, the ResponseHandler<String> approach works just fine.

For example, let's take a look at the Internet/Weather sample project. This implements an activity that retrieves weather data for your current location from the National Weather Service. (Note that this probably only works only for geographic locations in the United States.) That data is converted into an HTML page, which is poured into a WebKit widget for display. Rebuilding this demo using a ListView is left as an exercise for the reader. Also, since this sample is relatively long, we will only show relevant pieces of the Java code here in this chapter, though you can always download the full source code from the Apress web site.

To make this a bit more interesting, we use the Android location services to figure out where we are—well, sort of. The full details of how that works are left until Chapter 32.

In the onResume() method, we toggle on location updates, so we will be informed where we are now and when we move a significant distance (10 kilometers). When a location is available—either at the start or based on movement—we retrieve the National Weather Service data via our updateForecast() method:

```
private void updateForecast(Location loc) {
  String url=String.format(format, loc.getLatitude(),
                      loc.getLongitude());
  HttpGet getMethod=new HttpGet(url);

  try {
    ResponseHandler<String> responseHandler=new BasicResponseHandler();
    String responseBody=client.execute(getMethod,
                                 responseHandler);

    buildForecasts(responseBody);
```

```
    String page=generatePage();

    browser.loadDataWithBaseURL(null, page, "text/html",
                                "UTF-8", null);
  }
  catch (Throwable t) {
    Toast
      .makeText(this, "Request failed: "+t.toString(), 4000)
      .show();
  }
}
```

The updateForecast() method takes a Location as a parameter, obtained from the location update process. For now, all you need to know is that Location sports getLatitude() and getLongitude() methods, which return the latitude and longitude of the device's position, respectively.

We hold the URL to the National Weather Service XML in a string resource, and pour in the latitude and longitude at runtime. Given our HttpClient object created in onCreate(), we populate an HttpGet with that customized URL, and then execute that method. Given the resulting XML from the REST service, we build the forecast HTML page, as described next, and pour that into the WebKit widget. If the HttpClient blows up with an exception, we provide that error as a Toast.

Parsing Responses

The response you get will be formatted using some system—HTML, XML, JSON, or whatever. It is up to you, of course, to pick out the information you need and do something useful with it. In the case of the WeatherDemo, we need to extract the forecast time, temperature, and icon (indicating sky conditions and precipitation), and generate an HTML page from it.

Android includes three XML parsers: the traditional W3C DOM parser (org.w3c.dom), a SAX parser (org.xml.sax), and the XML pull parser (discussed in Chapter 20). It also has a JSON parser (org.json).

You are also welcome to use third-party Java code, where possible, to handle other formats, such as a dedicated RSS/Atom parser for a feed reader. The use of third-party Java code is discussed in Chapter 24.

For WeatherDemo, we use the W3C DOM parser in our buildForecasts() method:

```
void buildForecasts(String raw) throws Exception {
  DocumentBuilder builder=DocumentBuilderFactory
                            .newInstance()
                            .newDocumentBuilder();
  Document doc=builder.parse(new InputSource(new StringReader(raw)));
  NodeList times=doc.getElementsByTagName("start-valid-time");

  for (int i=0;i<times.getLength();i++) {
    Element time=(Element)times.item(i);
    Forecast forecast=new Forecast();
```

```
      forecasts.add(forecast);
      forecast.setTime(time.getFirstChild().getNodeValue());
    }

    NodeList temps=doc.getElementsByTagName("value");

    for (int i=0;i<temps.getLength();i++) {
      Element temp=(Element)temps.item(i);
      Forecast forecast=forecasts.get(i);

      forecast.setTemp(new Integer(temp.getFirstChild().getNodeValue()));
    }

    NodeList icons=doc.getElementsByTagName("icon-link");

    for (int i=0;i<icons.getLength();i++) {
      Element icon=(Element)icons.item(i);
      Forecast forecast=forecasts.get(i);

      forecast.setIcon(icon.getFirstChild().getNodeValue());
    }
  }
```

The National Weather Service XML format is curiously structured, relying heavily on sequential position in lists versus the more object-oriented style you find in formats like RSS or Atom. That being said, we can take a few liberties and simplify the parsing somewhat, taking advantage of the fact that the elements we want (start-valid-time for the forecast time, value for the temperature, and icon-link for the icon URL) are unique within the document.

The HTML comes in as an InputStream and is fed into the DOM parser. From there, we scan for the start-valid-time elements and populate a set of Forecast models using those start times. Then we find the temperature value elements and icon-link URLs and fill those in to the Forecast objects.

In turn, the generatePage() method creates a rudimentary HTML table with the forecasts:

```
String generatePage() {
  StringBuffer bufResult=new StringBuffer("<html><body><table>");

  bufResult.append("<tr><th width=\"50%\">Time</th>"+
                   "<th>Temperature</th><th>Forecast</th></tr>");

  for (Forecast forecast : forecasts) {
    bufResult.append("<tr><td align=\"center\">");
    bufResult.append(forecast.getTime());
    bufResult.append("</td><td align=\"center\">");
    bufResult.append(forecast.getTemp());
    bufResult.append("</td><td><img src=\"");
    bufResult.append(forecast.getIcon());
    bufResult.append("\"></td></tr>");
  }
```

```
bufResult.append("</table></body></html>");

    return(bufResult.toString());
}
```

The result looks like Figure 25–1.

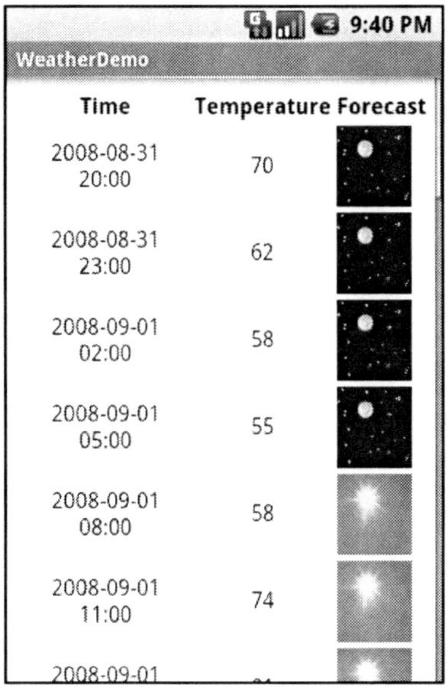

Figure 25–1. *The WeatherDemo sample application*

Stuff to Consider

If you need to use Secure Sockets Layer (SSL) protocol, bear in mind that the default HttpClient setup does not include SSL support. Mostly, this is because you need to decide how to handle SSL certificate presentation. Do you blindly accept all certificates, even self-signed or expired ones? Or do you want to ask the users if they really want to use some strange certificates?

Similarly, the HttpClient component, by default, is designed for single-threaded use. If you will be using HttpClient from a service or some other place where multiple threads might be an issue, you can readily set up HttpClient to support multiple threads.

For these sorts of topics, you are best served by checking out the HttpClient web site for documentation and support.

Chapter **26**

Using a Content Provider

Any Uri in Android that begins with the content:// scheme represents a resource served up by a content provider. Content providers offer data encapsulation using Uri instances as handles. You neither know nor care where the data represented by the Uri comes from, as long as it is available to you when needed. The data could be stored in a SQLite database, in flat files, or on some far-off server accessed over the Internet.

Given a Uri, you can perform basic CRUD (create, read, update, delete) operations using a content provider. Uri instances can represent either collections or individual pieces of content. Given a collection Uri, you can create new pieces of content via insert operations. Given an instance Uri, you can read data represented by the Uri, update that data, or delete the instance outright.

Android lets you use existing content providers or create your own. This chapter covers using content providers. Chapter 27 explains how you can serve up your own data using the content provider framework.

Pieces of Me

The simplified model of the construction of a content Uri is the scheme, the namespace of data, and, optionally, the instance identifier—all separated by slashes in URL-style notation. The scheme of a content Uri is always content://.

So, a content Uri of content://constants/5 represents the constants instance with an identifier of 5.

The combination of the scheme and the namespace is known as the base Uri of a content provider, or a set of data supported by a content provider. In the preceding example, content://constants is the base Uri for a content provider that serves up information about "constants" (in this case, physical constants).

The base Uri can be more complicated. For example, if the base Uri for contacts were content://contacts/people, the Contacts content provider may serve up other data using other base Uri values.

The base Uri represents a collection of instances. The base Uri combined with an instance identifier (e.g., 5) represents a single instance.

Most of the Android APIs expect these to be Uri objects, though in common discussion, it is simpler to think of them as strings. The Uri.parse() static method creates a Uri from the string representation.

Getting a Handle

So, where do these Uri instances come from?

The most popular starting point, if you know the type of data you want to work with, is to get the base Uri from the content provider itself in code. For example, CONTENT_URI is the base Uri for contacts represented as people; this maps to content://contacts/people. If you just need the collection, this Uri works as is. If you need an instance and know its identifier, you can call addId() on the Uri to inject it, so you have a Uri for the instance.

You might also get Uri instances handed to you from other sources, such as getting Uri handles for contacts via subactivities responding to ACTION_PICK intents. In this case, the Uri is truly an opaque handle, unless you decide to pick it apart using the various getters on the Uri class.

You can also hardwire literal String objects (e.g., "content://contacts/people") and convert them into Uri instances via Uri.parse(). This is not an ideal solution, as the base Uri values could conceivably change over time. For example, the Contacts content provider's base Uri is no longer content://contacts/people due to an overhaul of that subsystem.

Makin' Queries

Given a base Uri, you can run a query to return data from the content provider related to that Uri. This has much of the feel of SQL—you specify the "columns" to return, the constraints to determine which "rows" to return, a sort order, and so on. The difference is that this request is being made of a content provider, not directly of some database (e.g., SQLite).

The nexus of this is the managedQuery() method available to your activity. This method takes five parameters:

- The base Uri of the content provider to query, or the instance Uri of a specific object to query

- An array of properties of instances from that content provider that you want returned by the query

- A constraint statement, functioning like a SQL WHERE clause

- An optional set of parameters to bind into the constraint clause, replacing any ? characters that appear there

- An optional sort statement, functioning like a SQL ORDER BY clause

This method returns a Cursor object, which you can use to retrieve the data returned by the query.

Properties are to content providers as columns are to databases. In other words, each instance (row) returned by a query consists of a set of properties (columns), each representing some piece of data.

This should make more sense given an example.

Our content provider examples come from the ContentProvider/ConstantsPlus sample application, specifically the ConstantsBrowser class:

```
constantsCursor=managedQuery(Provider.Constants.CONTENT_URI,
                     PROJECTION, null, null, null);
```

In the call to managedQuery(), we provide the following:

- The Uri passed into the activity by the caller (CONTENT_URI); in this case, representing the collection of physical constants managed by the content provider

- A list of properties to retrieve

- Three null values, indicating that we do not need a constraint clause (the Uri represents the instance we need), nor parameters for the constraint, nor a sort order (we should get only one entry back)

```
private static final String[] PROJECTION = new String[] {
    Provider.Constants._ID, Provider.Constants.TITLE,
    Provider.Constants.VALUE};
```

The biggest "magic" here is the list of properties. The lineup of what properties are possible for a given content provider should be provided by the documentation (or source code) for the content provider itself. In this case, we define logical values on the Provider content provider implementation class that represent the various properties (namely, the unique identifier, the display name or title, and the value of the constant).

Adapting to the Circumstances

Now that we have a Cursor via managedQuery(), we have access to the query results and can do whatever we want with them. We might, for example, manually extract data from the Cursor to populate widgets or other objects.

However, if the goal of your query is to return a list from which the user should choose an item, you probably should consider using SimpleCursorAdapter. This class bridges between the Cursor and a selection widget, such as a ListView or Spinner. Pour the Cursor into a SimpleCursorAdapter, hand the adapter off to the widget, and you're set— your widget will show the available options.

For example, here is the onCreate() method from ConstantsBrowser, which gives the user a list of physical constants:

```
@Override
public void onCreate(Bundle savedInstanceState) {
  super.onCreate(savedInstanceState);

  constantsCursor=managedQuery(Provider.Constants.CONTENT_URI,
                         PROJECTION, null, null, null);

  ListAdapter adapter=new SimpleCursorAdapter(this,
                         R.layout.row, constantsCursor,
                         new String[] {Provider.Constants.TITLE,
                                   Provider.Constants.VALUE},
                         new int[] {R.id.title, R.id.value});

  setListAdapter(adapter);
  registerForContextMenu(getListView());
}
```

After executing the managedQuery() and getting the Cursor, ConstantsBrowser creates a SimpleCursorAdapter with the following parameters:

- The activity (or other Context) creating the adapter; in this case, the ConstantsBrowser itself

- The identifier for a layout to be used for rendering the list entries (R.layout.row)

- The cursor (constantsCursor)

- The properties to pull out of the cursor and use for configuring the list entry View instances (TITLE and VALUE)

- The corresponding identifiers of TextView widgets in the list entry layout that those properties should go into (R.id.title and R.id.value)

After that, we put the adapter into the ListView, and we get the result shown in Figure 26–1.

If you need more control over the views than you can reasonably achieve with the stock view construction logic, subclass SimpleCursorAdapter and override getView() to create your own widgets to go into the list, as demonstrated earlier in this book.

And, of course, you can manually manipulate the Cursor (e.g., moveToFirst(), getString()), as demonstrated in Chapter 22.

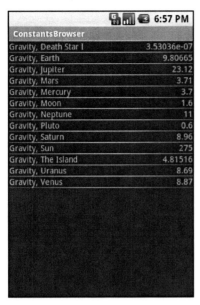

Figure 26–1. *ConstantsBrowser, showing a list of physical constants*

Give and Take

Of course, content providers would be astonishingly weak if you couldn't add or remove data from them, as well as update what is there. Fortunately, content providers offer these abilities.

To insert data into a content provider, you have two options available on the ContentProvider interface (available through getContentProvider() to your activity):

- Use insert() with a collection Uri and a ContentValues structure describing the initial set of data to put in the row.

- Use bulkInsert() with a collection Uri and an array of ContentValues structures to populate several rows at once.

The insert() method returns a Uri for you to use for future operations on that new object. The bulkInsert() method returns the number of created rows; you would need to do a query to retrieve the data you just inserted.

For example, here is a snippet of code from ConstantsBrowser to insert a new constant into the content provider, given a DialogWrapper that can provide access to the title and value of the constant:

```
private void processAdd(DialogWrapper wrapper) {
  ContentValues values=new ContentValues(2);

  values.put(Provider.Constants.TITLE, wrapper.getTitle());
  values.put(Provider.Constants.VALUE, wrapper.getValue());
```

```
    getContentResolver().insert(Provider.Constants.CONTENT_URI,
                                values);
    constantsCursor.requery();
}
```

Since we already have an outstanding `Cursor` for the content provider's contents, we call `requery()` on that to update the `Cursor`'s contents. This, in turn, will update any `SimpleCursorAdapter` you may have wrapping the `Cursor`, and that will update any selection widgets (e.g., `ListView`) you have using the adapter.

To delete one or more rows from the content provider, use the `delete()` method on `ContentResolver`. This works akin to a SQL `DELETE` statement and takes three parameters:

- A `Uri` representing the collection (or instance) you wish to update

- A constraint statement, functioning like a SQL `WHERE` clause, to determine which rows should be updated

- An optional set of parameters to bind into the constraint clause, replacing any ? characters that appear there

Beware of the BLOB!

Binary large objects (BLOBs) are supported in many databases, including SQLite. However, the Android model is more aimed at supporting such hunks of data via their own separate content `Uri` values. A content provider, therefore, does not provide direct access to binary data, like photos, via a `Cursor`. Rather, a property in the content provider will give you the content `Uri` for that particular BLOB. You can use `getInputStream()` and `getOutputStream()` on your `ContentProvider` to read and write the binary data.

Quite possibly, the rationale is to minimize unnecessary data copying. For example, the primary use of a photo in Android is to display it to the user. The `ImageView` widget can do just that, via a content `Uri` to a JPEG file. By storing the photo in a manner that has its own `Uri`, you do not need to copy data out of the content provider into some temporary holding area just to be able to display it—just use the `Uri`. The expectation, presumably, is that few Android applications will do much more than upload binary data and use widgets or built-in activities to display that data.

Chapter 27

Building a Content Provider

Building a content provider is probably the most complicated and tedious task in all of Android development. There are many requirements of a content provider, in terms of methods to implement and public data members to supply. And, until you try using your content provider, you have no great way of telling if you did it correctly (versus, say, building an activity and getting validation errors from the resource compiler).

That being said, building a content provider is of huge importance if your application wishes to make data available to other applications. If your application is keeping its data solely to itself, you may be able to avoid creating a content provider, and just access the data directly from your activities. But if you want your data to possibly be used by others—for example, you are building a feed reader and you want other programs to be able to access the feeds you are downloading and caching—then a content provider is right for you.

This chapter shows some sample bits of code from the ContentProvider/ConstantsPlus application. This is the same basic application as was first shown back in Chapter 22, but rewritten to pull the database logic into a content provider, which is then used by the activity.

First, Some Dissection

As discussed in the previous chapter, the content Uri is the linchpin behind accessing data inside a content provider. When using a content provider, all you really need to know is the provider's base Uri. From there, you can run queries as needed, or construct a Uri to a specific instance if you know the instance identifier.

However, when building a content provider, you need to know a bit more about the innards of the content Uri.

A content Uri has two to four pieces, depending on the situation:

- It always has a scheme (content://), indicating it is a content Uri instead of a Uri to a web resource (http://).

- It always has an authority, which is the first path segment after the scheme. The authority is a unique string identifying the content provider that handles the content associated with this Uri.

- It may have a data type path, which is the list of path segments after the authority and before the instance identifier (if any). The data type path can be empty, if the content provider handles only one type of content. It can be a single path segment (foo) or a chain of path segments (foo/bar/goo) as needed to handle whatever data access scenarios the content provider requires.

- It may have an instance identifier, which is an integer identifying a specific piece of content. A content Uri without an instance identifier refers to the collection of content represented by the authority (and, where provided, the data path).

For example, a content Uri could be as simple as content://sekrits, which would refer to the collection of content held by whatever content provider was tied to the sekrits authority (e.g., SecretsProvider). Or it could be as complex as content://sekrits/card/pin/17, which would refer to a piece of content (identified as 17) managed by the Sekrits content provider that is of the data type card/pin.

Next, Some Typing

Next, you need to come up with some MIME types corresponding with the content your content provider will provide.

Android uses both the content Uri and the MIME type as ways to identify content on the device. A collection content Uri—or, more accurately, the combination authority and data type path—should map to a pair of MIME types. One MIME type will represent the collection; the other will represent an instance. These map to the Uri patterns listed in the previous section for no-identifier and identifier, respectively. As you saw earlier in this book, you can fill a MIME type into an Intent to route the Intent to the proper activity (e.g., ACTION_PICK on a collection MIME type to call up a selection activity to pick an instance out of that collection).

The collection MIME type should be of the form vnd.X.cursor.dir/Y, where X is the name of your firm, organization, or project, and Y is a dot-delimited type name. So, for example, you might use vnd.tlagency.cursor.dir/sekrits.card.pin as the MIME type for your collection of secrets.

The instance MIME type should be of the form vnd.X.cursor.item/Y, usually for the same values of X and Y as you used for the collection MIME type (though that is not strictly required).

Creating Your Content Provider

Creating a content provider involves four basic steps: create a provider class, supply a Uri, declare the properties, and update the manifest.

Step 1: Create a Provider Class

Just as an activity and intent receiver are both Java classes, so is a content provider. So, the big step in creating a content provider is crafting its Java class, with a base class of ContentProvider.

In your subclass of ContentProvider, you are responsible for implementing six methods that, when combined, perform the services that a content provider is supposed to offer to activities wishing to create, read, update, or delete content.

onCreate()

As with an activity, the main entry point to a content provider is onCreate(). Here, you can do whatever initialization you want. In particular, here is where you should lazy-initialize your data store. For example, if you plan on storing your data in such-and-so directory on an SD card, with an XML file serving as a table of contents, you should check and see if that directory and XML file are there; if not, create them so the rest of your content provider knows they are out there and available for use.

Similarly, if you have rewritten your content provider sufficiently to cause the data store to shift structure, you should check to see what structure you have now and adjust it if what you have is out of date. You don't write your own "installer" program. This means that you have no great way of determining if, when onCreate() is called, this is the first time ever for the content provider, the first time for a new release of a content provider that was upgraded in place, or just a normal startup.

For example, here is the onCreate() method for Provider, from the ContentProvider/ConstantsPlus sample application:

```
@Override
public boolean onCreate() {
   db=(new DatabaseHelper(getContext())).getWritableDatabase();

   return (db == null) ? false : true;
}
```

While that doesn't seem all that special, the "magic" is in the private DatabaseHelper object, described in Chapter 22.

query()

As you might expect, the query() method is where your content provider gets details on a query some activity wants to perform. It is up to you to actually process said query.

The query method gets the following as parameters:

- A Uri representing the collection or instance being queried
- A String[] representing the list of properties that should be returned
- A String representing what amounts to a SQL WHERE clause, constraining which instances should be considered for the query results
- A String[] representing values to go in the WHERE clause, replacing any ? character found there
- A String representing what amounts to a SQL ORDER BY clause

You are responsible for interpreting these parameters however they make sense, and returning a Cursor that can be used to iterate over and access the data.

As you can imagine, these parameters are aimed toward people using a SQLite database for storage. You are welcome to ignore some of these parameters (e.g., you can elect not to try to roll your own SQL WHERE clause parser), but you need to document that fact so activities attempt to query you only by instance Uri, and not by using parameters you choose not to handle.

For SQLite-backed storage providers, however, the query() method implementation should be largely boilerplate. Use a SQLiteQueryBuilder to convert the various parameters into a single SQL statement, and then use query() on the builder to actually invoke the query and give you back a Cursor. The Cursor is what your query() method returns.

For example, here is query() from Provider:

```
@Override
public Cursor query(Uri url, String[] projection, String selection,
                    String[] selectionArgs, String sort) {
  SQLiteQueryBuilder qb=new SQLiteQueryBuilder();

  qb.setTables(getTableName());

  if (isCollectionUri(url)) {
    qb.setProjectionMap(getDefaultProjection());
  }
  else {
    qb.appendWhere(getIdColumnName()+"="+url.getPathSegments().get(1));
  }

  String orderBy;

  if (TextUtils.isEmpty(sort)) {
    orderBy=getDefaultSortOrder();
  } else {
    orderBy=sort;
  }

  Cursor c=qb.query(db, projection, selection, selectionArgs,
```

```
                    null, null, orderBy);
    c.setNotificationUri(getContext().getContentResolver(), url);
    return c;
  }
```

We create a `SQLiteQueryBuilder` and pour the query details into the builder. Note that the query could be based around either a collection or an instance `Uri`. In the latter case, we need to add the instance ID to the query. When done, we use the `query()` method on the builder to get a `Cursor` for the results.

insert()

Your `insert()` method will receive a `Uri` representing the collection and a `ContentValues` structure with the initial data for the new instance. You are responsible for creating the new instance, filling in the supplied data, and returning a `Uri` to the new instance.

If this is a SQLite-backed content provider, once again, the implementation is mostly boilerplate. You just need to validate that all required values were supplied by the activity, merge your own notion of default values with the supplied data, and call `insert()` on the database to actually create the instance.

For example, here is `insert()` from Provider:

```
@Override
public Uri insert(Uri url, ContentValues initialValues) {
  long rowID;
  ContentValues values;

  if (initialValues!=null) {
    values=new ContentValues(initialValues);
  } else {
    values=new ContentValues();
  }

  if (!isCollectionUri(url)) {
    throw new IllegalArgumentException("Unknown URL " + url);
  }

  for (String colName : getRequiredColumns()) {
    if (values.containsKey(colName) == false) {
      throw new IllegalArgumentException("Missing column: "+colName);
    }
  }

  populateDefaultValues(values);

  rowID=db.insert(getTableName(), getNullColumnHack(), values);
  if (rowID > 0) {
    Uri uri=ContentUris.withAppendedId(getContentUri(), rowID);
    getContext().getContentResolver().notifyChange(uri, null);
    return uri;
  }
```

```
      throw new SQLException("Failed to insert row into " + url);
   }
```

The pattern is the same as before: use the provider particulars plus the data to be inserted to actually do the insertion. Note the following regarding the example:

- You can insert only into a collection Uri, so we validate that by calling isCollectionUri().

- The provider also knows which columns are required (getRequiredColumns()), so we iterate over those and confirm our supplied values cover the requirements.

- The provider is also responsible for filling in any default values (populateDefaultValues()) for columns not supplied in the insert() call and not automatically handled by the SQLite table definition.

update()

Your update() method gets the Uri of the instance or collection to change, a ContentValues structure with the new values to apply, a String for a SQL WHERE clause, and a String[] with parameters to use to replace ? characters found in the WHERE clause. Your responsibility is to identify the instance(s) to be modified (based on the Uri and WHERE clause), and then replace those instances' current property values with the ones supplied.

This will be annoying, unless you're using SQLite for storage. Then you can pretty much pass all the parameters you received to the update() call to the database, although the update() call will vary slightly depending on whether you are updating one instance or several instances.

For example, here is update() from Provider:

```
@Override
public int update(Uri url, ContentValues values, String where, String[] whereArgs) {
   int count;

   if (isCollectionUri(url)) {
      count=db.update(getTableName(), values, where, whereArgs);
   }
   else {
      String segment=url.getPathSegments().get(1);
      count=db
         .update(getTableName(), values, getIdColumnName()+"="
            + segment
            + (!TextUtils.isEmpty(where) ? " AND (" + where
               + ')' : ""), whereArgs);
   }

   getContext().getContentResolver().notifyChange(url, null);
   return count;
}
```

In this case, updates can either be to a specific instance or applied across the entire collection, so we check the Uri (isCollectionUri()) and, if it is an update for the collection, just perform the update. If we are updating a single instance, we need to add a constraint to the WHERE clause to update only for the requested row.

delete()

As with update(), delete() receives a Uri representing the instance or collection to work with and a WHERE clause and parameters. If the activity is deleting a single instance, the Uri should represent that instance and the WHERE clause may be null. But the activity might be requesting to delete an open-ended set of instances, using the WHERE clause to constrain which ones to delete.

As with update(), this is simple if you are using SQLite for database storage (sense a theme?). You can let it handle the idiosyncrasies of parsing and applying the WHERE clause. All you need to do is call delete() on the database.

For example, here is delete() from Provider:

```
@Override
public int delete(Uri url, String where, String[] whereArgs) {
  int count;
  long rowId=0;

  if (isCollectionUri(url)) {
    count=db.delete(getTableName(), where, whereArgs);
  }
  else {
    String segment=url.getPathSegments().get(1);
    rowId=Long.parseLong(segment);
    count=db
        .delete(getTableName(), getIdColumnName()+"="
            + segment
            + (!TextUtils.isEmpty(where) ? " AND (" + where
                + ')' : ""), whereArgs);
  }

  getContext().getContentResolver().notifyChange(url, null);
  return count;
}
```

This is almost a clone of the update() implementation described in the preceding section, It either deletes a subset of the entire collection or deletes a single instance (if it also satisfies the supplied WHERE clause).

getType()

The last method you need to implement is getType(). This takes a Uri and returns the MIME type associated with that Uri. The Uri could be a collection or an instance Uri; you need to determine which was provided and return the corresponding MIME type.

For example, here is getType() from Provider:

```
@Override
public String getType(Uri url) {
  if (isCollectionUri(url)) {
    return(getCollectionType());
  }

  return(getSingleType());
}
```

As you can see, most of the logic delegates to private getCollectionType() and getSingleType() methods:

```
private String getCollectionType() {
  return("vnd.android.cursor.dir/vnd.commonsware.constant");
}

private String getSingleType() {
  return("vnd.android.cursor.item/vnd.commonsware.constant");
}
```

Step 2: Supply a Uri

You also need to add a public static member—somewhere—containing the Uri for each collection your content provider supports. Typically, this is a public static final Uri put on the content provider class itself:

```
public static final Uri CONTENT_URI
    =Uri.parse("content://com.commonsware.android.constants.Provider/constants");
```

You may wish to use the same namespace for the content Uri that you use for your Java classes, to reduce the chance of collision with others.

Step 3: Declare the Properties

Remember those properties you referenced when you were using a content provider, in the previous chapter? Well, you also need to have those for your own content provider.

Specifically, you want a public static class implementing BaseColumns that contains your property names, such as this example from Provider:

```
public static final class Constants implements BaseColumns {
  public static final Uri CONTENT_URI
      =Uri.parse("content://com.commonsware.android.constants.Provider/constants");
  public static final String DEFAULT_SORT_ORDER="title";
  public static final String TITLE="title";
  public static final String VALUE="value";
}
```

If you are using SQLite as a data store, the values for the property name constants should be the corresponding column names in the table, so you can just pass the projection (array of properties) to SQLite on a query(), or pass the ContentValues on an insert() or update().

Note that nothing in here stipulates the types of the properties. They could be strings, integers, or whatever. The biggest limitation is what a Cursor can provide access to via its property getters. The fact that there is nothing in code that enforces type safety means you should document the property types well, so people attempting to use your content provider know what they can expect.

Step 4: Update the Manifest

The glue tying the content provider implementation to the rest of your application resides in your AndroidManifest.xml file. Simply add a <provider> element as a child of the <application> element:

```
<?xml version="1.0" encoding="utf-8"?>
<manifest xmlns:android="http://schemas.android.com/apk/res/android"
  package="com.commonsware.android.constants">
  <application android:label="@string/app_name"
    android:icon="@drawable/cw">
    <provider android:name=".Provider"
            android:authorities="com.commonsware.android.constants.Provider" />
    <activity android:name=".ConstantsBrowser" android:label="@string/app_name">
      <intent-filter>
        <action android:name="android.intent.action.MAIN" />
        <category android:name="android.intent.category.LAUNCHER" />
      </intent-filter>
    </activity>
  </application>
</manifest>
```

The android:name property is the name of the content provider class, with a leading dot to indicate it is in the stock namespace for this application's classes (just like you use with activities).

The android:authorities property should be a semicolon-delimited list of the authority values supported by the content provider. As discussed earlier in this chapter, each content Uri is made up of a scheme, authority, data type path, and instance identifier. Each authority from each CONTENT_URI value should be included in the android:authorities list.

Now, when Android encounters a content Uri, it can sift through the providers registered through manifests to find a matching authority. That tells Android which application and class implement the content provider, and from there, Android can bridge between the calling activity and the content provider being called.

Notify-on-Change Support

An optional feature your content provider can offer to its clients is notify-on-change support. This means that your content provider will let clients know if the data for a given content Uri changes.

For example, suppose you have created a content provider that retrieves RSS and Atom feeds from the Internet based on the user's feed subscriptions (via OPML, perhaps). The content provider offers read-only access to the contents of the feeds, with an eye toward several applications on the phone using those feeds versus everyone implementing their own feed poll-fetch-and-cache system. You have also implemented a service that will get updates to those feeds asynchronously, updating the underlying data store. Your content provider could alert applications using the feeds that such-and-so feed was updated, so applications using that specific feed can refresh and get the latest data.

On the content provider side, to do this, call notifyChange() on your ContentResolver instance (available in your content provider via getContext().getContentResolver()). This takes two parameters: the Uri of the piece of content that changed and the ContentObserver that initiated the change. In many cases, the latter will be null; a non-null value simply means that the observer that initiated the change will not be notified of its own changes.

On the content consumer side, an activity can call registerContentObserver() on its ContentResolver (via getContentResolver()). This ties a ContentObserver instance to a supplied Uri, and the observer will be notified whenever notifyChange() is called for that specific Uri. When the consumer is done with the Uri, unregisterContentObserver() releases the connection.

Chapter 28

Requesting and Requiring Permissions

In the late 1990s, a wave of viruses spread through the Internet, delivered via e-mail, using contact information culled from Microsoft Outlook. A virus would simply e-mail copies of itself to each of the Outlook contacts that had an e-mail address. This was possible because, at the time, Outlook did not take any steps to protect data from programs using the Outlook API, since that API was designed for ordinary developers, not virus authors.

Nowadays, many applications that hold onto contact data secure that data by requiring that a user explicitly grant rights for other programs to access the contact information. Those rights could be granted on a case-by-case basis or a once at install time.

Android is no different, in that it requires permissions for applications to read or write contact data. Android's permission system is useful well beyond contact data, and for content providers and services other than those supplied by the Android framework.

You, as an Android developer, will frequently need to ensure your applications have the appropriate permissions to do what you want to do with other applications' data. You may also elect to require permissions for other applications to use your data or services, if you make those available to other Android components. This chapter covers how to accomplish both these ends.

Mother, May I?

Requesting the use of other applications' data or services requires the `uses-permission` element to be added to your `AndroidManifest.xml` file. Your manifest may have zero or more `uses-permission` elements, all as direct children of the root `manifest` element.

The uses-permission element takes a single attribute, android:name, which is the name of the permission your application requires:

```
<uses-permission
  android:name="android.permission.ACCESS_LOCATION" />
```

All of the stock system permissions begin with android.permission and are listed in the Android SDK documentation for Manifest.permission. Third-party applications may have their own permissions, which hopefully they have documented for you. Here are some of the more important built-in permissions:

- INTERNET, if your application wishes to access the Internet through any means, from raw Java sockets through the WebView widget

- READ_CALENDAR, READ_CONTACTS, and the like for reading data from the built-in content providers

- WRITE_CALENDAR, WRITE_CONTACTS, and the like for modifying data in the built-in content providers

Permissions are confirmed at the time the application is installed. The user will be prompted to confirm it is acceptable for your application to do what the permission calls for. Hence, it is important for you to ask for as few permissions as possible and to justify those you request, so users do not elect to skip installing your application because you ask for too many unnecessary permissions. This prompt is not available in the current emulator, however.

If you do not have the desired permission and try to do something that needs it, you may get a SecurityException informing you of the missing permission, but this is not a guarantee. Failures may come in other forms, depending on if something else is catching and trying to handle that exception. Note that you will fail on a permission check only if you forgot to ask for the permission; it is impossible for your application to be running and *not* have been granted your requested permissions.

Halt! Who Goes There?

The other side of the coin is to secure your own application. If your application is merely activities and intent receivers, security may be just an "outbound" thing, where you request the right to use resources of other applications. If, on the other hand, you put content providers or services in your application, you will want to implement "inbound" security to control which applications can do what with the data.

Note that the issue here is less about whether other applications might mess up your data, but rather about privacy of the user's information or use of services that might incur expense. That is where the stock permissions for built-in Android applications are focused: whether you can read or modify contacts, send messages, and so on. If your application does not store information that might be considered private, security is less of an issue. If, on the other hand, your application stores private data, such as medical information, security is much more important.

The first step to securing your own application using permissions is to declare said permissions, once again in the AndroidManifest.xml file. In this case, instead of uses-permission, you add permission elements. Once again, you can have zero or more permission elements, all as direct children of the root manifest element.

Declaring a permission is slightly more complicated than using a permission. You need to supply three pieces of information:

▓ *The symbolic name of the permission*: To keep your permissions from colliding with those from other applications, you should use your application's Java namespace as a prefix.

▓ *A label for the permission*: Something short that would be understandable by users.

▓ *A description for the permission*: Something a wee bit longer that is understandable by your users.

```
<permission
  android:name="vnd.tlagency.sekrits.SEE_SEKRITS"
  android:label="@string/see_sekrits_label"
  android:description="@string/see_sekrits_description" />
```

This does not enforce the permission. Rather, it indicates that it is a possible permission. Your application must still flag security violations as they occur.

There are two ways for your application to enforce permissions, dictating where and under which circumstances they are required. You can enforce permissions in your code, but the easier option is to indicate in the manifest where permissions are required.

Enforcing Permissions via the Manifest

Activities, services, and intent receivers can declare an attribute named android:permission, whose value is the name of the permission that is required to access those items:

```
<activity
  android:name=".SekritApp"
  android:label="Top Sekrit"
  android:permission="vnd.tlagency.sekrits.SEE_SEKRITS">
  <intent-filter>
    <action android:name="android.intent.action.MAIN" />
    <category
      android:name="android.intent.category.LAUNCHER" />
  </intent-filter>
</activity>
```

Only applications that have requested your indicated permission will be able to access the secured component. In this case, "access" means:

▓ Activities cannot be started without the permission.

▓ Services cannot be started, stopped, or bound to an activity without the permission.

■ Intent receivers ignore messages sent via sendBroadcast() unless the
sender has the permission.

Content providers offer two distinct attributes: readPermission and writePermission.

```
<provider
  android:name=".SekritProvider"
  android:authorities="vnd.tla.sekrits.SekritProvider"
  android:readPermission="vnd.tla.sekrits.SEE_SEKRITS"
  android:writePermission="vnd.tla.sekrits.MOD_SEKRITS" />
```

In this case, readPermission controls access to querying the content provider, and
writePermission controls access to insert, update, or delete data in the content
provider.

Enforcing Permissions Elsewhere

In your code, you have two additional ways to enforce permissions:

■ Your services can check permissions on a per-call basis via
checkCallingPermission(). This returns PERMISSION_GRANTED or
PERMISSION_DENIED, depending on whether the caller has the
permission you specified. For example, if your service implements
separate read and write methods, you could get the effect of
readPermission and writePermission in code by checking those
methods for the permissions you need from Java.

■ You can include a permission when you call sendBroadcast(). This
means that eligible receivers must hold that permission; those without
the permission are ineligible to receive it. For example, the Android
subsystem presumably includes the RECEIVE_SMS permission when it
broadcasts that an SMS message has arrived. This will restrict the
receivers of that intent to be only those authorized to receive SMS
messages.

May I See Your Documents?

There is no automatic discovery of permissions at compile time; all permission failures
occur at runtime. Hence, it is important that you document the permissions required for
your public APIs, including content providers, services, and activities intended for
launching from other activities. Otherwise, the programmers attempting to interface with
your application will need to find out the permission rules by trial and error.

Furthermore, you should expect that users of your application will be prompted to
confirm any permissions your application says it needs. Hence, you need to document
for your users what they should expect, lest they get confused by the question posed by
the phone and elect to not install or use your application.

Chapter 29

Creating a Service

As noted previously, Android services are for long-running processes that may need to keep running even when decoupled from any activity. Examples include playing music even if the player activity gets garbage-collected, polling the Internet for RSS/Atom feed updates, and maintaining an online chat connection even if the chat client loses focus due to an incoming phone call.

Services are created when manually started (via an API call) or when some activity tries connecting to the service via interprocess communication (IPC). Services will live until no longer needed and if RAM needs to be reclaimed, or until shut down (on their own volition or because no one is using them anymore). Running for a long time isn't without its costs, though, so services need to be careful not to use too much CPU or keep radios active too much of the time, lest the service cause the device's battery to get used up too quickly.

This chapter covers how you can create your own services. The next chapter covers how you can use such services from your activities or other contexts. Both chapters will analyze the Service/WeatherPlus sample application. This chapter focuses mostly on the WeatherPlusService implementation. WeatherPlusService extends the weather-fetching logic of the original Internet/Weather sample, by bundling it in a service that monitors changes in location, so the weather is updated as the emulator is "moved."

Service with Class

Creating a service implementation shares many characteristics with building an activity. You inherit from an Android-supplied base class, override some life-cycle methods, and hook the service into the system via the manifest.

So, the first step in creating a service is to extend the Service class—in our case, with our own WeatherPlusService subclass.

Just as activities have onCreate(), onResume(), onPause(), and the like, Service implementations have their own life-cycle methods, such as the following:

- onCreate(): As with activities, called when the service process is created, by any means.

- onStart(): Called each time the service is started via startService().

- onDestroy(): Called as the service is being shut down.

For example, here is the onCreate() method for WeatherPlusService:

```
@Override
public void onCreate() {
  super.onCreate();

  client=new DefaultHttpClient();
  format=getString(R.string.url);

  mgr=(LocationManager)getSystemService(Context.LOCATION_SERVICE);
  mgr.requestLocationUpdates(LocationManager.GPS_PROVIDER,
                       10000, 10000.0f, onLocationChange);
}
```

First, we chain upward to the superclass, so Android can do any setup work it needs to have done. Then we initialize our HttpClient component and format string as we did in the Weather demo. We then get the LocationManager instance for our application and request to get updates as our location changes, via the GPS LocationProvider, which will be discussed in greater detail in Chapter 32.

The onDestroy() method is much simpler:

```
@Override
public void onDestroy() {
  super.onDestroy();

  mgr.removeUpdates(onLocationChange);
}
```

Here, we just shut down the location-monitoring logic, in addition to chaining upward to the superclass for any Android internal bookkeeping that might be needed.

In addition to those life-cycle methods, your service also needs to implement onBind(). This method returns an IBinder, which is the linchpin behind the IPC mechanism. We will examine onBind() a bit more closely in the next section.

There Can Only Be One

Services, by default, run in the same process as all other components of the application, such as its activities. Hence, you can call API methods on the service object—if you can get your hands on it. Ideally, there would be some means, perhaps even type-safe, to ask Android to give you the local service object. Unfortunately, at the time of this writing, there is no such API. Hence, we are forced to cheat.

Any given service can, at most, have one copy running in memory. There might be zero copies in memory, if the service has not been started. But even if multiple activities try using the service, only one will actually be running. This is a fine implementation of the singleton pattern—all we need to do is expose the singleton itself, so other components can access the object.

We could expose the singleton via a public static data member or a public static getter method. However, then we run into some memory-management risks. Since everything referenced from a static context is immune to garbage collection, we would need to be very careful to set the static reference to null in our service's onDestroy(). Otherwise, our service, while disconnected from Android, would remain in memory indefinitely, until Android elected to shut down our process.

Fortunately, there is an alternative, and that is using onBind().

Binding allows a service to expose an API to activities (or other services) that bind to it. Much of this infrastructure is set up to support remote services, where the bound-to API is available via IPC, so one service can expose its API to other applications. However, the simple act of binding itself can be useful in situations where the service and its clients are all in the same application—the local service scenario.

To expose the service itself to activities via local binding, you must first create a public inner class that extends the android.os.Binder class:

```
public class LocalBinder extends Binder {
  WeatherPlusService getService() {
    return(WeatherPlusService.this);
  }
}
```

Here, our binder exposes one method: getService(), which returns the service itself. In a remote service scenario, this would not work, because the limitations of IPC prevent us from passing services between processes. However, for local services, this is a perfectly fine binder.

Next, we need to return that binder object in our onBind() method:

```
@Override
public IBinder onBind(Intent intent) {
  return(binder);
}
```

At this point, any client that binds to our service will be able to access the service object itself and call methods on it. We will go into this in greater detail in the next chapter.

Manifest Destiny

Finally, you need to add the service to your AndroidManifest.xml file, for it to be recognized as an available service for use. That is simply a matter of adding a service element as a child of the application element, providing android:name to reference your service class.

For example, here is the AndroidManifest.xml file for WeatherPlus:

```
<?xml version="1.0" encoding="utf-8"?>
<manifest xmlns:android="http://schemas.android.com/apk/res/android"
    package="com.commonsware.android.service">
  <uses-permission android:name="android.permission.INTERNET" />
  <uses-permission android:name="android.permission.ACCESS_COARSE_LOCATION" />
  <uses-permission android:name="android.permission.ACCESS_FINE_LOCATION" />
  <application android:label="@string/app_name"
    android:icon="@drawable/cw">
    <activity android:name=".WeatherPlus" android:label="@string/app_name">
      <intent-filter>
        <action android:name="android.intent.action.MAIN" />
        <category android:name="android.intent.category.LAUNCHER" />
      </intent-filter>
    </activity>
    <service android:name=".WeatherPlusService" />
  </application>
</manifest>
```

Since the service class is in the same Java namespace as everything else in this application, we can use the shorthand dot notation (".WeatherPlusService") to reference our class.

If you want to require some permission of those who wish to start or bind to the service, add an android:permission attribute naming the permission you are mandating. See Chapter 28 for more details.

Lobbing One Over the Fence

Sometimes, the service needs to asynchronously alert an activity of some occurrence.

For example, the theory behind the WeatherPlusService implementation is that the service gets "tickled" when the device (or emulator) position changes. At that point, the service calls out to the web service and generates a new forecast web page for the activity to display. Then the service needs to let the activity know that a new forecast is available, so the activity can load and display it.

To interoperate with components this way, there are two major alternatives: callbacks and broadcast Intents.

Note that if all your service needs to do is alert the user of some event, you may wish to consider using a notification (described in Chapter 31), as that is the more normal way to handle that requirement.

Callbacks

Since an activity can work with a local service directly, an activity could provide some sort of listener object to the service, which the service could then call when needed. To make this work, you would need to:

1. Define a Java interface for that listener object.

2. Give the service a public API to register and retract listeners.

3. Have the service use those listeners at appropriate times, to notify those who registered the listener of some event.

4. Have the activity register and retract a listener as needed.

5. Have the activity respond to the listener-based events in some suitable fashion.

The biggest catch is to make sure that the activity retracts the listeners when it is done. Listener objects generally know their activity, explicitly (via a data member) or implicitly (by being implemented as an inner class). If the service is holding onto defunct listener objects, the corresponding activities will linger in memory, even if the activities are no longer being used by Android. This represents a big memory leak. You may wish to use WeakReferences, SoftReferences, or similar constructs to ensure that if an activity is destroyed, any listeners it registers with your service will not keep that activity in memory.

Broadcast Intents

An alternative approach, first mentioned in Chapter 17, is to have the service send a broadcast Intent that can be picked up by the activity—assuming the activity is still around and is not paused. We will look at the client side of this exchange in Chapter 30. Here, let's examine how the service can send a broadcast.

The high-level implementation of the flow is packaged in FetchForecastTask, an AsyncTask implementation that allows us to move the Internet access to a background thread:

```
class FetchForecastTask extends AsyncTask<Location, Void, Void> {
  @Override
  protected Void doInBackground(Location... locs) {
    Location loc=locs[0];
    String url=String.format(format, loc.getLatitude(),
                             loc.getLongitude());
    HttpGet getMethod=new HttpGet(url);

    try {
      ResponseHandler<String> responseHandler=new BasicResponseHandler();
      String responseBody=client.execute(getMethod, responseHandler);
      String page=generatePage(buildForecasts(responseBody));
```

```
    synchronized(this) {
      forecast=page;
    }

    sendBroadcast(broadcast);
  }
  catch (Throwable t) {
    android.util.Log.e("WeatherPlus",
                       "Exception in updateForecast()", t);
  }

  return(null);
}

@Override
protected void onProgressUpdate(Void... unused) {
  // not needed here
}

@Override
protected void onPostExecute(Void unused) {
  // not needed here
}
}
```

Much of this is similar to the equivalent piece of the original Weather demo. It performs the HTTP request, converts that into a set of Forecast objects, and turn those into a web page. The first difference, besides the introduction of the AsyncTask, is that the web page is simply cached in the service, since the service cannot put the page directly into the activity's WebView. The second difference is that we call sendBroadcast(), which takes an Intent and sends it out to all interested parties. That Intent is declared up front in the class prologue:

```
private Intent broadcast=new Intent(BROADCAST_ACTION);
```

Here, BROADCAST_ACTION is simply a static String with a value that will distinguish this Intent from all others:

```
public static final String BROADCAST_ACTION=
        "com.commonsware.android.service.ForecastUpdateEvent";
```

Where's the Remote? And the Rest of the Code?

In Android, services can either be local or remote. Local services run in the same process as the launching activity. Remote services run in their own process. A detailed discussion of remote services can be found in *The Busy Coder's Guide to Advanced Android Development* (CommonsWare, 2009).

We will return to this service in Chapter 32, at which point we will flesh out how locations are tracked (and, in this case, mocked up).

Chapter 30

Invoking a Service

Services can be used by any application component that hangs around for a reasonable period of time. This includes activities, content providers, and other services. Notably, it does not include pure broadcast receivers (i.e., intent receivers that are not part of an activity), since those will get garbage collected immediately after each instance processes one incoming Intent.

To use a local service, you need to start the service, get access to the service object, and then call methods on that service. You can then stop the service when you are finished with it, or perhaps let the service stop itself. In this chapter, we will look at the client side of the Service/WeatherPlus sample application. The WeatherPlus activity looks a lot like the original Weather application. It's just a web page showing a weather forecast, as shown in Figure 30–1.

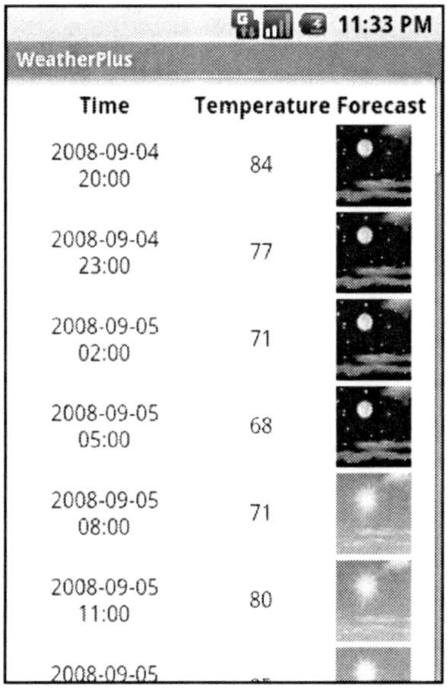

Figure 30–1. *The WeatherPlus service client*

The Ties That Bind

To start a service, one approach is to simply call startService(), providing the Intent specifying the service to start (again, the easiest way is probably to specify the service class, if it's your own service). Conversely, to stop a service started via startService(), call stopService() with the Intent you used in the corresponding startService() call.

Once the service is started, you need to communicate with it. It could be that all the communication you need can be via the extras you package in the Intent. Or, if it is a local service that offers a singleton, you can reference the singleton.

However, if you implemented onBind() as shown in the previous chapter, there is a different way to get at the service: through bindService().

When an activity binds to a service, it primarily is requesting to be able to access the public API exposed by that service via the service's binder, as returned by the service's onBind() method. When doing this, the activity can also indicate, via the BIND_AUTO_CREATE flag, to have Android automatically start up the service if it is not already running.

To use this technique with our WeatherPlus and WeatherPlusService classes, we first need to make a call to bindService() from onCreate():

```
@Override
public void onCreate(Bundle savedInstanceState) {
  super.onCreate(savedInstanceState);
  setContentView(R.layout.main);

  browser=(WebView)findViewById(R.id.webkit);
  bindService(new Intent(this, WeatherPlusService.class),
              onService, Context.BIND_AUTO_CREATE);
}
```

This bindService() call refers to an onService callback object, an instance of ServiceConnection:

```
private ServiceConnection onService=new ServiceConnection() {
  public void onServiceConnected(ComponentName className,
                                 IBinder rawBinder) {
    appService=((WeatherPlusService.LocalBinder)rawBinder).getService();
  }

  public void onServiceDisconnected(ComponentName className) {
    appService=null;
  }
};
```

Our onService object will be called with onServiceConnected() as soon as the WeatherPlusService is up and running. We are given an IBinder object, which is an opaque handle representing the service. We can use that to obtain the LocalBinder exposed by the WeatherPlusService, and from there to get the actual WeatherPlusService object itself, held as a private data member:

```
private WeatherPlusService appService=null;
```

We can then call methods on the `WeatherPlusService`, such as a call to get the forecast page when needed:

```
private void updateForecast() {
  try {
    String page=appService.getForecastPage();

    browser.loadDataWithBaseURL(null, page, "text/html",
                               "UTF-8", null);
  }
  catch (final Throwable t) {
    goBlooey(t);
  }
}
```

We also need to call `unbindService()` from `onDestroy()`, to release our binding to `WeatherPlusService`:

```
@Override
public void onDestroy() {
  super.onDestroy();

  unbindService(onService);
}
```

If there are no other bound clients to the service, Android will shut down the service as well, releasing its memory. Hence, we do not need to call `stopService()` ourselves, because Android handles that, if needed, as a side effect of unbinding.

This is a fair bit more code than simply using a public static singleton for the service object. However, this approach is less likely to result in memory leaks.

So to recap:

- To have a service start running, use `bindService()` with `BIND_AUTO_CREATE` (if you wish to communicate via the binding mechanism) or `startService()`.

- To have a service stop running, do the inverse of what you did to start it: `unbindService()` or `stopService()`.

Another possibility for stopping a service is to have the service call `stopSelf()` on itself. You might do this if you use `startService()` to have a service begin running and do some work on a background thread, so the service will stop itself when that background work is completed.

Catching the Lob

In the preceding chapter, you saw how the service sends a broadcast to let the `WeatherPlus` activity know a change was made to the forecast based on movement. Now, you'll see how the activity receives and uses that broadcast.

Here are the implementations of onResume() and onPause() for WeatherPlus:

```
@Override
public void onResume() {
  super.onResume();

  registerReceiver(receiver,
        new IntentFilter(WeatherPlusService.BROADCAST_ACTION));
}

@Override
public void onPause() {
  super.onPause();

  unregisterReceiver(receiver);
}
```

In onResume(), we register a static BroadcastReceiver to receive Intents matching the action declared by the service. In onPause(), we disable that BroadcastReceiver, since we will not be receiving any such Intents while paused.

The BroadcastReceiver, in turn, simply arranges to update the forecast:

```
private BroadcastReceiver receiver=new BroadcastReceiver() {
  public void onReceive(Context context, Intent intent) {
    updateForecast();
  }
};
```

Chapter 31

Alerting Users via Notifications

Pop-up messages, tray icons with their associated "bubble" messages, bouncing dock icons, and so on—you are no doubt used to programs trying to get your attention, sometimes for good reason. Your phone also probably chirps at you for more than just incoming calls: low battery, alarm clocks, appointment notifications, incoming text messages, and so on.

Not surprisingly, Android has a whole framework for dealing with these sorts of alerts, collectively called *notifications*, which is the subject of this chapter.

Types of Pestering

A service, running in the background, needs a way to let users know something of interest has occurred, such as when e-mail has been received. Moreover, the service may need some way to steer users to an activity where they can act on the event, such as reading a received message. For this, Android supplies status bar icons, flashing lights, and other indicators collectively known as "notifications".

Your current phone may already have such icons, to indicate battery life, signal strength, whether Bluetooth is enabled, and the like. With Android, applications can add their own status bar icons, with an eye toward having them appear only when needed (e.g., a message has arrived).

In Android, you can raise notifications via the `NotificationManager`. The `NotificationManager` is a system service. To use it, you need to get the service object via `getSystemService(NOTIFICATION_SERVICE)` from your activity.

The `NotificationManager` gives you three methods: one to pester (`notify()`) and two to stop pestering (`cancel()` and `cancelAll()`).

The notify() method takes a Notification, which is a data structure that spells out the form your pestering should take. The capabilities of this object are described in the following sections.

Hardware Notifications

You can flash LEDs on the device by setting lights to true, also specifying the color (as an #ARGB value in ledARGB) and the pattern in which the light should blink (by providing off/on durations in milliseconds for the light via ledOnMS and ledOffMS). Note, however, that Android devices will apply best efforts to meet your color request, meaning that different devices may give you different colors, or perhaps no control over color at all. For example, the Motorola CLIQ reportedly has only a white LED, so you can ask for any color you want, and you will still get white.

You can play a sound, using a Uri to a piece of content held, perhaps, by a ContentManager (sound). Think of this as a "ringtone" for your application.

You can vibrate the device, controlled via a long[] indicating the on/off patterns (in milliseconds) for the vibration (vibrate). You might do this by default, or you might make it an option the user can choose when circumstances require a more subtle notification than a ringtone. To use this approach, you will need to request the VIBRATE permission (see Chapter 28 for more on permissions).

Icons

While the flashing lights, sounds, and vibrations are aimed at getting users to look at the device, icons are designed to take them the next step and tell them what's so important.

To set up an icon for a Notification, you need to set two public fields: icon, where you provide the identifier of a Drawable resource representing the icon, and contentIntent, where you supply an PendingIntent to be raised when the icon is clicked. You should make sure the PendingIntent will be caught by something—perhaps your own application code—to take appropriate steps to let the user deal with the event triggering the notification. You can also supply a text blurb to appear when the icon is put on the status bar (tickerText).

If you want all three, the simpler approach is to call setLatestEventInfo(), which wraps an icon, contentIntent, and tickerText in a single call.

Seeing Pestering in Action

Let's now take a peek at the Notifications/Notify1 sample project, in particular the NotifyDemo class:

```
package com.commonsware.android.notify;

import android.app.Activity;
import android.app.Notification;
```

```java
import android.app.NotificationManager;
import android.app.PendingIntent;
import android.content.Intent;
import android.os.Bundle;
import android.view.View;
import android.widget.Button;
import java.util.Timer;
import java.util.TimerTask;

public class NotifyDemo extends Activity {
  private static final int NOTIFY_ME_ID=1337;
  private Timer timer=new Timer();
  private int count=0;

  @Override
  public void onCreate(Bundle savedInstanceState) {
    super.onCreate(savedInstanceState);
    setContentView(R.layout.main);

    Button btn=(Button)findViewById(R.id.notify);

    btn.setOnClickListener(new View.OnClickListener() {
      public void onClick(View view) {
        TimerTask task=new TimerTask() {
          public void run() {
            notifyMe();
          }
        };

        timer.schedule(task, 5000);
      }
    });

    btn=(Button)findViewById(R.id.cancel);

    btn.setOnClickListener(new View.OnClickListener() {
      public void onClick(View view) {
        NotificationManager mgr=
          (NotificationManager)getSystemService(NOTIFICATION_SERVICE);

        mgr.cancel(NOTIFY_ME_ID);
      }
    });
  }

  private void notifyMe() {
    final NotificationManager mgr=
      (NotificationManager)getSystemService(NOTIFICATION_SERVICE);
    Notification note=new Notification(R.drawable.red_ball,
                                       "Status message!",
                                       System.currentTimeMillis());
    PendingIntent i=PendingIntent.getActivity(this, 0,
                          new Intent(this, NotifyMessage.class),
                                     0);
```

```
        note.setLatestEventInfo(this, "Notification Title",
                                "This is the notification message", i);
        note.number=++count;

        mgr.notify(NOTIFY_ME_ID, note);
    }
}
```

As shown in Figure 31–1, this activity sports two large buttons: one to kick off a notification after a 5-second delay and one to cancel that notification (if it is active).

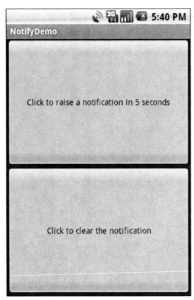

Figure 31–1. *The NotifyDemo activity main view*

Creating the notification, in notifyMe(), is accomplished in six steps:

1. Get access to the NotificationManager instance.

2. Create a Notification object with our icon (red ball), a message to flash on the status bar as the notification is raised, and the time associated with this event.

3. Create a PendingIntent that will trigger the display of another activity (NotifyMessage).

4. Use setLatestEventInfo() to specify that, when the notification is clicked, we are to display a certain title and message, and if that is clicked, we launch the PendingIntent.

5. Update the number associated with the notification.

6. Tell the NotificationManager to display the notification.

Hence, if we click the top button, after 5 seconds, our red ball icon will appear in the status bar, along with a brief display of our status message, as shown in Figure 31–2. The red ball will have our number (initially 1) superimposed on the lower-right corner (you might use this to signify the number of unread messages, for example).

Figure 32-2. *Our notification as it appears on the status bar, with our status message*

If you click the red ball, a drawer will appear beneath the status bar. Drag that drawer all the way to the bottom of the screen to see the outstanding notifications, including our own, as shown in Figure 32-3.

Figure 32-3. *The notifications drawer, fully expanded, with our notification*

If you click the notification entry in the drawer, you'll be taken to a trivial activity displaying a message. In a real application, this activity would do something useful based on the event that occurred (e.g., take users to the newly arrived mail messages).

Clicking the button to clear the notification will remove the red ball from the status bar.

Chapter 32

Accessing Location-Based Services

A popular feature on current mobile devices is GPS capability, so the device can tell you where you are at any point in time. While the most common uses of GPS services are for mapping and getting directions, there are other things you can do if you know your location. For example, you might set up a dynamic chat application based on physical location, so you're chatting with those people who are nearest to you. Or you could automatically geo-tag posts to Twitter or similar services.

GPS is not the only way a mobile device can identify your location. Alternatives include the following:

■ The European equivalent to GPS, called Galileo, which is still under development at the time of this writing

■ Cell tower triangulation, where your position is determined based on signal strength to nearby cell towers

■ Proximity to public Wi-Fi hotspots that have known geographic locations

Android devices may have one or more of these services available to them. You, as a developer, can ask the device for your location, plus details on which providers are available. There are even ways for you to simulate your location in the emulator, for use in testing your location-enabled applications.

Location Providers: They Know Where You're Hiding

Android devices can have access to several different means of determining your location. Some will have better accuracy than others. Some may be free, while others may have a cost associated with them. Some may be able to tell you more than just your current position, such as your elevation over sea level or your current speed.

Android has abstracted all this out into a set of LocationProvider objects. Your Android environment will have zero or more LocationProvider instances: one for each distinct locating service that is available on the device. Providers know not only your location, but also are aware of their own characteristics, in terms of accuracy, cost, and so on.

You, as a developer, will use a LocationManager, which holds the LocationProvider set, to figure out which LocationProvider is right for your particular circumstance. You will also need a permission in your application, or the various location APIs will fail due to a security violation. Depending on which location providers you wish to use, you may need ACCESS_COARSE_LOCATION, ACCESS_FINE_LOCATION, or both. (Permissions are discussed in Chapter 28.)

Finding Yourself

The obvious thing to do with a location service is to figure out where you are right now.

To determine your current location, first you need to get a LocationManager—call getSystemService(LOCATION_SERVICE) from your activity or service and cast it to be a LocationManager.

The next step is to get the name of the LocationProvider you want to use. Here, you have two main options:

- Ask the user to pick a provider.
- Find the best-match provider based on a set of criteria.

If you want the user to pick a provider, calling getProviders() on the LocationManager will give you a List of providers, which you can then present to the user for selection.

Alternatively, you can create and populate a Criteria object, stating the particulars of what you want out of a LocationProvider. Here are some of the criteria you can specify:

- setAltitudeRequired(): Indicates whether or not you need the current altitude.
- setAccuracy(): Sets a minimum level of accuracy, in meters, for the position.
- setCostAllowed(): Controls if the provider must be free or if it can incur a cost on behalf of the device user.

Given a filled-in Critieria object, call getBestProvider() on your LocationManager. Android will sift through the criteria and give you the best answer. Note that not all of your criteria may be met. All but the monetary cost criterion might be relaxed if nothing matches.

You are also welcome to hardwire in a LocationProvider name (e.g., GPS_PROVIDER), perhaps just for testing purposes.

Once you know the name of the LocationProvider, you can call getLastKnownPosition() to find out where you were recently. Note that "recently" might be fairly out of date (e.g., the phone was turned off) or even null if there has been no location recorded for that provider yet. Calling getLastKnownPosition() incurs no monetary or power cost, since the provider does not need to be activated to get the value.

This method returns a Location object, which can give you the latitude and longitude of the device in degrees as a Java double. If the particular location provider offers other data, you can get at that as well:

- For altitude, hasAltitude() will tell you if there is an altitude value, and getAltitude() will return the altitude in meters.

- For bearing (i.e., compass-style direction), hasBearing() will tell you if there is a bearing available, and getBearing() will return it as degrees east of true north.

- For speed, hasSpeed() will tell you if the speed is known and getSpeed() will return the speed in meters per second.

A more likely approach to getting the Location from a LocationProvider, though, is to register for updates, as described in the next section.

On the Move

Not all location providers are necessarily immediately responsive. GPS, for example, requires activating a radio and getting a fix from the satellites before you get a location. That is why Android does not offer a getMeMyCurrentLocationNow() method. Combine that with the fact that your users may want their movements to be reflected in your application, and you are probably best off registering for location updates and using that as your means of getting the current location.

The Weather and WeatherPlus sample applications show how to register for updates: call requestLocationUpdates() on your LocationManager instance. This method takes four parameters:

- The name of the location provider you wish to use

- How long, in milliseconds, must have elapsed before you might get a location update

- How far, in meters, the device must have moved before you might get a location update

- A LocationListener that will be notified of key location-related events

Here's an example of a LocationListener:

```
LocationListener onLocationChange=new LocationListener() {
  public void onLocationChanged(Location location) {
    updateForecast(location);
  }
```

```
    public void onProviderDisabled(String provider) {
      // required for interface, not used
    }

    public void onProviderEnabled(String provider) {
      // required for interface, not used
    }

    public void onStatusChanged(String provider, int status,
                                Bundle extras) {
      // required for interface, not used
    }
  };
```

Here, all we do is call updateForecast() with the Location supplied to the onLocationChanged() callback method. The updateForecast() implementation, as shown in Chapter 29, builds a web page with the current forecast for the location, and sends a broadcast so the activity knows an update is available.

When you no longer need the updates, call removeUpdates() with the LocationListener you registered. If you fail to do this, your application will continue receiving location updates even after all activities and such are closed up, which will also prevent Android from reclaiming your application's memory.

Are We There Yet? Are We There Yet? Are We There Yet?

Sometimes, you are not interested in where you are now, or even when you move, but want to know when you get to where you're going. This could be an end destination, or it could be getting to the next step on a set of directions, so you can give the user the next instruction.

To accomplish this, LocationManager offers addProximityAlert(). This registers an PendingIntent, which will be fired off when the device gets within a certain distance of a certain location. The addProximityAlert() method takes the following as parameters:

- The latitude and longitude of the position of interest

- A radius, specifying how close you should be to that position for the Intent to be raised

- A duration for the registration, in milliseconds (after this period, the registration automatically lapses); a value of -1 means the registration lasts until you manually remove it via removeProximityAlert()

- The PendingIntent to be raised when the device is within the target zone expressed by the position and radius

Note that it is not guaranteed that you will actually receive an Intent. There may be in an interruption in location services, or the device may not be in the target zone during the period of time the proximity alert is active. For example, if the position is off by a bit, and the radius is a little too tight, the device might only skirt the edge of the target zone, or it may go by the target zone so quickly that the device's location isn't sampled during that time.

It is up to you to arrange for an activity or intent receiver to respond to the Intent you register with the proximity alert. What you do when the Intent arrives is up to you. For example, you might set up a notification (e.g., vibrate the device), log the information to a content provider, or post a message to a web site.

Note that you will receive the Intent whenever the position is sampled and you are within the target zone, not just upon entering the zone. Hence, you will get the Intent several times—perhaps quite a few times, depending on the size of the target zone and the speed of the device's movement.

Testing...Testing...

The Android emulator does not have the ability to get a fix from GPS, triangulate your position from cell towers, or identify your location by some nearby Wi-Fi signal. So, if you want to simulate a moving device, you will need to have some means of providing mock location data to the emulator.

For whatever reason, this particular area has undergone significant changes as Android itself has evolved. It used to be that you could provide mock location data within your application, which was very handy for demonstration purposes. Alas, those options were removed in Android 1.0.

One likely option for supplying mock location data is the Dalvik Debug Monitor Service (DDMS). This is an external program, separate from the emulator, which can feed the emulator single location points or full routes to traverse, in a few different formats. DDMS is described in greater detail in Chapter 35.

Chapter 33

Mapping with MapView and MapActivity

One of Google's most popular services—after search, of course—is Google Maps, which lets you find everything from the nearest pizza parlor to directions from New York City to San Francisco (only 2,905 miles!), along with supplying street views and satellite imagery.

Most Android devices, not surprisingly, integrate Google Maps. For those that do, there is a mapping activity available to users directly from the main Android launcher. More relevant to you, as a developer, are `MapView` and `MapActivity`, which allow you to integrate maps into your own applications. Not only can you display maps, control the zoom level, and allow people to pan around, but you can tie in Android's location-based services (covered in Chapter 32) to show where the device is and where it is going.

Fortunately, integrating basic mapping features into your Android project is fairly easy. And there is also a fair bit of power available to you, if you want to get fancy.

Terms, Not of Endearment

Integrating Google Maps into your own application requires agreeing to a fairly lengthy set of legal terms. These terms include clauses that you may find unpalatable.

If you are considering Google Maps, please review these terms closely to determine if your intended use will not run afoul of any clauses. You are strongly recommended to seek professional legal counsel if there are any potential areas of conflict.

Also, keep your eyes peeled for other mapping options, based on other sources of map data, such as OpenStreetMap (http://www.openstreetmap.org/).

Piling On

As of Android 1.5, Google Maps is not strictly part of the Android SDK. Instead, it is part of the Google APIs add-on, an extension of the stock SDK. The Android add-on system provides hooks for other subsystems that may be part of some devices but not others.

> **NOTE:** Google Maps is not part of the Android open source project, and undoubtedly there will be some devices that lack Google Maps due to licensing issues. For example, at the time of this writing, the Archos 5 Android tablet does not have Google Maps.

By and large, the fact that Google Maps is in an add-on does not affect your day-to-day development. However, bear in mind the following:

- You will need to create your project with a suitable target to ensure the Google Maps APIs will be available.

- To test your Google Maps integration, you will also need an AVD that supports the Google Maps API.

The Bare Bones

Far and away the simplest way to get a map into your application is to create your own subclass of `MapActivity`. Like `ListActivity`, which wraps up some of the smarts behind having an activity dominated by a `ListView`, `MapActivity` handles some of the nuances of setting up an activity dominated by a `MapView`.

In your layout for the `MapActivity` subclass, you need to add an element named, at the time of this writing, `com.google.android.maps.MapView`. This is the "longhand" way to spell out the names of widget classes, by including the full package name along with the class name. This is necessary because `MapView` is not in the `com.google.android.widget` namespace. You can give the `MapView` widget whatever `android:id` attribute value you want, plus handle all the layout details to have it render properly alongside your other widgets.

However, you do need to have these two items:

- `android:apiKey`, which in production will need to be a Google Maps API key

- `android:clickable = "true"`, if you want users to be able to click and pan through your map

For example, from the `Maps/NooYawk` sample application, here is the main layout:

```
<?xml version="1.0" encoding="utf-8"?>
<RelativeLayout xmlns:android="http://schemas.android.com/apk/res/android"
  android:layout_width="fill_parent"
  android:layout_height="fill_parent">
  <com.google.android.maps.MapView android:id="@+id/map"
```

```
        android:layout_width="fill_parent"
        android:layout_height="fill_parent"
        android:apiKey="<YOUR_API_KEY>"
        android:clickable="true" />
</RelativeLayout>
```

We'll cover that mysterious apiKey later in this chapter, in the "The Key to It All" section.

In addition, you will need a couple of extra things in your AndroidManifest.xml file:

- The INTERNET and ACCESS_COARSE_LOCATION permissions (the latter for use with the MyLocationOverlay class, described later in this chapter)

- Inside your <application>, a <uses-library> element with android:name = "com.google.android.maps", to indicate you are using one of the optional Android APIs

Here is the AndroidManifest.xml file for NooYawk:

```
<?xml version="1.0" encoding="utf-8"?>
<manifest xmlns:android="http://schemas.android.com/apk/res/android"
  package="com.commonsware.android.maps">
  <uses-permission android:name="android.permission.INTERNET" />
  <uses-permission android:name="android.permission.ACCESS_COARSE_LOCATION" />

  <application android:label="@string/app_name"
    android:icon="@drawable/cw">
    <uses-library android:name="com.google.android.maps" />
    <activity android:name=".NooYawk" android:label="@string/app_name">
      <intent-filter>
        <action android:name="android.intent.action.MAIN" />
        <category android:name="android.intent.category.LAUNCHER" />
      </intent-filter>
    </activity>
  </application>
</manifest>
```

That is pretty much all you need for starters, plus to subclass your activity from MapActivity. If you were to do nothing else, and built that project and tossed it in the emulator, you would get a nice map of the world. Note, however, that MapActivity is abstract. You need to implement isRouteDisplayed() to indicate if you are supplying some sort of driving directions.

In theory, users could pan around the map using the D-pad. However, that's not terribly useful when they have the whole world in their hands.

Since a map of the world is not much good by itself, we need to add a few things, as described next.

Exercising Your Control

You can find your MapView widget by findViewById(), just as with any other widget. The widget itself offers a getMapController() method. Between the MapView and MapController, you have a fair bit of capability to determine what the map shows and how it behaves. The following sections cover zoom and center, the features you will most likely want to use.

Zoom

The map of the world you start with is rather broad. Usually, people looking at a map on a phone will be expecting something a bit narrower in scope, such as a few city blocks.

You can control the zoom level directly via the `setZoom()` method on the `MapController`. This takes an integer representing the level of zoom, where 1 is the world view and 21 is the tightest zoom you can get. Each level is a doubling of the effective resolution: 1 has the equator measuring 256 pixels wide, while 21 has the equator measuring 268,435,456 pixels wide. Since the phone's display probably doesn't have 268,435,456 pixels in either dimension, the user sees a small map focused on one tiny corner of the globe. A level of 16 will show several city blocks in each dimension, which is probably a reasonable starting point for experimentation.

If you wish to allow users to change the zoom level, call `setBuiltInZoomControls(true);`, and the user will be able to zoom in and out of the map via zoom controls found at the bottom center of the map.

Center

Typically, you will need to control what the map is showing, beyond the zoom level, such as the user's current location or a location saved with some data in your activity. To change the map's position, call `setCenter()` on the `MapController`.

The `setCenter()` method takes a `GeoPoint` as a parameter. A `GeoPoint` represents a location, via latitude and longitude. The catch is that the `GeoPoint` stores latitude and longitude as integers representing the actual latitude and longitude multiplied by 1E6. This saves a bit of memory versus storing a float or double, and it greatly speeds up some internal calculations Android needs to do to convert the `GeoPoint` into a map position. However, it does mean you must remember to multiply the real-world latitude and longitude by 1E6.

Rugged Terrain

Just as the Google Maps service you use on your full-size computer can display satellite imagery, so can Android maps.

`MapView` offers `toggleSatellite()`, which, as the name suggests, toggles on and off the satellite perspective on the area being viewed. You can have the user trigger these via an options menu or, in the case of NooYawk, via key presses:

```
@Override
  public boolean onKeyDown(int keyCode, KeyEvent event) {
    if (keyCode == KeyEvent.KEYCODE_S) {
      map.setSatellite(!map.isSatellite());
```

```
      return(true);
    }
    else if (keyCode == KeyEvent.KEYCODE_Z) {
      map.displayZoomControls(true);
      return(true);
    }

    return(super.onKeyDown(keyCode, event));
  }
```

Layers upon Layers

If you have ever used the full-size edition of Google Maps, you are probably used to seeing things overlaid atop the map itself, such as pushpins indicating businesses near the location being searched. In map parlance (and, for that matter, in many serious graphic editors), the pushpins are on a layer separate from than the map itself, and what you are seeing is the composition of the pushpin layer atop the map layer.

Android's mapping allows you to create layers as well, so you can mark up the maps as you need to based on user input and your application's purpose. For example, NooYawk uses a layer to show where select buildings are located in the island of Manhattan.

Overlay Classes

Any overlay you want to add to your map needs to be implemented as a subclass of Overlay. There is an ItemizedOverlay subclass available if you are looking to add pushpins or the like; ItemizedOverlay simplifies this process.

To attach an overlay class to your map, just call getOverlays() on your MapView and add() your Overlay instance to it, as we do here with a custom SitesOverlay:

```
marker.setBounds(0, 0, marker.getIntrinsicWidth(),
                     marker.getIntrinsicHeight());

map.getOverlays().add(new SitesOverlay(marker));
```

We will take a closer look at that marker in the next section.

Drawing the ItemizedOverlay

As the name suggests, ItemizedOverlay allows you to supply a list of points of interest to be displayed on the map—specifically, instances of OverlayItem. The overlay handles much of the drawing logic for you. Here are the minimum steps to make this work:

1. Override ItemizedOverlay<OverlayItem> as your own subclass (in this example, SitesOverlay).

2. In the constructor, build your roster of OverlayItem instances, and call populate() when they are ready for use by the overlay.

3. Implement `size()` to return the number of items to be handled by the overlay.

4. Override `createItem()` to return `OverlayItem` instances given an index.

5. When you instantiate your `ItemizedOverlay` subclass, provide it with a `Drawable` that represents the default icon (e.g., a pushpin) to display for each item.

The `marker` from the `NooYawk` constructor is the `Drawable` used for step 5. It shows a pushpin.

You may also wish to override `draw()` to do a better job of handling the shadow for your markers. While the map will handle casting a shadow for you, it appears you need to provide a bit of assistance for it to know where the bottom of your icon is, so it can draw the shadow appropriately.

For example, here is `SitesOverlay`:

```
private class SitesOverlay extends ItemizedOverlay<OverlayItem> {
  private List<OverlayItem> items=new ArrayList<OverlayItem>();
  private Drawable marker=null;

  public SitesOverlay(Drawable marker) {
    super(marker);
    this.marker=marker;

    items.add(new OverlayItem(getPoint(40.748963847316034,
                              -73.96807193756104),
                    "UN", "United Nations"));
    items.add(new OverlayItem(getPoint(40.76866299974387,
                              -73.98268461227417),
                    "Lincoln Center",
                    "Home of Jazz at Lincoln Center"));
    items.add(new OverlayItem(getPoint(40.765136435316755,
                              -73.97989511489868),
                    "Carnegie Hall",
              "Where you go with practice, practice, practice"));
    items.add(new OverlayItem(getPoint(40.70686417491799,
                              -74.01572942733765),
                    "The Downtown Club",
                "Original home of the Heisman Trophy"));

    populate();
  }

  @Override
  protected OverlayItem createItem(int i) {
    return(items.get(i));
  }

  @Override
  public void draw(Canvas canvas, MapView mapView,
                  boolean shadow) {
    super.draw(canvas, mapView, shadow);
```

```
    boundCenterBottom(marker);
  }

  @Override
  protected boolean onTap(int i) {
    Toast.makeText(NooYawk.this,
                items.get(i).getSnippet(),
                Toast.LENGTH_SHORT).show();

    return(true);
  }

  @Override
  public int size() {
    return(items.size());
  }
}
```

Handling Screen Taps

An Overlay subclass can also implement onTap(), to be notified when the user taps the map, so the overlay can adjust what it draws. For example, in full-size Google Maps, clicking a pushpin pops up a bubble with information about the business at that pin's location. With onTap(), you can do much the same in Android.

The onTap() method for ItemizedOverlay receives the index of the OverlayItem that was clicked. It is up to you to do something worthwhile with this event.

In the case of SitesOverlay, as shown in the preceding section, onTap() looks like this:

```
@Override
protected boolean onTap(int i) {
  Toast.makeText(NooYawk.this,
              items.get(i).getSnippet(),
              Toast.LENGTH_SHORT).show();

  return(true);
}
```

Here, we just toss up a short Toast with the snippet from the OverlayItem, returning true to indicate we handled the tap.

My, Myself, and MyLocationOverlay

Android has a built-in overlay to handle two common scenarios:

- Showing where you are on the map, based on GPS or other location-providing logic

- Showing where you are pointed, based on the built-in compass sensor, where available

All you need to do is create a `MyLocationOverlay` instance, add it to your `MapView`'s list of overlays, and enable and disable the desired features at appropriate times.

The "at appropriate times" notion is for maximizing battery life. There is no sense in updating locations or directions when the activity is paused, so it is recommended that you enable these features in `onResume()` and disable them in `onPause()`.

For example, NooYawk will display a compass rose using `MyLocationOverlay`. To do this, we first need to create the overlay and add it to the list of overlays:

```
me=new MyLocationOverlay(this, map);
map.getOverlays().add(me);
```

Then we enable and disable the compass rose as appropriate:

```
@Override
public void onResume() {
  super.onResume();

  me.enableCompass();
}

@Override
public void onPause() {
  super.onPause();

  me.disableCompass();
}
```

The Key to It All

If you actually download the source code for the book, compile the NooYawk project, install it in your emulator, and run it, you will probably see a screen with a grid and a couple of pushpins, but no actual maps.

That's because the API key in the source code is invalid for your development machine. Instead, you will need to generate your own API key(s) for use with your application.

Full instructions for generating API keys for development and production use can be found on the Android web site (http://code.google.com/android/add-ons/google-apis/mapkey.html). In the interest of brevity, let's focus on the narrow case of getting NooYawk running in your emulator. Doing this requires the following steps:

1.   Visit the API key signup page and review the terms of service.

2.   Reread those terms of service and make really sure you want to agree to them.

3.   Find the MD5 digest of the certificate used for signing your debug-mode applications.

4.   On the API key signup page, paste in that MD5 signature and submit the form.

5. On the resulting page, copy the API key and paste it as the value of apiKey in your MapView-using layout.

The trickiest part is finding the MD5 signature of the certificate used for signing your debug-mode applications. Actually, much of the complexity is merely in making sense of the concept.

All Android applications are signed using a digital signature generated from a certificate. You are automatically given a debug certificate when you set up the SDK, and there is a separate process for creating a self-signed certificate for use in your production applications. This signature process involves the use of the Java keytool and jarsigner utilities. For the purposes of getting your API key, you only need to worry about keytool.

To get your MD5 digest of your debug certificate, if you are on Mac OS X or Linux, use the following command:

```
keytool -list -alias androiddebugkey -keystore ~/.android/debug.keystore -storepass
android -keypass android
```

On other development platforms, you will need to replace the value of the -keystore switch with the location for your platform and user account:

- On Windows XP, use C:\Documents and Settings\<user>\.android\debug.keystore.

- On Windows Vista/Windows 7, use C:\Users\<user>\.android\debug.keystore (where <user> is your account name).

The second line of the output contains your MD5 digest, as a series of pairs of hex digits separated by colons.

Chapter **34**

Handling Telephone Calls

Many, if not most, Android devices will be phones. As such, not only will users be expecting to place and receive calls using Android, but you will have the opportunity to help them place calls, if you wish.

Why might you want to?

- Maybe you are writing an Android interface to a sales management application (*a la* Salesforce.com) and you want to offer users the ability to call prospects with a single button click, and without them needing to keep those contacts both in your application and in the phone's contacts application.

- Maybe you are writing a social networking application, and the roster of phone numbers that you can access shifts constantly, so rather than try to synchronize the social network contacts with the phone's contact database, you let people place calls directly from your application.

- Maybe you are creating an alternative interface to the existing contacts system, perhaps for users with reduced motor control (e.g., the elderly), sporting big buttons and the like to make it easier for them to place calls.

Whatever the reason, Android has the means to let you manipulate the phone just like any other piece of the Android system.

Report to the Manager

To get at much of the phone API, you use the `TelephonyManager`. That class lets you do things like the following:

- Determine if the phone is in use via `getCallState()`, with return values of `CALL_STATE_IDLE` (phone not in use), `CALL_STATE_RINGING` (call requested but still being connected), and `CALL_STATE_OFFHOOK` (call in progress).

- Find out the SIM ID (IMSI) via getSubscriberId().

- Find out the phone type (e.g., GSM) via getPhoneType(), or find out the data connection type (e.g., GPRS or EDGE) via getNetworkType().

You Make the Call!

You can also initiate a call from your application, such as from a phone number you obtained through your own web service. To do this, simply craft an ACTION_DIAL Intent with a Uri of the form tel:NNNNN (where NNNNN is the phone number to dial) and use that Intent with startActivity(). This will not actually dial the phone; rather, it activates the dialer activity, from which the user can press a button to place the call.

For example, let's look at the Phone/Dialer sample application. Here's the crude (but effective) layout:

```
<?xml version="1.0" encoding="utf-8"?>
<LinearLayout xmlns:android="http://schemas.android.com/apk/res/android"
    android:orientation="vertical"
    android:layout_width="fill_parent"
    android:layout_height="fill_parent"
    >
  <LinearLayout
    android:orientation="horizontal"
    android:layout_width="fill_parent"
    android:layout_height="wrap_content"
    >
    <TextView
      android:layout_width="wrap_content"
      android:layout_height="wrap_content"
      android:text="Number to dial:"
      />
    <EditText android:id="@+id/number"
      android:layout_width="fill_parent"
      android:layout_height="wrap_content"
      android:cursorVisible="true"
      android:editable="true"
      android:singleLine="true"
    />
  </LinearLayout>
  <Button android:id="@+id/dial"
    android:layout_width="fill_parent"
    android:layout_height="wrap_content"
    android:layout_weight="1"
    android:text="Dial It!"
  />
</LinearLayout>
```

We have a labeled field for typing in a phone number, plus a button for dialing that number.

The Java code simply launches the dialer using the phone number from the field:

```
package com.commonsware.android.dialer;

import android.app.Activity;
import android.content.Intent;
import android.net.Uri;
import android.os.Bundle;
import android.view.View;
import android.widget.Button;
import android.widget.EditText;

public class DialerDemo extends Activity {
  @Override
  public void onCreate(Bundle icicle) {
    super.onCreate(icicle);
    setContentView(R.layout.main);

    final EditText number=(EditText)findViewById(R.id.number);
    Button dial=(Button)findViewById(R.id.dial);

    dial.setOnClickListener(new Button.OnClickListener() {
      public void onClick(View v) {
        String toDial="tel:"+number.getText().toString();

        startActivity(new Intent(Intent.ACTION_DIAL,
                                 Uri.parse(toDial)));
      }
    });
  }
}
```

The activity's own UI is not that impressive, as you can see in Figure 34–1.

Figure 34–1. *The DialerDemo sample application, as initially launched*

However, the dialer you get from clicking the dial button is better, showing you the number you are about to dial, as shown in Figure 34–2.

Figure 34–2. *The Android Dialer activity, as launched from DialerDemo*

Chapter 35

Development Tools

The Android SDK is more than a library of Java classes and API calls. It also includes a number of tools to assist in application development.

Much of the focus has been on the Eclipse plug-in, to integrate Android development with that IDE. Secondary emphasis has been placed on the plug-in's equivalents for use in other IDEs or without an IDE, such as adb for communicating with a running emulator.

This chapter will cover other tools beyond those two groups.

Hierarchical Management

Android comes with a Hierarchy Viewer tool, designed to help you visualize your layouts as they are seen in a running activity in a running emulator. So, for example, you can determine how much space a certain widget is taking up, or try to find where a widget that does not appear on the screen is hiding.

To use Hierarchy Viewer, you first need to fire up your emulator, install your application, launch your activity, and navigate to spot you wish to examine. Note that you cannot use Hierarchy Viewer with a production Android device (e.g., T-Mobile G1). For illustration purposes, we'll use the ReadWrite demo application introduced back in Chapter 23, as shown in Figure 35–1.

You can launch Hierarchy Viewer via the hierarchyviewer program, found in the tools/ directory in your Android SDK installation. This brings up the main Hierarchy Viewer window, as shown in Figure 35–2.

Figure 35–1. *ReadWrite demo application*

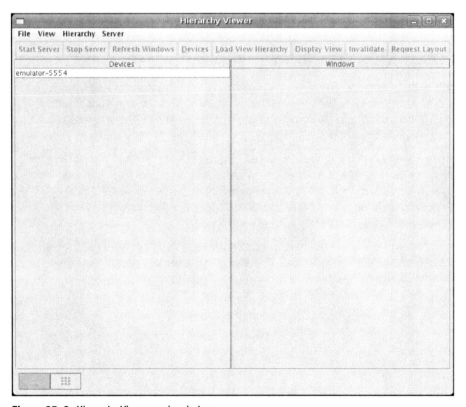

Figure 35–2. *Hierarchy Viewer main window*

The list on the left shows the various emulators you have opened. The number after the hyphen should line up with the number in parentheses in your emulator's title bar.

When you click an emulator, the list of windows available for examination appears on the right, as shown in Figure 35–3.

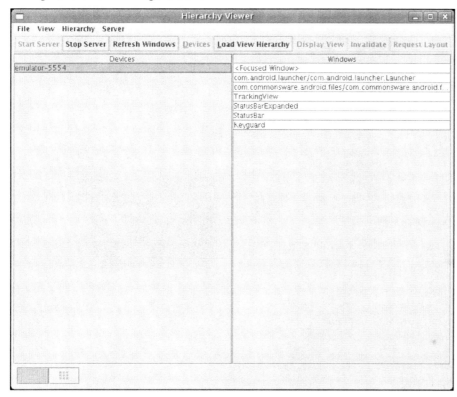

Figure 35–3. *Hierarchy Viewer list of available windows*

Notice how there are many other windows besides our open activity, including the Launcher window (i.e., the home screen), the Keyguard window (i.e., the "Press Menu to Unlock" black screen you get when first opening the emulator), and so on. Your activity will be identified by application package and class (e.g., com.commonsware.android.files/...).

Things get interesting when you choose a window and click Load View Hierarchy. After a few seconds, the details spring into view, in a perspective called the Layout view, as shown in Figure 35–4.

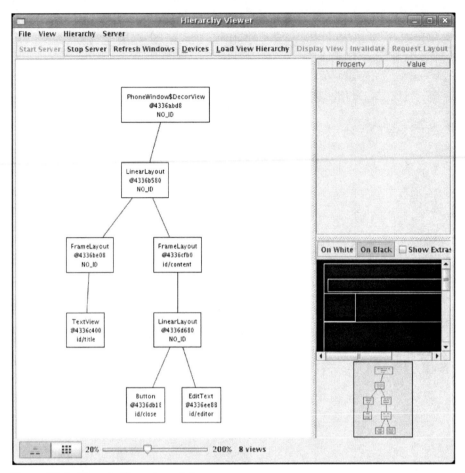

Figure 35–4. *Hierarchy Viewer Layout view*

The main area of the Layout view shows a tree of the various views that make up your activity, starting from the overall system window and driving down into the individual UI widgets. You will see, on the lower-right branch of the tree, the LinearLayout, Button, and EditText shown in the preceding code listing. All of the remaining views, including the title bar, are supplied by the system.

Clicking one of the views adds more information to this perspective, as shown in Figure 35–5.

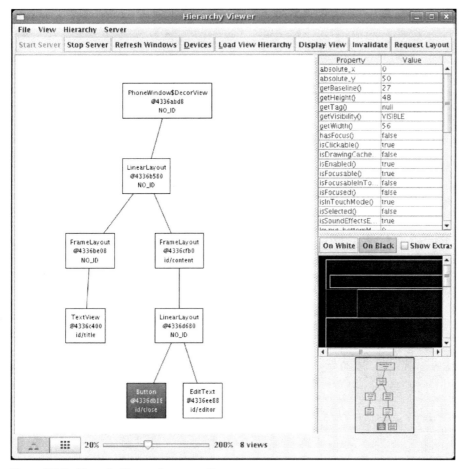

Figure 35–5. *Hierarchy Viewer view properties*

Now, in the upper-right region of the viewer, you see properties of the selected widget—in this case, the Button. Alas, these properties do not appear to be editable.

Also, the widget is highlighted in red in the wireframe of the activity, shown beneath the properties (by default, views are shown as white outlines on a black background). This can help you ensure you have selected the correct widget, if, say, you have several buttons and cannot readily tell from the tree what is what.

If you double-click a view in the tree, you will see a pop-up pane showing just that view (and its children), isolated from the rest of your activity.

Down in the lower-left corner, you will see two toggle buttons, with the tree button initially selected. Clicking the grid button puts the viewer in a whole new perspective, called the Pixel Perfect view, as shown in Figure 35–6.

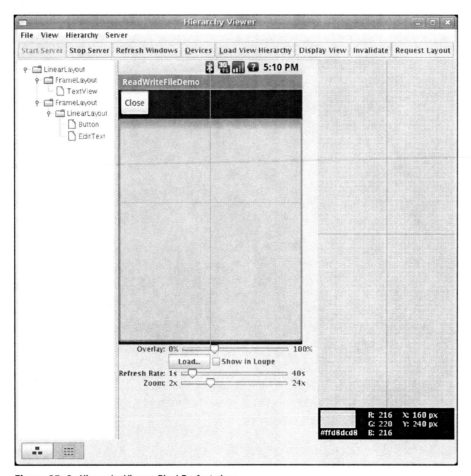

Figure 35–6. *Hierarchy Viewer Pixel Perfect view*

On the left, you see a tree representing the widgets and other views in your activity. In the middle, you see your activity (the Normal view), and on the right, you see a zoomed edition of your activity (the Loupe view).

What may not be initially obvious is that this imagery is live. Your activity is polled every so often, controlled by the Refresh Rate slider. Anything you do in the activity will then be reflected in the Pixel Perfect view's Normal and Loupe views.

The hairlines (cyan) overlaying the activity show the position being zoomed. Just click a new area to change where the Loupe view is inspecting. And, of course, there is another slider to adjust how much the Loupe view is zoomed.

Delightful Dalvik Debugging Detailed, Demoed

Another tool in the Android developer's arsenal is the Dalvik Debug Monitor Service (DDMS). This is like a Swiss army knife, allowing you to do everything from browse log files, update the GPS location provided by emulator, simulate incoming calls and messages, and browse the on-emulator storage to push and pull files.

DDMS has a wide range of uses. Here, I will introduce some of the most useful features.

To launch DDMS, run the ddms program inside the tools/ directory in your Android SDK distribution. It will initially display just a tree of emulators and running programs on the left, as shown in Figure 35–7.

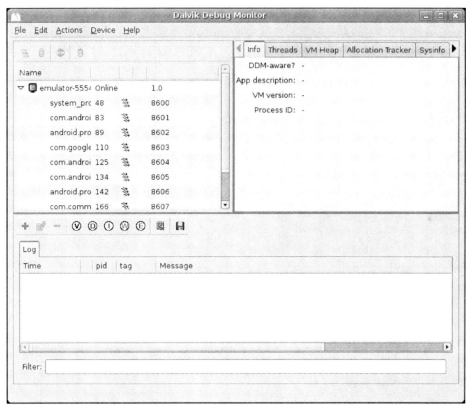

Figure 35–7. *DDMS initial view*

Clicking an emulator allows you to browse the event log on the bottom and manipulate the emulator via the tabs on the right, as shown in Figure 35–8.

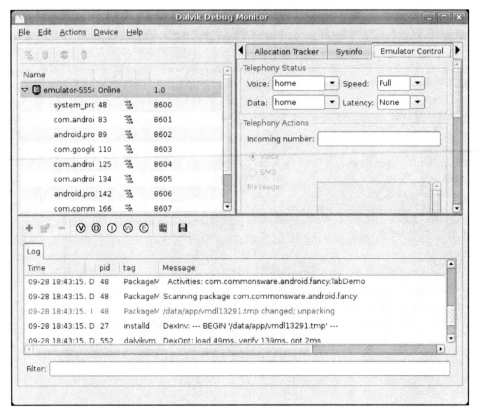

Figure 35–8. *DDMS, with emulator selected*

Logging

Rather than use `adb logcat`, DDMS lets you view your logging information in a scrollable table. Just highlight the emulator or device you want to monitor, and the bottom half of the screen shows the logs.

In addition, you can do the following:

- Filter the Log tab by any of the five logging levels, shown as the V through E toolbar buttons.

- Create a custom filter, so you can view only those entries tagged with your application's tag, by pressing the + toolbar button and completing the form (see Figure 35–9). The name you enter in the form will be used as the name of another logging output tab in the bottom portion of the DDMS main window.

- Save the log information to a text file for later perusal, or for searching.

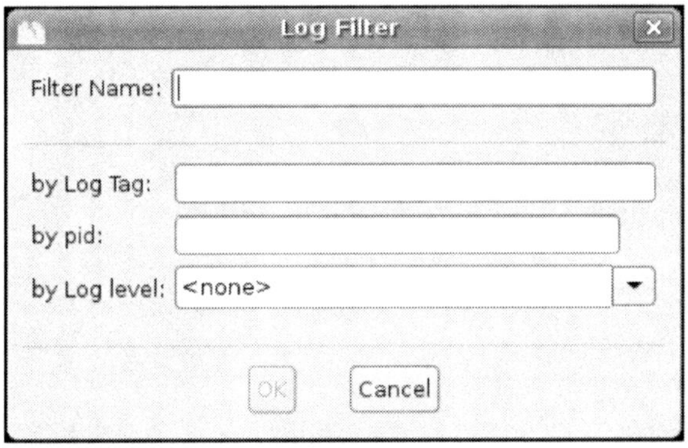

Figure 35–9. *DDMS logging filter*

File Push and Pull

While you can use `adb pull` and `adb push` to get files to and from an emulator or device, DDMS lets you do that visually. Just highlight the emulator or device you wish to work with, and then choose Device ➤ File Explorer from the main menu. That will bring up your typical directory browser, as shown in Figure 35–10.

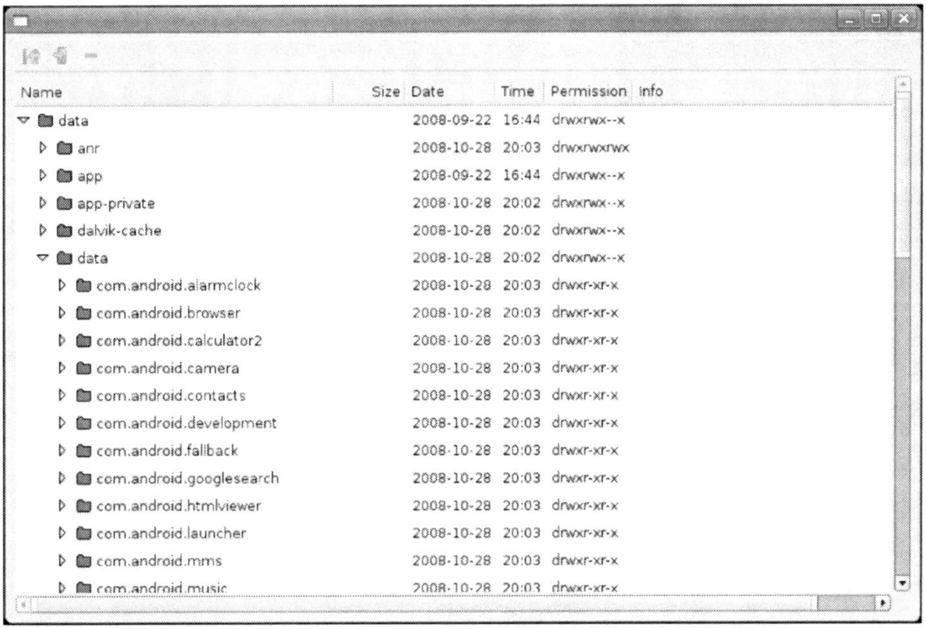

Figure 35–10. *DDMS File Explorer*

Just browse to the file you want and click either the pull (leftmost) or push (middle) toolbar button to transfer the file to or from your development machine. To delete a file, click the delete (rightmost) toolbar button.

There are a few caveats to using File Explorer:

- You cannot create directories through this tool. You will either need to use adb shell or create them from within your application.

- While you can putter through most of the files on an emulator, you can access very little outside /sdcard on an actual device, due to Android security restrictions.

Screenshots

To take a screenshot of the Android emulator or device, simply press Ctrl+S or choose Device ➤ Screen Capture from the main menu. This will bring up a dialog box containing an image of the current screen, as shown in Figure 35–11.

Figure 35–11. *DDMS screen capture*

From here, you can do the following:

- Click Save to save the image as a PNG file somewhere on your development machine.

- Click Refresh to update the image based on the current state of the emulator or device.

- Click Done to close the dialog box.

Location Updates

To use DDMS to supply location updates to your application, the first thing you must do is have your application use the gps LocationProvider, as that is the one that DDMS is set to update.

Next, click the Emulator Control tab and scroll down to the Location Controls section. Here, you will find a smaller tabbed pane with three options for specifying locations: Manual, GPX, and KML, as shown in Figure 35–12.

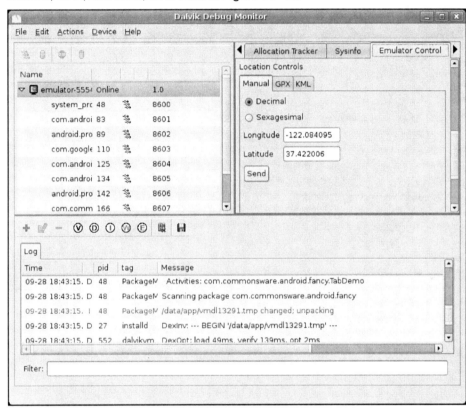

Figure 35–12. *DDMS location controls*

To use the Manual tab, provide a latitude and longitude and click the Send button to submit that location to the emulator. The emulator will notify any location listeners of the new position.

The other tabs allow you to specify locations using GPS Exchange (GPX) format or Keyhole Markup Language (KML) format.

Placing Calls and Messages

If you want to simulate incoming calls or SMS messages to the Android emulator, DDMS can handle that as well.

On the Emulator Control tab, above the Location Controls group, is the Telephony Actions group, as shown in Figure 35–13.

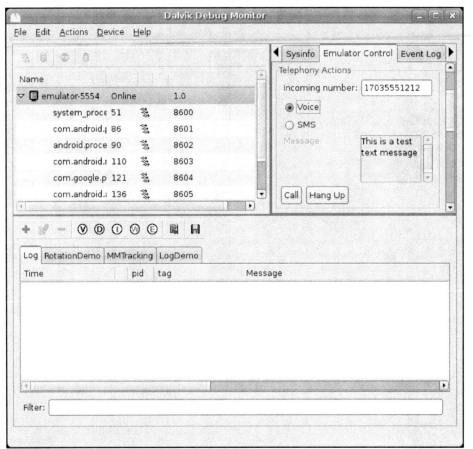

Figure 35–13. *DDMS telephony controls*

To simulate an incoming call, fill in a phone number, choose the Voice radio button, and click Call. At that point, the emulator will show the incoming call, allowing you to accept it (via the green phone button) or reject it (via the red phone button), as shown in Figure 35–14.

Figure 35–14. *Simulated incoming call*

To simulate an incoming text message, fill in a phone number, choose the SMS radio button, enter a message in the provided text area, and click Send. The text message will then appear as a notification, as shown in Figure 35–15.

Figure 35–15. *Simulated text message*

And, of course, you can click the notification to view the message in the full-fledged messaging application, as shown in Figure 35–16.

Figure 35–16. *Simulated text message, in messaging application*

Put It on My Card

The T-Mobile G1 has a microSD card slot. Many other Android devices are likely to have similar forms of removable storage, which the Android platform refers to generically as an SD card.

It's strongly recommended that developers use SD cards as the holding pen for large data sets: images, movie clips, audio files, and so on. The T-Mobile G1, in particular, has a relatively paltry amount of on-board flash memory, so the more you can store on an SD card, the better.

Of course, the challenge is that, while the G1 has an SD card by default, the emulator does not. To make the emulator work like the G1, you need to create and "insert" an SD card into the emulator.

Creating a Card Image

Rather than require emulators to somehow have access to an actual SD card reader and use actual SD cards, Android is set up to use card images. A card image is simply a file that the emulator will treat as if it were an SD card volume. If you are used to disk images used with virtualization tools (e.g., VirtualBox), the concept is the same. Android uses a disk image representing the SD card contents.

To create such an image, use the `mksdcard` utility, provided in the `tools/` directory of your SDK installation. This takes two main parameters:

- The size of the image, and hence the size of the resulting "card." If you just supply a number, it is interpreted as a size in bytes. Alternatively, you can append `K` or `M` to the number to indicate a size in kilobytes or megabytes, respectively.

- The filename under which to store the image.

So, for example, to create a 1GB SD card image, to simulate the G1's SD card in the emulator, you could run the following:

```
mksdcard 1024M sdcard.img
```

Inserting the Card

To have your emulator use this SD card image, start the emulator with the `-sdcard` switch, containing a fully qualified path to the image file you created using `mksdcard`. While there will be no visible impact—you won't see an icon or anything else in Android showing that you have a card mounted—the `/sdcard` path will now be available for reading and writing.

To put files on the `/sdcard`, either use File Explorer in DDMS or `adb push` and `adb pull` from the console.

Chapter 36

Handling Multiple Screen Sizes

For the first year or so since Android 1.0 was released, all production Android devices had the same screen resolution (HVGA, 320 by 480) and size (around 3.5 inches, or 9 centimeters). Starting in the fall of 2009, though, devices have been arriving with widely disparate screen sizes and resolutions, from tiny QVGA (240 by 320) screens to much larger WVGA (480 by 800) screens.

Of course, users will be expecting your application to be functional on all of these screens, and perhaps take advantage of larger screen sizes to add greater value. To that end, Android 1.6 added new capabilities to help better support these different screen sizes and resolutions.

The Android documentation has extensive coverage of the mechanics of handling multiple screen sizes (http://d.android.com/guide/practices/screens_support.html). You are encouraged to read that information along with this chapter, to get the best understanding of how to cope with, and perhaps take advantage of, multiple screen sizes.

After a number of sections discussing the screen size options and theory, the chapter wraps with an in-depth look at making a fairly simple application that handles multiple screen sizes well.

Taking the Default

Let's suppose that you start off by totally ignoring the issue of screen sizes and resolutions. What happens?

If your application is compiled for Android 1.5 or lower, Android will assume your application was designed to look good on the classic screen size and resolution. If your application is installed on a device with a larger screen, Android automatically will run your application in compatibility mode, scaling everything based on the actual screen size.

For example, suppose you have a 24-pixel square PNG file, and Android installs and runs your application on a device with the standard physical size but a WVGA resolution (a so-called high-density screen). Android might scale your PNG file to be 36 pixels, so it will take up the same visible space on the screen. On the plus side, Android handles this automatically. On the minus side, bitmap-scaling algorithms tend to make the images a bit fuzzy.

Additionally, Android will block your application from running on a device with a smaller screen. Hence, QVGA devices, like the HTC Tattoo, will be unable to get your application, even if it is available on the Android Market.

If your application is compiled for Android 1.6 or higher, Android assumes that you are properly handling all screen sizes, and therefore will not run your application in compatibility mode. You will see how to tailor this in a later section.

Whole in One

The simplest approach to handling multiple screen sizes in Android is to design your UIs so that they automatically scale for the screen size, without any size-specific code or resources. In other words, "it just works."

This implies, though, that everything you use in your UI can be gracefully scaled by Android and that everything will fit, even on a QVGA screen.

The following sections contain some tips for achieving this all in one solution.

Think About Rules, Rather Than Positions

Some developers, perhaps those coming from the drag-and-drop school of UI development, think first and foremost about the positions of widgets. They think that they want particular widgets to be certain fixed sizes at certain fixed locations. They get frustrated with Android layout managers (containers) and may gravitate to the deprecated AbsoluteLayout as a way to design UIs in a familiar way.

That approach rarely works well—even on desktops—as can be seen by applications that do a poor job of window resizing. Similarly, it will not work on mobile devices, particularly Android, with their wide range of screen sizes and resolutions.

Instead of thinking about positions, think about rules. You need to teach Android the business rules about where widgets should be sized and placed, and then Android will interpret those rules based on what the device's screen actually supports in terms of resolution.

The simplest rules are the fill_parent and wrap_content values for android:layout_width and android:layout_height. Those do not specify specific sizes, but rather adapt to the space available.

The richest environment for easily specifying rules is to use RelativeLayout (discussed in Chapter 6). While complicated on the surface, RelativeLayout does an excellent job of letting you control your layout while still adapting it to other screen sizes. For example, you can do the following:

- Explicitly anchor widgets to the bottom or right side of the screen, rather than hoping they will wind up there courtesy of some other layout.

- Control the distances between widgets that are connected (e.g., a label for a field that should be to the left of the field) without needing to rely on padding or margins.

The greatest control for specifying rules is to create your own layout class. For example, suppose you are creating a series of applications that implement card games. You may want to have a layout class that knows about playing cards—how they overlap, which are face up versus face down, how big to be to handle varying number of cards, and so on. While you could achieve the desired look with, say, a RelativeLayout, you may be better served implementing a PlayingCardLayout or something that is more explicitly tailored for your application. Unfortunately, creating custom layout classes is underdocumented at this point in time.

Consider Physical Dimensions

Android offers a wide range of available units of measure for dimensions. The most popular has been the pixel (px), because it is easy to wrap your head around the concept. After all, each Android device will have a screen with a certain number of pixels in each direction.

However, pixels start to become troublesome as screen density changes. As the number of pixels in a given screen size increases, the pixels effectively shrink. A 32-pixel icon on a traditional Android device might be finger-friendly, but on a high-density device (say, WVGA in a mobile phone form factor), 32 pixels may be a bit small for use with a finger.

If you have something intrinsically scalable (e.g., a Button) where you had been specifying a size in pixels, you might consider switching to using millimeters (mm) or inches (in) as the unit of measure—10 millimeters are 10 millimeters, regardless of the screen resolution or the screen size. This way, you can ensure that your widget is sized to be finger-friendly, regardless of the number of pixels that might take.

Avoid Real Pixels

In some circumstances, using millimeters for dimensions will not make sense. Then you may wish to consider using other units of measure while still avoiding real pixels.

Android offers dimensions measured in density-independent pixels (dip). These map 1:1 to pixels for a 160-dpi screen (e.g., a classic HVGA Android device) and scale from there. For example, on a 240-dpi device (e.g., a phone-sized WVGA device), the ratio is 2:3, so 50dip = 50px at 160 dpi = 75px at 240 dpi. The advantage to the user of going with dip is that the actual size of the dimension stays the same, so visibly there is no difference between 50dip at 160 dpi and 50dip at 240 dpi.

Android also offers dimensions measured in scaled pixels (sp). Scaled pixels, in theory, are scaled based on the user's choice of font size (FONT_SCALE value in System.Settings).

Choose Scalable Drawables

Classic bitmaps—PNG, JPG, and GIF—are not intrinsically scalable. If you are not running in compatibility mode, Android will not even try to scale them for you based on screen resolution and size. Whatever size of bitmap you supply is the size it will be, even if that makes the image too large or too small on some screens.

One way to address this is to try to avoid static bitmaps, using nine-patch bitmaps and XML-defined drawables (e.g., GradientDrawable) as alternatives. A nine-patch bitmap is a PNG file specially encoded to have rules indicating how that image can be stretched to take up more space. XML-defined drawables use a quasi-SVG XML language to define shapes, their strokes and fills, and so on.

Tailor-Made, Just for You (and You, and You, and...)

There will be times when you want to have different looks or behaviors based on screen size or density. Android has ways for you to switch out resources or code blocks based on the environment in which your application runs. When properly used in combination with the techniques discussed in the previous section, achieving screen size- and density-independence is eminently possible, at least for devices running Android 1.6 and newer.

Add <supports-screens>

The first step to proactively supporting screen sizes is to add the <supports-screens> element to your AndroidManifest.xml file. This specifies which screen sizes you explicitly support and which you do not. Those that you do not explicitly support will be handled by the automatic compatibility mode described previously.

Here is a manifest containing a <supports-screens> element:

```
<?xml version="1.0" encoding="utf-8"?>
<manifest xmlns:android="http://schemas.android.com/apk/res/android"
  package="com.commonsware.android.eu4you"
  android:versionCode="1"
  android:versionName="1.0">
  <supports-screens
    android:largeScreens="true"
    android:normalScreens="true"
    android:smallScreens="true"
    android:anyDensity="true"
  />
```

```
  <application android:label="@string/app_name"
    android:icon="@drawable/cw">
    <activity android:name=".EU4You"
              android:label="@string/app_name">
      <intent-filter>
        <action android:name="android.intent.action.MAIN" />
        <category android:name="android.intent.category.LAUNCHER" />
      </intent-filter>
    </activity>
  </application>
</manifest>
```

Each of the attributes `android:smallScreens`, `android:normalScreens`, and `android:largeScreens` takes a Boolean value indicating if your application explicitly supports those screens (`true`) or requires compatibility mode assistance (`false`).

The `android:anyDensity` attribute indicates whether you are taking density into account in your calculations (`true`) or not (`false`). If `false`, Android will behave as though all of your dimensions (e.g., 4px) were for a normal-density (160-dpi) screen. If your application is running on a screen with lower or higher density, Android will scale your dimensions accordingly. If you indicate that `android:anyDensity = "true"`, you are telling Android not to do that, putting the onus on you to use density-independent units, such as `dip`, `mm`, or `in`.

Resources and Resource Sets

The primary way to toggle different things based on screen size or density is to create resource sets. By creating resource sets that are specific to different device characteristics, you teach Android how to render each, with Android switching among those sets automatically.

Default Scaling

By default, Android will scale all drawable resources. Those that are intrinsically scalable will scale nicely. Ordinary bitmaps will be scaled using a normal scaling algorithm, which may or may not give you great results. It also may slow things down a bit. If you wish to avoid this, you will need to set up separate resource sets containing your nonscalable bitmaps.

Density-Based Sets

If you wish to have different layouts, dimensions, or the like based on different screen densities, you can use the `-ldpi`, `-mdpi`, and `-hdpi` resource set labels. For example, `res/values-hdpi/dimens.xml` would contain dimensions used in high-density devices.

Size-Based Sets

Similarly, if you wish to have different resource sets based on screen size, Android offers `-small`, `-normal`, and `-large` resource set labels. Creating `res/layout-large-land/` would indicate layouts to use on large screens (e.g., WVGA) in landscape orientation.

Version-Based Sets

There may be times when earlier versions of Android get confused by newer resource set labels. To help with that, you can include a version label to your resource set, of the form `-vN`, where `N` is an API level. Hence, `res/drawable-large-v4/` indicates these drawables should be used on large screens at API level 4 (Android 1.6) and newer.

Android has had the ability to filter on version from early on, and so this technique will work going back to Android 1.5 (and perhaps earlier).

So, if you find that Android 1.5 emulators or devices are grabbing the wrong resource sets, consider adding `-v4` to their resource set names to filter them out.

Finding Your Size

If you need to take different actions in your Java code based on screen size or density, you have a few options.

If there is something distinctive in your resource sets, you can sniff on that and branch accordingly in your code. For example, as will be seen in the code sample later in this chapter, you can have extra widgets in some layouts (e.g., `res/layout-large/main.xml`); simply seeing if an extra widget exists will tell you if you are running a large screen.

You can also find out your screen size class via a `Configuration` object, typically obtained by an `Activity` via `getResources().getConfiguration()`. A `Configuration` object has a public field named `screenLayout` that is a bitmask indicating the type of screen on which the application is running. You can test to see if your screen is small, normal, or large, or if it is long (where long indicates a 16:9 or similar aspect ratio, compared to 4:3). For example, here we test to see if we are running on a large screen:

```
if (getResources().getConfiguration().screenLayout
      & Configuration.SCREENLAYOUT_SIZE_LARGE)
    ==Configuration.SCREENLAYOUT_SIZE_LARGE) {
  // yes, we are large
}
else {
  // no, we are not
}
```

There does not appear to be an easy way to find out your screen density in a similar fashion. If you absolutely need to know that, a hack would be to create `res/values-ldpi/`, `res/values-mdpi/`, and `res/values-hdpi/` directories in your project, and add a `strings.xml` file to each. Put a string resource in `strings.xml` that has a common name across all three resource sets and has a distinctive value (e.g., name it `density`, with values of ldpi, mdpi, and hdpi, respectively). Then test the value of the string resource at runtime. This is inelegant but should work.

Ain't Nothing Like the Real Thing

The Android emulators will help you test your application on different screen sizes. However, that will get you only so far, because mobile device LCDs have different characteristics than your desktop or notebook, such as the following:

- Mobile device LCDs may have a much higher density than that of your development machine.

- A mouse allows for much more precise touchscreen input than does an actual fingertip.

Where possible, you are going to need to either use the emulator in new and exciting ways or try to get your hands on actual devices with alternative screen resolutions.

Density Differs

The Motorola DROID has a 240-dpi, 3.7-inch, 480-by-854 pixel screen (an FWVGA display). To emulate a DROID screen, based on pixel count, takes up one third of a 19-inch, 1280-by-1024 LCD monitor, because the LCD monitor's density is much lower than that of the DROID—around 96 dpi. So, when you fire up your Android emulator for an FWVGA display like that of the DROID, you will get a massive emulator window.

This is still perfectly fine for determining the overall look of your application in an FWVGA environment. Regardless of density, widgets will still align the same, sizes will have the same relationships (e.g., widget A might be twice as tall as widget B, and that will be true regardless of density), and so on.

However, these issues may come up:

- Things that might appear to be a suitable size when viewed on a 19-inch LCD may be entirely too small on a mobile device screen of the same resolution.

- Things that you can easily click with a mouse in the emulator may be much too small to pick out on a physically smaller and denser screen when used with a finger.

Adjusting the Density

By default, the emulator will keep the pixel count accurate at the expense of density, which is why you get the really big emulator window. You do have an option of keeping the density accurate at the expense of pixel count.

The easiest way to do this is to use the Android AVD Manager, introduced in Android 1.6. The Android 2.0 edition of this tool has a Launch Options dialog that pops up when you go to start an emulator instance via the Start button, as shown in Figure 36–1.

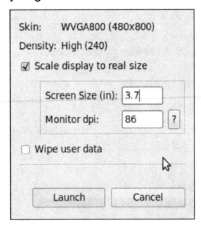

Figure 36–1. *The Launch Options dialog*

By default, the "Scale display to real size" check box is unchecked, and Android will open the emulator window normally. You can check that check box, and then provide two bits of scaling information:

- The screen size of the device you wish to emulate, in inches (e.g., 3.7 for the Motorola DROID)

- The dots-per-inch resolution of your monitor (click the ? button to bring up a calculator to help you determine that value)

This will give you an emulator window that more accurately depicts what your UI will look like on a physical device, at least in terms of sizes. However, since the emulator is using far fewer pixels than will a device, fonts may be difficult to read, images may be blocky, and so forth.

Accessing Actual Devices

Of course, the best possible way to see what your application looks like on different devices is to actually test it on different devices. You do not necessarily need to get every Android device ever made, but you may want to have access to ones with distinctive hardware that impacts your application, and screen size impacts just about everyone. Here are some suggestions:

- Virtually test devices using services like DeviceAnywhere (http://www.deviceanywhere.com/). This is an improvement over the emulator, but it is not free and certainly cannot test everything (e.g., changes in location).

- Purchase devices, perhaps through back channels like eBay. Unlocked GSM phones can readily share a SIM when you need to test telephony operations or go SIM-less otherwise.

- If you live in or near a city, you may be able to set up some form of a user group, and use that group for testing applications on your collective set of hardware.

- Take the user-testing route, releasing your application as a free beta or something, and then letting user feedback guide adjustments. You may wish to distribute this outside the Android Market, lest beta test feedback harm your application's market rating.

Ruthlessly Exploiting the Situation

So far, we have focused on how you can ensure your layouts look decent on other screen sizes. And, for smaller screens than the norm (e.g., QVGA), that is perhaps all you can achieve.

Once we get into larger screens, though, another possibility emerges: using different layouts designed to take advantage of the extra screen space. This is particularly useful when the physical screen size is larger (e.g., a 5-inch LCD like on the Archos 5 Android tablet), rather than simply having more pixels in the same physical space.

The following sections describe some ways you might take advantage of additional space.

Replace Menus with Buttons

An option menu selection requires two physical actions: press the Menu button, and then tap on the appropriate menu choice. A context menu selection requires two physical actions as well: long-tap on the widget, and then tap on the menu choice. Context menus have the additional problem of being effectively invisible; for example, users may not realize that your ListView has a context menu.

You might consider augmenting your UI to provide direct on-screen ways of accomplishing things that might otherwise be hidden away on a menu. Not only does this reduce the number of steps a user needs to take to do things, but it also makes those options more obvious.

For example, suppose you are creating a media player application, and you want to offer manual playlist management. You have an activity that displays the songs in a playlist in a ListView. On an option menu, you have an Add choice, to add a new song from the ones on the device to the playlist. On a context menu on the ListView, you have a Remove choice, plus Move Up and Move Down choices to reorder the songs in the list. On a large screen, you might consider adding four ImageButton widgets to your UI for these four options, with the three from the context menu enabled only when a row is selected by the D-pad or trackball. On regular or small screens, you would stick with just using the menus.

Replace Tabs with a Simple Activity

You may have introduced a TabHost into your UI to allow you to display more widgets in the available screen space. As long as the widget space you save by moving them to a separate tab is more than the space taken up by the tabs themselves, you win. However, having multiple tabs means more user steps to navigate your UI, particularly if the user needs to flip back and forth between tabs frequently.

If you have only two tabs, consider changing your UI to offer a large-screen layout that removes the tabs and puts all the widgets on one screen. This places everything in front of the user, without needing to switch tabs all the time.

If you have three or more tabs, you probably will lack screen space to put all those tabs' contents on one activity. However, you might consider going half and half: have popular widgets be on the activity all of the time, leaving your TabHost to handle the rest on (roughly) half of the screen.

Consolidate Multiple Activities

The most powerful technique is to use a larger screen to get rid of activity transitions outright. For example, if you have a ListActivity where clicking an item brings up that item's details in a separate activity, consider supporting a large-screen layout where the details are on the same activity as the ListView (e.g., ListView on the left, details on the right, in a landscape layout). This eliminates the user having to constantly press the Back button to leave one set of details before viewing another.

You will see this technique applied in the sample code presented in the following section.

Example: EU4You

To examine how to use some of the techniques discussed so far, let's look at the ScreenSizes/EU4You sample application. This application has one activity (EU4You) that contains a ListView with the roster of European Union (EU) members and their respective flags (http://www.wpclipart.com/flags/Countries/index.html). Clicking one of the countries brings up the mobile Wikipedia page for that country.

In the source code to this book, you will find four versions of this application. We start with an application that is ignorant of screen size and slowly add in more screen-related features.

The First Cut

First, here is our AndroidManifest.xml file, which looks distinctly like one shown earlier in this chapter:

```
<?xml version="1.0" encoding="utf-8"?>
<manifest xmlns:android="http://schemas.android.com/apk/res/android"
  package="com.commonsware.android.eu4you"
```

```
      android:versionCode="1"
      android:versionName="1.0">
      <supports-screens
        android:largeScreens="true"
        android:normalScreens="true"
        android:smallScreens="true"
        android:anyDensity="true"
      />
      <application android:label="@string/app_name"
        android:icon="@drawable/cw">
        <activity android:name=".EU4You"
                  android:label="@string/app_name">
          <intent-filter>
            <action android:name="android.intent.action.MAIN" />
            <category android:name="android.intent.category.LAUNCHER" />
          </intent-filter>
        </activity>
      </application>
  </manifest>
```

Notice we have the `<supports-screens>` element, saying that we do indeed support all screen sizes. This blocks most of the automatic scaling that Android would do if we said we did not support certain screen sizes.

Our main layout is size-independent, as it is just a full-screen `ListView`:

```
<?xml version="1.0" encoding="utf-8"?>
<ListView xmlns:android="http://schemas.android.com/apk/res/android"
  android:id="@android:id/list"
  android:layout_width="fill_parent"
  android:layout_height="fill_parent"
/>
```

Our row, though, will eventually need some tweaking:

```
<?xml version="1.0" encoding="utf-8"?>
<LinearLayout xmlns:android="http://schemas.android.com/apk/res/android"
  android:layout_width="fill_parent"
  android:layout_height="wrap_content"
  android:padding="2dip"
  android:minHeight="?android:attr/listPreferredItemHeight"
>
  <ImageView android:id="@+id/flag"
    android:layout_width="wrap_content"
    android:layout_height="wrap_content"
    android:layout_gravity="center_vertical|left"
    android:paddingRight="4px"
  />
  <TextView android:id="@+id/name"
    android:layout_width="wrap_content"
    android:layout_height="wrap_content"
    android:layout_gravity="center_vertical|right"
    android:textSize="20px"
  />
</LinearLayout>
```

For example, right now, our font size is set to 20px, which will not vary by screen size or density.

Our EU4You activity is a bit verbose, mostly because there are a lot of EU members, and we need to have the smarts to display the flag and the text in the row:

```
package com.commonsware.android.eu4you;

import android.app.ListActivity;
import android.content.Intent;
import android.net.Uri;
import android.os.Bundle;
import android.view.View;
import android.view.ViewGroup;
import android.widget.ArrayAdapter;
import android.widget.ImageView;
import android.widget.ListView;
import android.widget.TextView;
import java.util.ArrayList;

public class EU4You extends ListActivity {
  static private ArrayList<Country> EU=new ArrayList<Country>();

  static {
    EU.add(new Country(R.string.austria, R.drawable.austria,
                       R.string.austria_url));
    EU.add(new Country(R.string.belgium, R.drawable.belgium,
                       R.string.belgium_url));
    EU.add(new Country(R.string.bulgaria, R.drawable.bulgaria,
                       R.string.bulgaria_url));
    EU.add(new Country(R.string.cyprus, R.drawable.cyprus,
                       R.string.cyprus_url));
    EU.add(new Country(R.string.czech_republic,
                       R.drawable.czech_republic,
                       R.string.czech_republic_url));
    EU.add(new Country(R.string.denmark, R.drawable.denmark,
                       R.string.denmark_url));
    EU.add(new Country(R.string.estonia, R.drawable.estonia,
                       R.string.estonia_url));
    EU.add(new Country(R.string.finland, R.drawable.finland,
                       R.string.finland_url));
    EU.add(new Country(R.string.france, R.drawable.france,
                       R.string.france_url));
    EU.add(new Country(R.string.germany, R.drawable.germany,
                       R.string.germany_url));
    EU.add(new Country(R.string.greece, R.drawable.greece,
                       R.string.greece_url));
    EU.add(new Country(R.string.hungary, R.drawable.hungary,
                       R.string.hungary_url));
    EU.add(new Country(R.string.ireland, R.drawable.ireland,
                       R.string.ireland_url));
    EU.add(new Country(R.string.italy, R.drawable.italy,
                       R.string.italy_url));
    EU.add(new Country(R.string.latvia, R.drawable.latvia,
                       R.string.latvia_url));
```

```
EU.add(new Country(R.string.lithuania, R.drawable.lithuania,
                   R.string.lithuania_url));
EU.add(new Country(R.string.luxembourg, R.drawable.luxembourg,
                   R.string.luxembourg_url));
EU.add(new Country(R.string.malta, R.drawable.malta,
                   R.string.malta_url));
EU.add(new Country(R.string.netherlands, R.drawable.netherlands,
                   R.string.netherlands_url));
EU.add(new Country(R.string.poland, R.drawable.poland,
                   R.string.poland_url));
EU.add(new Country(R.string.portugal, R.drawable.portugal,
                   R.string.portugal_url));
EU.add(new Country(R.string.romania, R.drawable.romania,
                   R.string.romania_url));
EU.add(new Country(R.string.slovakia, R.drawable.slovakia,
                   R.string.slovakia_url));
EU.add(new Country(R.string.slovenia, R.drawable.slovenia,
                   R.string.slovenia_url));
EU.add(new Country(R.string.spain, R.drawable.spain,
                   R.string.spain_url));
EU.add(new Country(R.string.sweden, R.drawable.sweden,
                   R.string.sweden_url));
EU.add(new Country(R.string.united_kingdom,
                   R.drawable.united_kingdom,
                   R.string.united_kingdom_url));
}

@Override
public void onCreate(Bundle savedInstanceState) {
  super.onCreate(savedInstanceState);
  setContentView(R.layout.main);
  setListAdapter(new CountryAdapter());
}

@Override
protected void onListItemClick(ListView l, View v,
                               int position, long id) {
  startActivity(new Intent(Intent.ACTION_VIEW,
                       Uri.parse(getString(EU.get(position).url))));
}

static class Country {
  int name;
  int flag;
  int url;

  Country(int name, int flag, int url) {
    this.name=name;
    this.flag=flag;
    this.url=url;
  }
}

class CountryAdapter extends ArrayAdapter<Country> {
  CountryAdapter() {
```

```
      super(EU4You.this, R.layout.row, R.id.name, EU);
    }

    @Override
    public View getView(int position, View convertView,
                        ViewGroup parent) {
      CountryWrapper wrapper=null;

      if (convertView==null) {
        convertView=getLayoutInflater().inflate(R.layout.row, null);
        wrapper=new CountryWrapper(convertView);
        convertView.setTag(wrapper);
      }
      else {
        wrapper=(CountryWrapper)convertView.getTag();
      }

      wrapper.populateFrom(getItem(position));

      return(convertView);
    }
  }

  class CountryWrapper {
    private TextView name=null;
    private ImageView flag=null;
    private View row=null;

    CountryWrapper(View row) {
      this.row=row;
    }

    TextView getName() {
      if (name==null) {
        name=(TextView)row.findViewById(R.id.name);
      }

      return(name);
    }

    ImageView getFlag() {
      if (flag==null) {
        flag=(ImageView)row.findViewById(R.id.flag);
      }

      return(flag);
    }

    void populateFrom(Country nation) {
      getName().setText(nation.name);
      getFlag().setImageResource(nation.flag);
    }
  }
}
```

Figures 36–2, 36–3, and 36–4 show what the activity looks like in an ordinary HVGA emulator, a WVGA emulator, and a QVGA screen.

Figure 36–2. *EU4You, original version, HVGA*

Figure 36–3. *EU4You, original version, WVGA (800x480 pixels)*

Figure 36–44. *EU4You, original version, QVGA*

Fixing the Fonts

The first problem that should be fixed is the font size. As you can see, with a fixed 20-pixel size, the font ranges from big to tiny, depending on screen size and density. For a WVGA screen, the font may be rather difficult to read.

We could put the dimension as a resource (res/values/dimens.xml) and have different versions of that resource based on screen size or density. However, it is simpler to just specify a density-independent size, such as 5mm, as seen in the ScreenSizes/EU4You_2 project:

```xml
<?xml version="1.0" encoding="utf-8"?>
<LinearLayout xmlns:android="http://schemas.android.com/apk/res/android"
  android:layout_width="fill_parent"
  android:layout_height="wrap_content"
  android:padding="2dip"
  android:minHeight="?android:attr/listPreferredItemHeight"
>
  <ImageView android:id="@+id/flag"
    android:layout_width="wrap_content"
    android:layout_height="wrap_content"
    android:layout_gravity="center_vertical|left"
    android:paddingRight="4px"
  />
  <TextView android:id="@+id/name"
    android:layout_width="wrap_content"
    android:layout_height="wrap_content"
    android:layout_gravity="center_vertical|right"
    android:textSize="5mm"
  />
</LinearLayout>
```

Figures 36–5, 36–6, and 36–7 shows the results on HVGA, WVGA, and QVGA screens.

Figure 36–5. *EU4You, 5mm font version, HVGA*

Figure 36–6. *EU4You, 5mm font version, WVGA (800x480 pixels)*

Figure 36–7. *EU4You, 5mm font version, QVGA*

Now our font is a consistent size and large enough to match the flags.

Fixing the Icons

So, what about those icons? They should be varying in size as well, since they are the same for all three emulators.

However, Android automatically scales bitmap resources, even with `<supports-screens>` and its attributes set to `true`. On the plus side, this means you may not need to do anything with these bitmaps. However, you are relying on a device to do the scaling, which definitely costs CPU time (and, hence, battery life). Also, the scaling algorithms that the device uses may not be optimal, compared to what you can do with graphics tools on your development machine.

The `ScreenSizes/EU4You_3` project creates `res/drawable-ldpi` and `res/drawable-hdpi`, putting in smaller and larger renditions of the flags, respectively. This project also renames `res/drawable` to `res/drawable-mdpi`. Android will use the flags for the appropriate screen density, depending on what the device or emulator needs.

Using the Space

While the activity looks fine on WVGA in portrait mode, it really wastes a lot of space in landscape mode, as shown in Figure 36–8.

Figure 36–8. *EU4You, landscape WVGA (800x480 pixels)*

We can put that to better use by having the Wikipedia content appear directly on the main activity when in large-screen landscape mode, instead of needing to spawn a separate browser activity.

To do this, we first must clone the main.xml layout into a res/layout-large-land rendition that incorporates a WebView widget, as seen in ScreenSizes/EU4You_4:

```xml
<?xml version="1.0" encoding="utf-8"?>
<LinearLayout xmlns:android="http://schemas.android.com/apk/res/android"
  android:layout_width="fill_parent"
  android:layout_height="fill_parent"
>
  <ListView
    android:id="@android:id/list"
    android:layout_width="fill_parent"
    android:layout_height="fill_parent"
    android:layout_weight="1"
  />
  <WebView
    android:id="@+id/browser"
    android:layout_width="fill_parent"
    android:layout_height="fill_parent"
    android:layout_weight="1"
  />
</LinearLayout>
```

Then we need to adjust our activity to look for that WebView and use it when found; otherwise, it will default to launching a browser activity:

```java
@Override
public void onCreate(Bundle savedInstanceState) {
  super.onCreate(savedInstanceState);
  setContentView(R.layout.main);

  browser=(WebView)findViewById(R.id.browser);

  setListAdapter(new CountryAdapter());
}

@Override
```

```
protected void onListItemClick(ListView l, View v,
                               int position, long id) {
    String url=getString(EU.get(position).url);

    if (browser==null) {
        startActivity(new Intent(Intent.ACTION_VIEW,
                                 Uri.parse(url)));
    }
    else {
        browser.loadUrl(url);
    }
}
```

This gives us a more space-efficient edition of the activity, as shown in Figure 36–9.

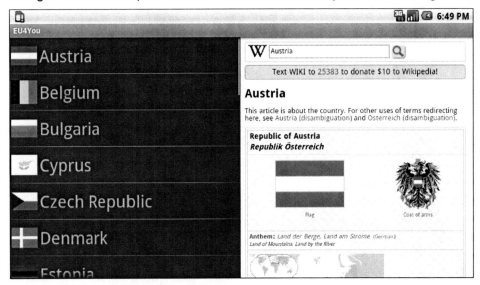

Figure 36–9. *EU4You, landscape WVGA (800x480 pixels), set for normal density, and showing the embedded WebView*

When the user clicks a link in the Wikipedia page, a full browser opens, for easier surfing.

Note that to test this version of the activity, and see this behavior, requires a bit of extra emulator work. By default, Android sets up WVGA devices as being high-density, meaning WVGA is not large in terms of resource sets, but rather normal. You will need to create a different emulator AVD that is set for normal (medium) density, which will result in a large screen size.

What If It's Not a Browser?

Of course, EU4You does cheat a bit. The second activity is a browser (or WebView in the embedded form), not some activity of your own creation. Things get slightly more complicated if the second activity is some activity of yours, with many widgets in a layout, and you want to use it both as an activity (for smaller screens) and have it embedded in your main activity UI (for larger screens).

Here is one pattern to deal with this scenario:

1. Initially develop and test the second activity as an activity.

2. Have all of the second activity's life-cycle methods delegate their logic to an inner class. Move all data members of the activity that are needed by only the inner class to that inner class, and ensure that still works.

3. Pull the inner class out into a separate public class, and ensure that still works.

4. For your first (or main) activity, create a separate layout for large screens and use the <include> directive to blend in the contents of your second activity's layout into the proper spot in the large-screen first activity's layout.

5. In the first activity, if it finds the second activity's layout has been inflated as part of its own (e.g., by checking for the existence of some widget via findViewById()), create an instance of the public class you created in step 3 and have it deal with all of those widgets. Adjust your code to reference that class directly, rather than start the second activity as shown in the previous section.

In short, use a public class and reusable layout to keep your code and resources in one place, yet use them from both a stand-alone activity and as part of a large-screen version of the main activity.

What Are a Few Bugs Among Friends?

The Motorola DROID, which shipped with Android 2.0, had two bugs of relevance for screen sizes:

- It had incorrect values for the screen density, both horizontal and vertical. This means it incorrectly scaled dimensions based on physical sizes: pt, mm, and in.

- It had Android 2.0 as API level 6 instead of level 5, so version-specific resource directories need to use the -v6 suffix instead of -v5

Both of these bugs are fixed in Android 2.0.1 and later, and no other devices should ship with Android 2.0 or be affected by these bugs.

Chapter 37

Dealing with Devices

Android is "free as in beer" for device manufacturers, as it is an open source project. Hence, device manufacturers have *carte blanche* to do what they want with Android as they put it on their devices. This means a breadth of choices for device users, who will be able to have Android devices in all shapes, sizes, and colors. This also means developers will have some device differences and idiosyncrasies to take into account.

This chapter will give you some tips and advice for dealing with these device-specific issues, to go along with the screen size material in Chapter 36.

This App Contains Explicit Instructions

Originally, the only Android device was the T-Mobile G1. Hence, if you were writing an Android application, you could assume the existence of a hardware QWERTY keyboard, a trackball for navigation, and so on. Now, other devices (e.g., HTC Magic) exist with different hardware capabilities (e.g., no keyboard).

Ideally, your application can work regardless of the existence of various types of hardware. Some applications, though, will be unusable without certain hardware characteristics. For example, a full-screen game may rely on a hardware keyboard or trackball to indicate player actions—soft keyboards and touchscreens may be insufficient.

Fortunately, starting with Android 1.5, you can add explicit instructions telling Android what you need, so your application is not installed on devices lacking such hardware.

In addition to using the target ID system to indicate the level of device that your project is targeting, you can use a new `AndroidManifest.xml` element to specify hardware that is required for your application to run properly. You can add one or more `<uses-configuration>` elements inside the `<manifest>` element. Each `<uses-configuration>` element specifies one valid configuration of hardware with which your application will work. At the present time, there are five possible hardware requirements you can specify this way:

- `android:reqFiveWayNav`: Indicates you need a five-way navigation pointing device of some form (e.g., `android:reqFiveWayNav = "true"`).

- android:reqNavigation: Restricts the five-way navigation pointing device to a specific type (e.g., android:reqNavigation = "trackball").

- android:reqHardKeyboard: Specifies if a hardware (physical) keyboard is required (e.g., android:reqHardKeyboard = "true").

- android:reqKeyboardType: Used in conjunction with android:reqHardKeyboard, indicates a specific type of hardware keyboard is required (e.g., android:reqKeyboardType = "qwerty").

- android:reqTouchScreen: Indicates what type of touchscreen is required, if any (e.g., android:reqTouchScreen = "finger").

Starting in Android 1.6, there is a similar manifest element, <uses-feature>, which is designed to document requirements an application has for other optional features on Android devices. Specifically, the following attributes can be placed in a <uses-feature> element:

- android:glEsVersion: Indicates that your application requires OpenGL, where the value of the attribute indicates the level of OpenGL support (e.g., 0x00010002 for OpenGL 1.2 or higher).

- android:name = "android.hardware.camera": Indicates that your application needs a camera.

- android:name = "android.hardware.camera.autofocus": Indicates that your application specifically needs an autofocus camera.

Button, Button, Who's Got the Button?

There are few, if any, requirements on device manufacturers as to what buttons are available as physical buttons, versus on-screen soft keys, versus simply not being available on a given Android device.

For example, the HTC Dream (a.k.a., T-Mobile G1) has call, end call, home, back, menu, and camera buttons, along with a volume control and a dedicated search button on its QWERTY keyboard. The HTC Magic (a.k.a., T-Mobile myTouch 3G) lacks the camera button, putting the search button in its place. The Archos 5 Android Internet Tablet has no hardware buttons at all beyond the volume control, with soft keys for home, back, and menu.

Therefore, you should be careful about assuming the existence or placement of hardware buttons. Provide alternative means of performing operations that you tie to buttons. For example, if you override the volume control to serve as page-up/page-down keys, make sure there is some other way for the user to move between pages.

A Guaranteed Market

As mentioned in the introduction to the chapter, Android is open source. Specifically, it is mostly available under the Apache Software License 2.0. This license places few restrictions on device manufacturers. Therefore, it is very possible for a device manufacturer to create a device that, frankly, does not run Android very well. It might work fine for standard applications shipped on the device but do a poor job of handling third-party applications, like the ones you might write.

To help address this, Google has some applications, such as the Android Market, that it has not released as open source. While these applications are available to device manufacturers, the devices that run the Android Market are tested first, to help ensure that a user's experience with the device will be reasonable.

A Google engineer cited one case where a device manufacturer was readying a phone that had a QVGA screen, before the release of Android 1.6 where QVGA support was officially added to the platform. While that manufacturer had arranged for the built-in applications to work acceptably on the smaller-resolution screen, third-party applications were a mess. Google apparently declined to provide the Android Market to the manufacturer for this device.

Hence, the existence of the Android Market on a device, beyond providing a distribution means for your applications, also serves as a bit of a seal of approval that the device should support well-written third-party applications.

The Down and Dirty Details

Unfortunately, the Android Market does not guarantee problem-free deployment on Market-enabled devices, nor does it prevent manufacturers from shipping Android devices without going through the Market. Inevitably, devices will have some quirks or idiosyncrasies that might have a negative impact on your applications. The following is a selection of some Android devices, in the order of their public availability, and ways that they differ from more standard devices.

Archos 5 Android Internet Tablet

The Archos 5 Android Internet Tablet is the first mainstream device to be based purely on the Android open source project. Unlike the phones from HTC, Motorola, and others, the Archos 5 is not a Google Experience device and does not have the Android Market, Google Maps, or other proprietary Google applications.

The Archos 5 is a WVGA device, but shipped with Android 1.5. Hence, an original Archos 5 will not honor the new -large resource set designation as documented in Chapter 36. Given that this device is not selling in major quantities, you may wind up with it simply having an unoptimized UI until the Archos 5 has Android 1.6 support.

The Archos 5's touchscreen is resistive, not capacitive. This means users will be using fingernails or styli to manipulate the screen, more so than fingertips. Bear this in mind when designing finger-friendly UIs.

The Archos 5, as of firmware 1.1.01, returned a somewhat invalid value for `ANDROID_ID` (a unique ID assigned to each Android device). `ANDROID_ID` is `null` in the emulator and is supposed to be a hex string in devices. On the Archos 5, `ANRDROID_ID` is a non-null but non-hex string. If all you care about is `null` versus non-`null`, then the Archos 5 is fine; if you need a hex value for `ANDROID_ID`, you will experience some problems.

Since the Archos 5 is not a phone, all telephony-related features, such as dialing via `ACTION_DIAL`, are unavailable. Similarly, since the Archos 5 lacks a camera, all camera-related features are unavailable. As noted earlier, the Archos 5 lacks Google Maps, the Android Market, and other proprietary Google applications.

Also, the Archos IMEI value is fake, since it is not a phone.

Motorola CLIQ/DEXT

The Motorola CLIQ (or DEXT, as it is known outside the United States) is an HVGA device, originally shipping with Android 1.5.

The CLIQ has a D-pad for non-touchscreen navigation. However, the D-pad is on a side-slider QWERTY keyboard, and as such, the D-pad is not available to users when the device is in portrait mode, unless you force portrait mode for your activity via the manifest and force users to use their CLIQ with the keyboard slid out. Do not write applications that assume the D-pad is always available.

The CLIQ also ships with MOTOBLUR, Motorola's social media presentation layer. This means that the home application, contacts, and select other features that Android normally ships with have been replaced by MOTOBLUR-specific features. This should not cause too many problems if you stick to the SDK. The one area that does get a bit interesting is that not all MOTOBLUR contacts will be available to you via the Android Contacts content provider. For example, Facebook contacts are available to MOTOBLUR, but not to third-party applications, perhaps for licensing reasons. This situation may change when the CLIQ is updated to the new `ContactsContract` system with Android 2.0.1 and beyond.

Motorola DROID/Milestone

The Motorola DROID (or Milestone, as it is known outside the United States) is a WVGA854 device, originally shipping with Android 2.0, though most of these devices will now be running Android 2.0.1.

The DROID, like the CLIQ, has a D-pad on the side-slider keyboard, meaning the D-pad is not readily available to users when the device is in portrait mode.

Because the DROID has a WVGA854 screen on a normal phone-sized device, Android will consider the DROID to have a high-density screen, so `-hdpi` resource sets will be used.

Google/HTC Nexus One

The Nexus One—built by HTC and sold by Google—is a WVGA800 device, originally shipping with Android 2.1.

Like the DROID, the Nexus One will be a high-density (-hdpi) device.

Motorola BACKFLIP

The Motorola BACKFLIP has yet another take on pointing devices. Rather than a trackball or a D-pad, the BACKFLIP has two non-touchscreen navigation options:

- The QWERTY keyboard has PC-style arrow keys, which should generate standard DPAD key events.

- The BACKFLIP touchpad on the reverse side of the touchscreen will generate trackball events (or DPAD key events, if the trackball events are not consumed).

Chapter 38

Handling Platform Changes

Android will continue to rapidly evolve over the next few years. Perhaps, in time, the rate of change will decline some. However, for the here and now, you should assume that there will be significant Android releases every 6 to 12 months, and changes to the lineup of possible Android hardware on an ongoing basis. So, while right now, the focus of Android is phones, soon you will see Android netbooks, Android tablets, Android media players, and so on.

Many of these changes will have little impact on your existing code. However, some will necessitate at least new rounds of testing for your applications, and perhaps changes to those applications based on the test results.

This chapter covers a number of the areas that may cause you trouble in the future as Android evolves, with some suggestions on how to deal with them.

Brand Management

As of the time of this writing, the Android devices that have been released have been Google Experience phones. This means they get the standard Android interface—the things you find in the emulator—along with the standard roster of add-on applications like Google Maps and Gmail. In turn, manufacturers are allowed to put the "with Google" brand on the device. But not all devices will be this way.

Some manufacturers will take Android as a base and change what is included, adding some of their own applications and perhaps even changing the look and feel (menu icons, home screen structure, etc.).

Others may use Android solely from the open source repository, and while they may ship with the standard look and feel, they will lack the commercial add-on applications.

Even today, some devices have a different mix of applications based on where they are distributed. US recipients of the T-Mobile G1 have an Amazon MP3 store application; not all international recipients do.

If your application is independent of all of this, then it should run anywhere. However, if your application code or documentation assumes the existence of Google Maps, Gmail, Amazon MP3 store, and the like, you may run into trouble. Be certain to test your application thoroughly in environments where these applications are not available.

More Things That Make You Go Boom

Most of the items noted in the previous section focused on hardware changes. Now, let's examine some ways in which Android can cause difficulty to you when the operating system itself changes.

View Hierarchy

Android is not designed to handle arbitrarily complicated view hierarchies. Here, *view hierarchy* means containers holding containers holding containers holding widgets.

The Hierarchy Viewer program, described in Chapter 35, depicts such view hierarchies well, as shown in Figure 38–1. In this example, you see a five-layer-deep hierarchy, because the longest chain of containers and widgets is five (from PhoneWindow$DecorView through to Button).

Android has always had limits as to how deep the view hierarchy can be. In Android 1.5, though, the limit was reduced, so some applications that worked fine on Android 1.1 would crash with a StackOverflowException in the newer Android. This, of course, was frustrating to developers who never realized there was an issue with view hierarchy depth and then got caught by this change.

The lessons to take from this are as follows:

- Keep your view hierarchies shallow. Once you drift into double-digit depth, you are increasingly likely to run out of stack space.

- If you encounter a StackOverflowException, and the stack trace looks like it is somewhere in the middle of drawing your widgets, your view hierarchy is probably too complex.

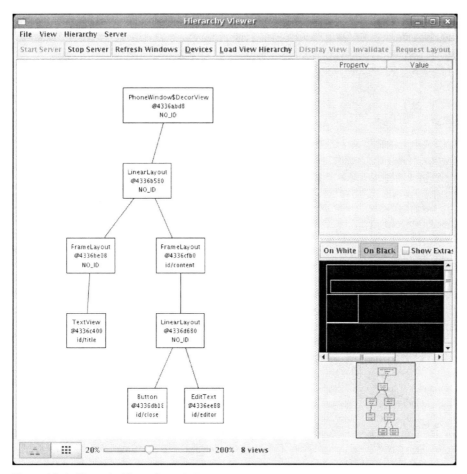

Figure 38–1. *Hierarchy Viewer Layout view*

Changing Resources

The core Android team may change resources with an Android upgrade, and those may have unexpected effects in your application. For example, in Android 1.5, they changed the stock Button background, to allow for smaller buttons. However, applications that implicitly relied on the former larger minimum size wound up breaking and needing some UI adjustment.

Similarly, applications can reuse public resources, such as icons, available inside of Android proper. While doing so saves some storage space, many of these resources are public by necessity and are not considered part of the SDK. For example, hardware manufacturers may change the icons to fit some alternative UI look and feel. Relying on the existing ones to always look as they do is a bit dangerous. You are better served copying those resources out of the Android open source project (http://source.android.com/) into your own code base.

Handling API Changes

The core Android team has generally done a good job of keeping APIs stable, and supporting a deprecation model when they change APIs. In Android, being *deprecated* does not mean it is going away—just that its continued use is discouraged. And, of course, new APIs are released with every new Android update. Changes to the APIs are well documented with each release via an API differences report.

Unfortunately, the Android Market (the primary distribution channel for Android applications) allows you to upload only one APK file for each application. Hence, you need that one APK file to deal with as many Android versions as possible. Many times, your code will "just work" and not require changing. Other times, though, you will need to make adjustments, particularly if you want to support new APIs on new versions while not breaking old versions. Let's examine some techniques for handling these cases.

Detecting the Version

If you just want to take different branches in your code based on version, the easiest thing to do is inspect `android.os.VERSION.SDK_INT`. This public static integer value will reflect the same API level as you use when creating AVDs and specifying API levels in the manifest. So, you can compare that value to, say, `android.os.VERSION_CODES.DONUT` to see whether you are running on Android 1.6 or newer.

Wrapping the API

So long as the APIs you try to use exist across all Android versions you are supporting, just branching may be sufficient. Where things get troublesome is when the APIs change, such as when there are new parameters to methods, new methods, or even new classes. You need code that will work regardless of Android version, yet lets you take advantage of new APIs where available.

There is a recommended trick for dealing with this: reflection, plus a wee bit of caching.

For example, back in Chapter 8, we used `getTag()` and `setTag()` to associate an arbitrary object with a `View`. Specifically, we used this to associate a wrapper object that would lazy-find all necessary widgets. You also learned that about the new versions of `getTag()` and `setTag()` that are indexed, taking a resource ID as a parameter.

However, these new indexed methods do not exist on Android 1.5. If you want to use this new technique, you need to wait until you are willing to support only Android 1.6 and beyond, or you will need to use reflection. Specifically, on Android 1.5, you could associate an `ArrayList<Object>` as the tag, and have your own `getTag()`/`setTag()` pair that takes the index.

This seems straightforward enough, so let's look at `APIVersions/Tagger`. Our activity has a simple layout, with just a `TextView`:

```
<?xml version="1.0" encoding="utf-8"?>
<LinearLayout xmlns:android="http://schemas.android.com/apk/res/android"
```

```
    android:orientation="vertical"
    android:layout_width="fill_parent"
    android:layout_height="fill_parent"
    >
<TextView android:id="@+id/test"
    android:layout_width="fill_parent"
    android:layout_height="wrap_content"
    />
</LinearLayout>
```

The source code to our Tagger activity looks at the API version we are running, and routes our getTag() and setTag() operations to either the native indexed one (for Android 1.6 and above) or to the original nonindexed getTag() and setTag(), where we use a HashMap to track all of the individual indexed objects:

```java
package com.commonsware.android.api.tag;

import android.app.Activity;
import android.os.Build;
import android.os.Bundle;
import android.util.Log;
import android.view.View;
import android.widget.TextView;
import java.util.HashMap;
import java.util.Date;

public class Tagger extends Activity {
  private static final String LOG_KEY="Tagger";

  @Override
  public void onCreate(Bundle savedInstanceState) {
    super.onCreate(savedInstanceState);
    setContentView(R.layout.main);

    TextView view=(TextView)findViewById(R.id.test);

    setTag(view, R.id.test, new Date());

    view.setText(getTag(view, R.id.test).toString());
  }

  public void setTag(View v, int key, Object value) {
    if (Build.VERSION.SDK_INT>=Build.VERSION_CODES.DONUT) {
      v.setTag(key, value);
    }
    else {
      HashMap<Integer, Object> meta=(HashMap<Integer, Object>)v.getTag();

      if (meta==null) {
        meta=new HashMap<Integer, Object>();
      }

      meta.put(key, value);
    }
  }
```

```
  public Object getTag(View v, int key) {
    Object result=null;

    if (Build.VERSION.SDK_INT>=Build.VERSION_CODES.DONUT) {
      result=v.getTag(key);
    }
    else {
      HashMap<Integer, Object> meta=(HashMap<Integer, Object>)v.getTag();

      if (meta==null) {
        meta=new HashMap<Integer, Object>();
      }

      result=meta.get(key);
    }

    return(result);
  }
}
```

This looks great, and if we build it and deploy it on a Android 1.6 or greater emulator or device, it runs like a champ, showing the current time in the activity.

If we build it and deploy it on an Android 1.5 emulator or device, and try to run it, it blows up with a VerifyError. VerifyError, in this case, basically means we are referring to things that do not exist in our version of Android, specifically:

- We are referring to SDK_INT, which was not introduced until Android 1.6.

- We are referring to the indexed versions of getTag() and setTag(). Even though we will not execute that code, the classloader still wants to resolve those methods and fails.

So, we need to use some reflection.

Take a look at APIVersions/Tagger2. This is the same project with the same layout, but we have a more elaborate version of the Java source:

```
package com.commonsware.android.api.tag;

import android.app.Activity;
import android.os.Build;
import android.os.Bundle;
import android.util.Log;
import android.view.View;
import android.widget.TextView;
import java.lang.reflect.Method;
import java.util.HashMap;
import java.util.Date;

public class Tagger extends Activity {
  private static final String LOG_KEY="Tagger";
  private static Method _setTag=null;
  private static Method _getTag=null;
```

```
static {
  int sdk=new Integer(Build.VERSION.SDK).intValue();

  if (sdk>=4) {
    try {
      _setTag=View.class.getMethod("setTag",
                            new Class[] {Integer.TYPE,
                                          Object.class});
      _getTag=View.class.getMethod("getTag",
                            new Class[] {Integer.TYPE});
    }
    catch (Throwable t) {
      Log.e(LOG_KEY, "Could not initialize 1.6 accessors", t);
    }
  }
};

@Override
public void onCreate(Bundle savedInstanceState) {
  super.onCreate(savedInstanceState);
  setContentView(R.layout.main);

  TextView view=(TextView)findViewById(R.id.test);

  setTag(view, R.id.test, new Date());

  view.setText(getTag(view, R.id.test).toString());
}

public void setTag(View v, int key, Object value) {
  if (_setTag!=null) {
    try {
      _setTag.invoke(v, key, value);
    }
    catch (Throwable t) {
      Log.e(LOG_KEY, "Could not use 1.6 setTag()", t);
    }
  }
  else {
    HashMap<Integer, Object> meta=(HashMap<Integer, Object>)v.getTag();

    if (meta==null) {
      meta=new HashMap<Integer, Object>();
      v.setTag(meta);
    }

    meta.put(key, value);
  }
}

public Object getTag(View v, int key) {
  Object result=null;

  if (_getTag!=null) {
    try {
```

```
        result=_getTag.invoke(v, key);
      }
      catch (Throwable t) {
        Log.e(LOG_KEY, "Could not use 1.6 getTag()", t);
      }
    }
  }
  else {
    HashMap<Integer, Object> meta=(HashMap<Integer, Object>)v.getTag();

    if (meta==null) {
      meta=new HashMap<Integer, Object>();
      v.setTag(meta);
    }

    result=meta.get(key);
  }

  return(result);
  }
}
```

First, when the class is initially loaded, the static initialization routines run. Here, we see what version of Android we are running, using the old SDK String instead of the new SDK_INT integer. If we are on Android 1.6 or newer, we use reflection to attempt to find the indexed getTag() and setTag() methods, and we cache those results. Since those methods should not change during the lifetime of our application, it is safe to cache them in static variables.

Then, when it comes time to actually use getTag() or setTag(), we look to see if the cached Method objects exist or are null. If they are null, we assume we need to use the old versions of those methods. If the Method objects exist, we use them instead, to take advantage of the native indexed versions.

This version of the application works fine on Android 1.5 and above. Android 1.6 and above uses the built-in indexed methods, and Android 1.5 uses our fake version of the indexed methods.

There is a little extra overhead for going through the Method-based reflection, but it may be worth it in some cases, to access APIs that exist in newer versions of Android, rather than restricting ourselves to only the older APIs.. There are even ways to use this technique for cases where entire classes are new to newer Android versions (see http://android-developers.blogspot.com/2009/04/backward-compatibility-for-android.html).

Chapter 39

Where Do We Go from Here?

Obviously, this book does not cover everything. And while your main resource (besides the book) is the Android SDK documentation, you are likely to need more information.

Searching online for "android" and a class name is a good way to turn up tutorials that reference a given Android class. However, bear in mind that tutorials written before late August 2008 are probably written for the M5 SDK and, as such, will require considerable adjustment to work properly in current SDKs.

Beyond randomly hunting around for tutorials, you can use some of the resources outlined in this chapter.

Questions—Sometimes with Answers

The official places to get assistance with Android are the Android Google Groups. With respect to the SDK, there are three to consider:

- android-beginners, a great place to ask entry-level questions

- android-developers, best suited for more complicated questions or ones that delve into less-used portions of the SDK

- android-discuss, designed for free-form discussion of anything Android-related, not necessarily for programming questions and answers

You might also consider these resources:

- The Android tutorials and programming forums over at `http://anddev.org`

- The Open Mob for Android wiki (`http://wiki.andmob.org/`)

- The #android IRC channel on freenode

- StackOverflow's android and android-sdk tags
- The Android board on JavaRanch

Heading to the Source

The source code to Android is now available. Mostly, this is for people looking to enhance, improve, or otherwise fuss with the insides of the Android operating system. But it is possible that you will find the answers you seek in that code, particularly if you want to see how some built-in Android component does its thing.

The source code and related resources can be found at http://source.android.com. Here, you can do the following:

- Download or browse the source code.
- File bug reports against the operating system itself.
- Submit patches and learn about the process for how such patches are evaluated and approved.
- Join a separate set of Google Groups for Android platform development.

Rather than download the multigigabyte Android source code snapshot, you may wish to use Google Code Search instead (http://www.google.com/codesearch). Just add the android:package constraint to your search query, and it will search only in Android and related projects.

Getting Your News Fix

Ed Burnette, a nice guy who happened to write his own Android book, is also the manager of Planet Android (http://www.planetandroid.com/), a feed aggregator for a number of Android-related blogs. Subscribing to the planet's feed will let you monitor Android-related blog posts, though not exclusively related to programming.

To try to focus more on programming-related, Android-referencing blog posts, you can search DZone for "android" and subscribe to a feed based on that search.

Index

■ Symbols and Numerics

■ A

H

■N

name property, 273, 354
National Weather Service XML format, 256
navigation
    specifying hardware requirements, 353
    WebView widget, 144
netbooks, Android
    handling platform changes, 359–366
networks
    Android development features, 3
    getNetworkType method, 312
newCursor method, SQLite, 235
newView method, CursorAdapter, 94
nextFocusXyz properties, 37
Nexus One *see* Google/HTC Nexus One
nine-patch bitmaps
    automatically scaling UI to screen size,
        334
NooYawk application, 302
normalScreens attribute, 335
NotificationManager class, 289, 292
notifications, 289–294
    see also alerts
    contentIntent, 290
    encountering error during background
        processing, 165
    hardware notifications, 290
    icons, 290
    notify method, 290
    paused state, 167
    PendingIntent, 290
    raising notifications, 289
    services alerting activities, 282
    setLatestEventInfo method, 290
    status bar icons, 289
    stopped state, 168
    tickerText, 290
notify method, notifications, 290
Notify1 project, 290
notifyChange method, 274
NotifyDemo activity, 292
notifyMe method, 292
notify-on-change support, 273, 274
Now.java file, 17, 18
NowRedux project, 24, 26
numColumns property, GridView, 66
numericShortcut attribute, item element, 135

■O

obtainMessage method, 156
onActivityResult callback, intents, 179
onBind method, services, 280
    communicating with services, 286
    exposing API through binding, 281
OnCheckedChangeListener, 34
    LinearLayout example, 44
onClick attribute, buttons, 30
onClick method, 19
OnClickListener, 30
    alert example, 152
    date and time, 97
    trapping button clicks within activity, 19
onConfigurationChanged method, 191, 193
onContextItemSelected method, menus,
        127, 130
onCreate method
    ConstantsBrowser, 262
    ContentProvider, 267
    handling screen rotation, 185, 189, 193
    invoking loadUrl() on WebView, 142
    invoking, activities, 19
    LinearLayout example, 44
    menus, 125, 130
    services, 280
    SQLite, 228, 230
    transitions between states, 168
onCreateContextMenu method, 127, 130
onCreateOptionsMenu method, 125, 127,
        130
onCreatePanelMenu method, 127
OnDateChangedListener, 95
OnDateSetListener, 95, 97
onDestroy method
    services, 280
    transitions between states, 168
OnItemSelectedListener, 65
online help, 367
onListItemClick method
    changes to list selection, 61
    combining RatingBar with ListView, 86
onOptionsItemSelected method, 126, 127,
        130
onPause method
    activity receiving/using broadcast, 288
    transitions between states, 169
    unregistering receivers, 175
    updating locations/directions, 308
    writeable application data files, 243

setOnItemSelectedListener method, 60, 64, 65, 67
    Spinner, 63–66
sendBroadcast method
    broadcast intents, 284
    enforcing permissions, 278
sendMessage method, 156
sendMessageAtFrontOfQueue method, 156
sendMessageAtTime method, 156
sendMessageDelayed method, 156
Service class, 279
service elements, 11
ServiceConnection instance, 286
services
    accessing location-based services, 295
    accessing service object, 280
    adding to AndroidManifest.xml, 281
    Android application components, 3
    asynchronously alerting activities, 282
    binding to, 286
    broadcast intents, 283–284
    callbacks, 283
    creating, 279–282
    description, 279
    exposing API through binding, 281
    exposing service object, 281
    GPS services, 295
    implementation of singleton pattern, 281
    invoking, 285
    life-cycle methods, 279
    local services, 284, 285
    location service, 296
    permissions, 277
    remote services, 284
    running costs, 279
    starting, 279, 286
    stopping, 286
setAccuracy method, LocationProvider, 296
setAdapter method
    AutoCompleteTextView widget, 70
    combining RatingBar with ListView, 93
    GridView widget, 67
    ListView widget, 60
    Spinner widget, 64
setAlphabeticShortcut method, menus, 126
setAltitudeRequired method, 296
setBuiltInZoomControls method, 304
setCenter method, MapController, 304
setCheckable method, MenuItem, 126
setChecked method
    CheckBox, 34

RadioButton, 37
setChoiceMode method, ListView, 62
setColumnXyz method, TableLayout, 53
setContent method, TabSpec, 104, 105, 106
setContentView method
    attaching XML layout file to Java, 25
    creating skeleton application, 19
    XML layout file, 26
setCostAllowed method, 296
setCurrentTab method, 105
setDefaultFontSize method, 147
setDropDownViewResource method, 64, 65
setEnabled method, 38
    MenuItem class, 134
setFantasyFontFamily method, 147
setFlipInterval method, 113
setGravity method, LinearLayout, 41
setGroupCheckable method, 126
setGroupEnabled method, 134
setGroupVisible method, Menu, 135
setIcon method, Builder, 150
setImageURI method, 31
setIndeterminate method, ProgressBar, 101
setIndicator method, TabSpec, 104, 105
setJavaScriptEnabled method, 143, 147
setLatestEventInfo method, 290, 292
setListAdapter method, 61
setMessage method, Builder, 150
setNegativeButton method, Builder, 150
setNeutralButton method, Builder, 150, 152
setNumericShortcut method, menus, 126
setOnCheckedChangeListener method, 44
setOnClickListener
    adding tabs during runtime, 107
    writeable application data files, 243
setOnEditorActionListener, 123
setOnItemSelectedListener method, 64, 65
    GridView widget, 67
    ListView widget, 60
setOnSeekBarChangeListener, 102
setOrientation method, 40
setPadding method, 41
setPositiveButton method, Builder, 150
setProgress method, 101
setQwertyMode method, menus, 126
setResult method, intents, 179
setTag method, View objects
    combining RatingBar with ListView, 87
    ListView with icons and text, 82, 83
    wrapping API, 362, 363, 364, 366
setTitle method, Builder, 150, 152

Y

Z

X